"The Klan of the 1920s, less violent but far more widespread, is a different story, and one that offers some chilling comparisons to the present day. . . . A thoughtful explanation of the Klan's appeal in the fast-urbanizing America of the 1920s, which was leaving behind an earlier nation based, in imagined memory, on self-sufficient yeoman farmers, proud blue-collar workers, and virtuous small-town businessmen, all of them going to the same white-steepled church on Sunday."

—Adam Hoschschild, *New York Review of Books*

"Illuminating and timely. . . . Part cautionary tale, part exposé, *The Second Coming of the KKK* illustrates how a potent and unyielding undercurrent in American life was methodically aroused and unleashed. By following a thread that courses through history, Gordon reveals why a dangerous movement, disdained and underestimated by some intellectual elites, powerfully appealed to a wide swath of white America."

—Pamela Newkirk, *Washington Post*

"It's hard to finish a single page in Gordon's book without a slight tingle of fearful familiarity, of reverberations in rhetoric and public opinion—a recognition that, maybe, it has always been thus. . . . They say the job of an anthropologist is to make the familiar strange and the strange familiar, and something similar goes for the historian. I can think of few books that accomplish this task as well as Gordon's: In her telling, the second Klan is at once utterly bizarre and undeniably American. The 2010s may not be the 1920s, but for anyone concerned with our present condition, *The Second Coming of the KKK* should be required reading."

—Clay Risen, *New York Times Book Review*

"A must-read. . . . Gordon documents not only the mechanics of how the Ku Klux Klan roared back to power, both socially and politically, in the 1920s but why. . . . Histories like Gordon's should help Americans understand the roots of these toxic ideologies, as well as the circumstances that help them flourish, in order to better spot them when they sprout."

—Erin Keane, *Salon*

"*The Second Coming of the KKK* illustrates how the 1920s reboot of the Ku Klux Klan was regarded as rather ordinary and respectable, much like today's efforts to make everyday racism, sexism, and anti-Semitism acceptable again." —Deborah Douglas, *VICE*

"Set aside your preconceptions about the Klan, from the era of Reconstruction. As the distinguished historian Linda Gordon demonstrates in this chilling account, the KKK of the 1920s was urban, northern, and modern. Its wizards and dragons used the latest tools of mass advertising to spread their message of 'true Americanism': racial purity, religious intolerance, and opposition to immigration. Its members, one in six of whom were women, favored women's suffrage. Its campaign of terror ended not long after it began, but it left on American politics its dark mark."

—Jill Lepore, author of *The Secret History of Wonder Woman*

"Vital and engaging. . . . Gordon's work succeeds brilliantly in showing us that the Klan is '100 percent American,' and that racist and nativist movements are a powerful and enduring feature of our political history, even if sometimes dormant." —Charles Reichmann, *San Francisco Chronicle*

"Gordon is a thorough and perceptive historian. . . . There's more to *The Second Coming of the KKK* than grim déjà vu. There are lessons, too."

—Randy Dotinga, *Christian Science Monitor*

"*The Second Coming of the KKK* reminds us that we Americans bid good riddance to serial aberrations in the civic and social life of our republic repeatedly, only to learn that these phenomena are as American as apple pie. Gordon's timely, crisply written, indispensable primer helps explain why another aberration is now upon us."

—David Levering Lewis, Pulitzer Prize–winning author of
W.E.B. Du Bois: A Biography

"A first-rate historian can show us the past in a way that clarifies the present. That's what Linda Gordon does here. . . . [*The Second Coming of the KKK*] reminds us that the sentiments that powered the reprise of the Klan have never been entirely absent from American life, and cannot be understood as an aberrant strain that might be entirely eliminated from the national character."
—Nicholas Lemann, author of *Redemption:
The Last Battle of the Civil War*

"An excellent historical treatment of an almost forgotten yet very dangerous period of hate in America. What a history lesson for today's electorate."
—Morris Dees, cofounder of the Southern Poverty Law Center

"Sharply argued. . . . [Gordon] encourages readers to draw bold lines between the political milieu of the Second Klan and our current predicament."
—Todd Moye, *Texas Observer*

"At once thoughtful, fair, and deeply troubling, *The Second Coming of the KKK* exhibits the analytical wisdom of a master historian who sharply reminds us that popular mass mobilizations can be instruments of depredation."   —Ira Katznelson, author of the Bancroft Prize–winning *Fear Itself*

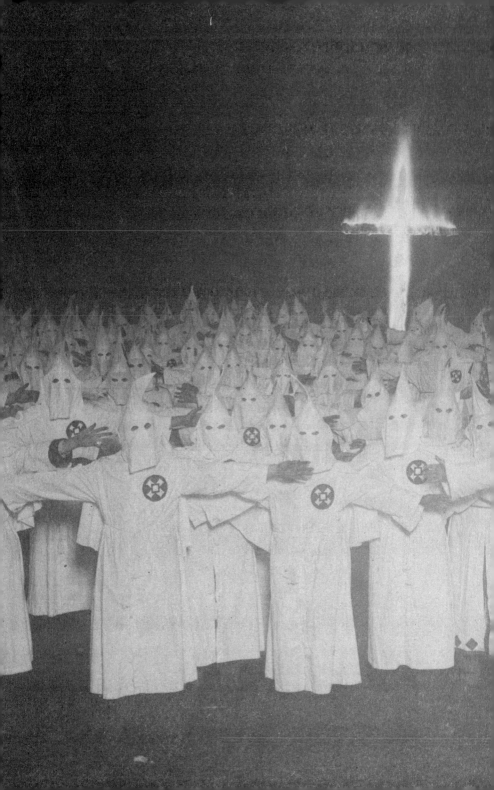

THE
SECOND
COMING
OF THE
KKK

The Ku Klux Klan
of the 1920s and the
American Political Tradition

LINDA GORDON

LIVERIGHT
PUBLISHING CORPORATION
A DIVISION OF W. W. NORTON & COMPANY
Independent Publishers Since 1923
NEW YORK LONDON

In memory of my friend, collaborator, and radical guru,
the late Ros Baxandall

And to my beloved partner, Allen Hunter

For information about permission to reproduce selections from this book,
write to Permissions, Liveright Publishing Corporation, a division of
W. W. Norton & Company, Inc., 500 Fifth Avenue, New York, NY 10110

For information about special discounts for bulk purchases, please contact
W. W. Norton Special Sales at specialsales@wwnorton.com or 800-233-4830

Manufacturing by LSC Communications, Harrisonburg
Book design by Lovedog Studio
Production manager: Anna Oler

Library of Congress Cataloging-in-Publication Data

Names: Gordon, Linda, author.
Title: The second coming of the KKK : the Ku Klux Klan of the 1920s
and the American political tradition / Linda Gordon.
Description: First edition. | New York, NY : Liveright Publishing
Corporation, 2017. | Includes bibliographical references and index.
Identifiers: LCCN 2017037229 | ISBN 9781631493690 (hardcover)
Subjects: LCSH: Ku Klux Klan (1915–)—History—20th century. |
Racism—United States—History—20th century. | Hate groups—
United States—History—20th century. | Political culture—
United States—History—20th century. | United States—
Race relations—History—20th century.
Classification: LCC HS2330.K63 G63 2017 | DDC 322.4/2097309042—dc23
LG record available at https://lccn.loc.gov/2017037229

ISBN 978-1-63149-492-5 pbk.

Liveright Publishing Corporation, 500 Fifth Avenue, New York, N.Y. 10110
www.wwnorton.com

W. W. Norton & Company Ltd., 15 Carlisle Street, London W1D 3BS

3 4 5 6 7 8 9 0

OTHER BOOKS BY LINDA GORDON

Feminism Unfinished:
A Short, Surprising History of American Women's Movements
(with Dorothy Sue Cobble and Astrid Henry)

Dorothea Lange: A Life Beyond Limits

Impounded: Dorothea Lange and the Censored Images
of Japanese American Internment
(coedited with Gary Y. Okihiro)

The Moral Property of Women:
A History of Birth Control Politics in America

The Great Arizona Orphan Abduction

Pitied but Not Entitled:
Single Mothers and the History of Welfare

Heroes of Their Own Lives:
The Politics and History of Family Violence

Cossack Rebellions:
Social Turmoil in the Sixteenth-Century Ukraine

CONTENTS

PREFACE AND
ACKNOWLEDGMENTS

In writing this book I was able to stand on the sturdy shoulders of many other scholars. Not only rigorous, they are also scholars who cared enough about freedom, justice, and our nation of immigrants to spend time studying something as unpleasant as the Ku Klux Klan. They understood that we Americans need a full and honest accounting of all our past, especially when it continues to shape our present. (But then, when doesn't it?)

The work of these scholars is cited repeatedly in the endnotes, but I want to offer here particular thanks to Kathleen Blee, David A. Horowitz, Allen Hunter, and Nancy MacLean. I am grateful also that I could rely on work by Charles Alexander, Kelly Baker, Betty Brenner, Newell Bringhurst, Dana Caldemeyer, David Chalmers, John Craig, Sarah Doherty, Glenn Feldman, Craig Fox, David J. Goldberg, Robert Alan Goldberg, Elizabeth Hatle, Thomas Heuterman, Kenneth Jackson, William Jenkins, Robert Johnston, Kelli Kerbawy, John T. Kneebone, Jeff LaLande, Elinor Langer, Shawn Lay, Rory McVeigh, Richard Melching, Tim Messer-Kruse, Leonard Moore, Thomas Pegram, Tom Rice, Mark Richard, Chris Rhomberg, Allen Safianow, Michael Schuyler, Wendy Thorson, Eckard Toy, William Trollinger Jr.,

Todd Tucker, Frances Valenti, and Wyn Wade. These people did the hard work and hard thinking that guided me. I hope I have done them justice.

I want also to thank the Radcliffe Institute for Advanced Study and the NYU Graduate School for giving me time that helped me write this book, and the NYU History Department for providing such a stimulating and supportive place to work.

Several scholar friends also did me the favor of reading parts of this text. Much gratitude to Kathleen Blee, Allen Hunter, Rosie Hunter, Michael Kazin, Nancy MacLean, and Charles Postel. Whatever mistakes remain, despite their best efforts, are mine alone.

I am appreciative of the many colleagues, friends, and acquaintances with whom I have discussed right-wing populism, social movements, democracy, and feminism. I am particularly indebted to the late Ros Baxandall, as well as to Suzanne Desan, Sara Evans, Susan Stanford Friedman, Michael Kazin, Linda Kerber, Alice Kessler-Harris, Elinor Langer, Judith Walzer Leavitt, Elaine Tyler May, Michele Mitchell, Maria Montoya, Erika Munk, Andrew Needham, Molly Nolan, Guy Ortolano, Ros Petchesky, Frances Fox Piven, Katha Pollitt, Charles Postel, Liz Schneider, Barbara Weinstein, Judith Vichniac, and Marilyn Young. Please do not blame any of them for whatever errors can be found here.

I continue to admire and be daunted by the energy, skill, and indomitable spirit of my longtime agent, Charlotte Sheedy. She took me on as a client in the 1970s, a time when publishers were leery of feminist books. Her sharp intelligence, ethical commitment, and passion for good books are inspiring. Her friendship over these many decades has been a blessing.

Charlotte also brought me the gift of a superb and learned editor, Robert Weil of Norton. He is an intellectual of great perspicacity and integrity. His enormous capacity for work and superb skills as a reader and editor have made several of my books much better. He pushed me to finish this manuscript quickly, for very good reason, and then worked overtime to read every word of it; an editor of a sort that is rare these days, he offered me not only textual editing but substantive historical suggestions. I could not fulfill all his hopes, but the book is vastly better than it would have been without him. I am deeply grateful, Bob.

Several others helped me greatly, reconfirming why I like working with W. W. Norton. It takes a team to publish a book. Because I hurried to produce this one, and finished it while teaching, Norton staff had to put up with my occasional inattentiveness and muddled queries. Particular thanks to Marie Pantojan, who patiently and efficiently answered questions, fielded requests, and shepherded the manuscript with care. My masterful assistant in gathering photographs, Elyse Rieder, not only coped with my disorganized record-keeping and indecisiveness but also offered sage advice. I benefited from the work of a fine copy editor, India Cooper. Not content merely to catch my errors and omissions, she found substantive mistakes and then did the research necessary to correct them. Her rephrasings often made my text more graceful. I am sure they will all be relieved when this book is finally in print. I am very grateful to everyone at Norton, and hope that they will be able to take some pride in the final product.

This book began as a chapter of a larger work in progress on twentieth-century American social movements. Expanding that chapter into a book shortly before and just after the 2016 election reconfirmed my sense of the importance of understanding movements like the Klan. Readers may find here similarities with some contemporary political movements, and may note the continuing influence of Klannish impulses and ideology.

Kathleen Blee wrote that scholars should not use right-wing groups as a "foil" against which we can define ourselves as more virtuous. I have tried, no doubt imperfectly, to live up to that admonition.

Linda Gordon
April 2017

THE SECOND COMING OF THE KKK

"100%
AMERICANISM"

A JULY 4 PICNIC IN KOKOMO, INDIANA, HELD IN 1923,
was the town's event of the decade, a lollapalooza of a carnival: some
said fifty thousand came, while others said two hundred thousand—no
doubt a wild exaggeration but one that reflected the celebratory mood.
Reserved train cars brought in people from throughout Indiana and
nearby states. This giant gathering made its participants feel part of
something vast, patriotic, and noble—a celebration of Americanism.
The food was so plentiful it required several rows of tables, each extending the distance of a block. In addition to the heaps of casseroles and
desserts that women brought, the organizers provided five thousand
cases of pop and near beer, fifty-five thousand buns, and six tons of
beef, not to mention the two hundred and fifty pounds of coffee and
twenty-five hundred pies. To entertain the kids, organizers had set up
a children's area with games and sports. Grown-ups could watch a six-
round boxing match, a boys' singing quartet, circus performers, and an
evening film, then known as a talkie. An airplane circled overhead with
a huge white cross flashing from the bottom of the fuselage while an
acrobat performed daredevil feats on its wings.[1]

Another Indiana mass pow-wow advertised like this:

BIG BARBECUE 20 BRASS BANDS
High Tight Wire Walking, 100 Feet in the Air
Wild Bronco Busting — Outlaw Horses — Imported Texas Cowboys
National Speakers — 200 Horsemen — Evening Fire Works
Illustrated Parades — Visit Valparaiso University[2]
The Sand Dunes — See the Calumet Region[3]

These quintessentially American celebrations were Ku Klux Klan affairs, held frequently during the peak of its power in the 1920s. If we are to understand this second coming of the Klan, we must surrender some of our preconceptions about it. Those come mainly from the first Ku Klux Klan, established after the Civil War as a secret fraternity with the aim of reimposing servitude on African Americans after the end of slavery. Its tools were lynchings, torture, and other forms of terrorism designed to inhibit any challenge to white supremacy. It had never entirely disappeared, but faded somewhat after achieving its goal: electoral disfranchisement and economic subjugation of black people.

This "second Klan," as it has been called, took pride in its namesake and its commitment to white supremacy. But it differed significantly from its parent. It was stronger in the North than in the South. It spread above the Mason-Dixon Line by adding Catholics, Jews, immigrants, and bootleggers to its list of enemies and pariahs, in part because African Americans were less numerous in the North. Its leaders tried to prohibit violence, though they could not always enforce the ban. Unlike the first Klan, which operated mainly at night, meeting in hard-to-find locations, the second operated in daylight and organized mass public events. Never a secret organization, it published recruiting ads in newspapers, its members boasted their affiliation, and it elected hundreds of its members to public office. It was vastly bigger than the first Klan, claiming, in what was almost certainly an exaggeration, four million to six million members.[4] It owned or controlled about 150 magazines or newspapers, two colleges, and the Cavalier Motion Picture Company, dedicated to countering Hollywood's immoral influence.[5]

Most important, the 1920s Klan's program was embraced by millions who were not members, possibly even a majority of Americans. Far from appearing disreputable or extreme in its ideology, the 1920s Klan seemed ordinary and respectable to its contemporaries. At many of its events, elected officials spoke. Its members included both the well and the poorly educated, professionals, businesspeople, farmers, and wage workers, but lower-middle-class and skilled working-class people formed its core constituency. In addition to providing fraternalism and sisterhood, it conferred prestige on its members and delivered business networking opportunities; for these reasons, many joined in the hopes of raising their social and economic status or identity. Thus membership in the Klan could appear to offer a route into the middle class. Although it claimed to represent the soul of America, its prestige rosé from its exclusiveness. During its relatively brief period of strength, its members were proud to belong.

The Klan built a politics of resentment, reflecting but also fomenting antipathy toward those who it defined as threatening Americanism. To understand its strength we need to notice which groups it identified as enemies. By blaming immigrants and non-Protestants for stealing jobs and government from "true" Americans, it stayed away from criticism of those who wielded economic power. Devoted to a business ethic, revering the pursuit of profit as confirmation of individual independence and manliness, the Klan respected men of great wealth and considered their social position earned and deserved. Instead it blamed "elites," typically presented as big-city liberal professionals, secular urbanites who promoted cosmopolitanism (and were thus insufficiently patriotic) and looked down on Klanspeople as stupid and/or irrational and/or out of step with modernity. This disrespect for the Klan only intensified its hostility and sense of righteousness. Simultaneously the

Klan denounced corruption, which it considered a uniquely big-city and non-Protestant phenomenon, and complained especially that big-city governments and police were venal and lazy.

These Klan targets were always racialized. Its anti-elitism focused on Jews, all of whom appeared in Klan talk either as snobbish, over-educated, effete professionals or money-grubbing merchants out to fleece innocent consumers. Thus large populations of urban poor and working-class Jews did not exist in Klan social analysis. Political corruption it blamed on Catholics, the Irish and Italians especially, and here too the Klan did not acknowledge the masses of non-Protestant working-class people who were as much fleeced by corruption as were Klan members.

In the last few decades, that understanding of elites, albeit with less anti-Semitism or anti-Catholicism, has once again become common in political rhetoric. Today's anti-elitism provides insight into the popularity of the Klan, and illustrates particularly the difficulty of placing it on a conventional left-right spectrum. True, Klanspeople typically preached distinctly right-wing principles, such as anti-Communism, though concern about political radicals played only a minor part in its diatribes. Of course, bigotry has long been characteristic of the Right. But Klan anger was also directed at what it considered immorality. This resentment did not always coincide with actual economic insecurity: some Klansmen felt their economic position slipping, but others were upwardly mobile. Racial and religious bigotry may have been provoked by economic anxiety but also arose from independent, long-standing American traditions. Goading members into racial and religious anger might not have worked without preexisting prejudices. Also challenging a neat left-right distinction is the fact that most traditional conservatives denounced the Klan, out of fear that mass social movements could lead to dangerous mob rule. Many ministers in mainstream Protestant denominations similarly denounced Klanspeople's evangelical and occasionally fundamentalist theology as the symptom of a primitive, ignorant mindset. Further blurring the left-right distinction was the Klan's endorsement of some progressive causes; however opportunist these endorsements, the Klan argued for more aid to public schools and welcomed the woman suffrage amendment.

Status anxiety, another diagnosis of the Klan's appeal, saturated Klan rhetoric, notably in the chorus of fake-news stories about how Catholics and Jews were taking over government. Its claim to be losing status and respect is not easily proved or disproved; we lack both historical evidence for anxiety and parameters for measuring it. Moreover, Klan rhetoric about the threat to American values also suggests a more immediate cause: the skillful demagoguery of leaders. The enthusiasm they engendered did not come exclusively from preexisting grievances. Because enlarging itself was the Klan's highest priority, it fielded scores of traveling speakers who delivered the message that the country faced a total crisis—of morals, government, and religion. They deployed hyperbole and allegations of terrifying conspiracies to bring in more members and described themselves as part of a team committed to rescuing the country from its internal enemies. Klan speakers, many of whom were ministers skilled in stirring listeners, drew hundreds and occasionally thousands into membership. (Attending lectures was then a standard leisure-time activity.) That speakers stood to profit personally, as we will see below, gave them further motivation to hone their rhetorical skill. We cannot afford to underestimate the power of this rhetoric in building the mass social movement what was the Ku Klux Klan in the 1920s. As sociologists Kathleen Blee and Alberto Melucci remind us, we should understand those grievances as not only intensified but actually produced by this social movement.[6]

Examining the Klan opens a window into a less familiar 1920s. A decade often called the "Roaring Twenties," it has been represented through the "flapper" who drank, smoked, danced, and wore short skirts, through the hot new consumer culture, the birth of commercial radio, and the decade's most important new product, automobiles—the number of cars on the road, 7.5 million by 1920, reached 23 million by 1929. And cars were implicated in the alleged immorality, because they provided not only mobility but sexual privacy for so many young Americans. The Klan thrived by exaggerating these stereotypes of cultural license, and its claim that the country was being led to moral depravity expanded its following.

But these carefree and edgy images sometimes obscure the fact that the vast majority of Americans did not participate in that "roaring" culture. While Jay Gatsby's crowd was dancing the lindy hop, actual voters supported President Harding's promised "return to normalcy," never mind the unprecedented corruption of his administration. His successor, "Silent Cal" Coolidge, combined stodgy respectability with an ideology that "the business of America is business," leaving predatory capitalism entirely unregulated. And his successor, Herbert Hoover, once a hero of wartime relief, stubbornly opposed government action and as a result found himself presiding helplessly over a disastrous economic depression. The Ku Klux Klan supported these presidents. Its politics were mainstream.

It may seem peculiar to label the KKK a social movement, since the better-known movements have been on the political left, such as civil rights and feminism. But almost any of the many scholarly definitions of "social movement" require recognizing it as such.[7] True, many social movements lack central organization; many have no top-down leadership; many do not engage in electoral politics. But many do all of these things. I think of "social movement" as a cluster concept, meaning that it may share some but not necessarily all of many characteristics. These include the active participation of large numbers, acting to produce social change through challenges to elites, developing strong solidarity and reshaping identities, and using strategies and tactics beyond the standard state-governed channels such as electioneering and lobbying. Such movements may be built from the top, even operated as businesses, but once they evoke large-scale grassroots identification and participation, they can become social movements—and may even escape the control of their founders.

The second Klan waned as rapidly as it arose and by 1926 had but a fraction of its peak strength (though it continues today). But many social movements, good and bad, are short-lived. Moreover, although internal rivalries and moral scandals repelled many Klan members, their movement won significant victories. Federal immigration-restriction and anti-miscegenation laws passed by some thirty states institutionalized a significant part of the Klan agenda. Immigration restriction installed the same hierarchy of desirable and undesirable populations that the Klan promoted. The Klan's greatest achievement may have been its influence on political consciousness: its redefinition of Americanness, and thereby of un-Americanism, would long continue to influence the country's political culture.

Precisely because the second Klan was so mainstream, examining it also reveals continuing currents in American history, currents at times rising to the surface, at other times remaining subterranean. Developed during a resurgence of this conservative populism, this book reflects its contemporary context, and is meant to do so. It rests on scholarly research, but like all scholarship, it reflects the politics of its time. In my discussion of the Ku Klux Klan I am not neutral, and like all historians, I cannot and do not wish to discard my values in interpreting the past. Moreover, in my interpretation of the 1920s I could not avoid the influence of later developments, such as European Nazism and fascism in the 1930s, and neo-Nazis, McCarthyists, and Tea Party and Trump supporters.[8] As a result, the question of fascism lurks not far beneath the surface of this investigation, and I will address it briefly at the end of the book. Besides, the fact that I am one of those the Klan detested—a Jew, an intellectual, a leftist, a feminist, a lover of diversity—no doubt also informs this book. I am offering an interpretation, not a scholarly monograph.

But my goal in this interpretation is to understand, not to conduct an argument or mount an attack. Readers in search of ringing denunciations of the Klan's evil may be disappointed. As a student of social movements I am less interested in condemnation than in explanation. Explaining requires that the historian avoid cheap shots and try to understand why perfectly reasonable people supported the Klan. Because the Klan was the biggest social movement of the early twentieth century, and because its ideas echo again today, examining it in order to grasp its attractions seems worthwhile. In what follows, I consider the Ku Klux Klan's methods of recruitment, the satisfactions it brought to its members, and the deep structures of its ideology. Its allures were manifold: they included the rewards of being an insider, of belonging to a community, of expressing and acting on resentments, of participating in drama, of feeling religiously and morally righteous, of turning a profit.

Poster for the film *Birth of a Nation*, which did so much to build the KKK.
(*Everett Historical/Shutterstock*)

Chapter 1

REBIRTH

TWO MEDIA EVENTS AND ONE LYNCHING CATALYZED the eruption of the second Ku Klux Klan. First came the film *Birth of a Nation*, released in 1915 as the adaptation of Thomas Dixon's 1905 novel *The Clansman*.[1] The film showed newly freed slaves rampaging, aiming to rape white women, with the collusion of northern "carpetbaggers." In it, the first Ku Klux Klan stars as the defender of "white womanhood." The film reached a large audience, including President Woodrow Wilson, who showed it at the White House—the first time any movie was shown there—and praised it effusively: "It is like writing history with lightning. And my only regret is that it is all so terribly true."[2] Second, later in 1915, came the lynching of Leo Frank, a Jewish Atlanta businessman falsely accused of rape and murder. Then, two publications contributed: In 1920, Henry Ford published the "Protocols of the Elders of Zion," and distributed half a million copies. A forgery, the "Protocols" claimed to be the minutes of a late nineteenth-century meeting where Jewish leaders discussed their drive for global domination through control of the world's finances and press. Then Ford went on to publish a ninety-one-article series, "The International Jew: The World's Problem," in his newspaper, the *Dearborn Independent*. These articles constituted an extended anti-Semitic rant along the same lines as the "Protocols."[3]

One of the film's viewers was Atlanta physician William Joseph Simmons, a southern racist Spanish-American War veteran (though one who never saw action—his unit reached Cuba only after the war ended) turned self-proclaimed minister. (See figure 2.) Hired as an itinerant preacher by a Methodist Episcopal Church, he was promptly fired for "inefficiency," a trait he duplicated in the Klan.[4] Afterward he drifted among occupations: garter salesman, teacher, and paid organizer for a number of fraternal orders. Seemingly addicted to joining organizations in search of a livelihood—he belonged to several churches and fifteen different fraternal orders—he decided to create his own fraternal group. Inspired by *Birth of a Nation* and the Leo Frank lynching, Simmons began studying up on the first Klan. (He later claimed that the idea came to him in a mystical vision in 1901, but if so, he did not act on it for fourteen years.) He got a copy of the original Klan's "Prescript" and used it, as well as Masonic rites, as a basis for a new ritual. It repeated the first Klan's chorus of hatred and fear of African Americans, arguing that "no new environment" could ever overcome their "hereditary handicap."[5] His propaganda also reflected the anti-radical hysteria of the World War I era. "Startling and indisputable facts," he claimed, showed that "the hairy claw of Bolshevism, Socialism, Syndicalism, I.W.W.ism and other isms . . . are seeking in an insidious but powerful manner to undermine the very fundamentals of the Nation."[6] Governmental actions—framing and executing anarchist immigrants Sacco and Vanzetti, and deporting more than five hundred immigrant citizens accused of disloyalty—created a model for the Klan's fight to exclude the "wrong kind" of people from belonging in America.

In 1915 Simmons advertised, inviting men into a new Ku Klux Klan, which he characterized as "A Classy Order of the Highest Class, No 'Rough Necks,' 'Rowdies,' nor 'Yellow Streaks.' . . . REAL MEN whose oaths are inviolate are needed."[7] He managed to gather a few dozen joiners, including several elderly men who had been members of the first Klan.[8] He appointed himself the Imperial Wizard of the Knights of the Ku Klux Klan. But like the fraternals he knew, his group developed rituals but no plan of action.

Simmons seems to have been somewhat delusional. Among his fabrications was a claim to have been a secret investigator for the federal government during the war, a boast that brought US Secret Service agents to investigate. He maintained, a few years later, that this experience led him to plan a "secret service" of fifty thousand Klansmen who would act as moles, reporting to him on immoral behavior in every community in the United States, behavior the Klan could then correct.[9] He made a disastrous move in buying the financially struggling Baptist Lanier University in Atlanta, which then promised to admit only "real Americans." Each state would build its own building, and poor students would be admitted gratis. Only twenty-five enrolled; forced into bankruptcy, he had to sell it.[10]

Proving not much of an organizer, in five years Simmons managed to collect only a few hundred Klansmen. Moreover, his principles proved weak. Needing an income, in his application to register his new Ku Klux Klan he labeled it a private "bottle club," thus evading Prohibition. He never even produced a roster of members, and his liquor sales were not profitable. His Klan conducted only one public action, at a veterans parade in 1919—and a photo of "his group" in that parade turned out to show twenty African Americans he had paid to dress up in sheets. By 1920 his small new group had stagnated.[11]

The Klan became a power by shifting to a less parochial and more strategic approach, which Simmons developed under the influence of some experienced PR people, Elizabeth Tyler and Edward Young Clarke. Their business, the Southern Publicity Association, was already in the Klan's network because it had contracted to promote the Prohibitionist Anti-Saloon League. Their partnership was a cross-class alliance between the social top and bottom: Clarke's father, who had been a Confederate colonel, owned the *Atlanta Constitution* and occupied a central position among Atlanta's power elite. Clarke's brother managed the paper. Edward Clarke was a college graduate but seems to have been a laid-back young man, a dabbler, never a hard worker, accustomed to a privileged life. He held a sinecure as religion editor for the paper but soon tired of the work. His life changed when he met "Bessie" Tyler. From a poor family of six children, barely educated, married at fifteen, a mother at sixteen, soon widowed, she exhibited unusual ambition and would become one of the country's most powerful and influential women, and one of the very richest.

The team saw a lucrative client in Simmons's new Klan group. "The minute we said Ku Klux," Tyler recalled, "editors from all over the United States began literally pressing us for publicity." By 1920 she and Clarke had convinced Simmons that they could grow his new Klan, that it had national potential. To realize that potential it had to multiply its bigotry. The alleged threat from black people would not reverberate among northerners at a time when so few African Americans lived outside the Southeast. So Simmons hired them, signing a contract that gave Clarke and Tyler an astonishing 80 percent of any revenue they brought in from new recruits.[12] Since Simmons had got nowhere with his new organization, he undoubtedly thought that he had nothing to lose in giving them four-fifths of anything they could bring in.

Tyler and Clarke became, in practice, head of the Klan for two years. (Some historians cite only Clarke in discussing their work for the KKK, revealing what I suspect is an unconscious assumption that the woman would naturally play only a secondary role in the business.) They turned Simmons into a polished speaker. Engendering and exploiting fear, he would warn that "degenerative" forces were destroying the American way of life. These were not only black people but also Jews, Catholics, and immigrants, the big-city dwellers who were tempting Americans with immoral pleasures—sex, alcohol, and music, notably jazz.[13] Only a fusion of racial purity and evangelical Christian morality could save the country. But the old Klan's "white" supremacy over blacks was no longer up to the task; only the supremacy of Anglo-Saxon Protestants, aka "100% Americans," could save the country. "The Anglo-Saxon is the typeman of history. To him must yield the self-centered Hebrew, the cultured Greek, the virile Roman, the mystic Oriental."[14] The second Klan took off by melding racism and ethnic bigotry with evangelical Protestant morality.

Clarke and Tyler used several modern techniques. They "offered" newspapers private interviews with Simmons, who turned out to be a charming and eloquent spinner of his propaganda. They placed advertisements that included membership application forms in newspapers. They sent out press releases that tied the Klan to any remotely relevant news story. They offered free memberships to ministers, presented to each as a rare honor. By January 1921 they had allegedly trained and deployed over a thousand recruiters; by that summer they claimed 850,000 new members.[15] A contemporary observer estimated the Klan's growth at a hundred thousand new members a week.[16] (These were probably exaggerations, but they convey contemporary observers' amazement at its exponential growth.) The team also turned this new fraternal order into a serious moneymaker, through dues and the sale of regalia. Simmons got a $33,000 home in Atlanta, known as Klankrest, two expensive cars, and a bonus of $25,000 ($300,000 today). He also purchased the Peachtree Creek Civil War battleground, sacred to the Confederacy, planning to build a university there—another of his unrealized fantasies. Tyler and Clarke profited handsomely, too, allegedly taking in more than $850,000 in their first fifteen months on the job.[17]

By late 1921, some of the new Klan members were complaining about this profiteering, while other leaders objected to Simmons's morals: never a hard-line social-purity man, he liked horse races and prizefights, and his partying was making him a noticeable drunkard.[18] Two regional Klan leaders—Hiram Evans from Texas and David Stephenson from Indiana—came to see Simmons as an obstacle to further development. So together with Tyler and Clarke, they executed a coup: they deceived Simmons into accepting the title "emperor" but ceding control. They had to buy Simmons out, for $140,000, since the Klan was legally his wholly owned business.[19] When he realized that he had been ousted, he started another fraternal order, Knights of the Flaming Sword (Klanspeople loved medieval martial titles), which flopped; then still another racist group, the White Band; but died in obscurity in 1945.[20] These early leadership conflicts presaged the rivalries that would terminally undermine the Klan by the end of the decade.

Hiram Evans became the Imperial Wizard in November 1922. (See figure 3.) A man of boundless vision, ambition, and confidence, Evans hailed from Alabama but grew up in Texas. Like Clarke, he was well born, the son of a judge; unlike Clarke he had an elite education, at Vanderbilt. His first career, as a dentist, might seem modest—one of his rivals liked to call him a "tooth-puller"—and he took advantage of this impression, calling himself "the most average man in America," so as to normalize the Klan.[21] His short, plump stature added to his everyman image. In fact, he was capable of serious violence: in Dallas, where he joined the Klan in 1920, he had organized "black squads" that kidnapped and tortured at least one black man.[22] In 1921, recognizing his aggressive leadership, Clarke and Tyler asked him to take charge of membership recruitment, offering him a guaranteed base salary of $7,500 plus commissions. In return, after becoming Imperial Wizard, he fired them. They had made the Klan a national force, and he had no further need for their services—certainly no need to give them their astounding 80 percent of Klan revenue. (Still, Tyler and Clarke continued to profit from the KKK, opening a realty business to handle Klan properties in Atlanta.[23])

As Klan boss, Evans became a reformer. He imagined the Klan as a political party and made electoral politics his top priority. To accomplish this he made the Klan fully national, moved its headquarters to

Washington, DC, and sold the Atlanta "Imperial Palace"—to the
Catholic Church! He held up ex-presidents Grover Cleveland and
Woodrow Wilson as Klan heroes. He hired professional speechwriters
and attorneys and established numerous publications. One of them
was a stealth magazine, *Fellowship Forum*, designed to promote "pure
Americanism" among those who "shy away from the mention of the Ku
Klux Klan."[24] Acknowledging the need to purify the Klan, he tried to
combat drinking and other moral infractions among members, threatening sinners with expulsion. He denounced violence and revised the
oath to make recruits swear to uphold the law. He urged members to
avoid using their masks when not participating in formal rituals. In the
hopes of cleansing the Klan of corruption, he put recruiters on salary
rather than commission. He urged recruiters to investigate potential
members more carefully. Some complied. The LaGrande, Oregon,
Klan minutes listed those rejected: "Howard Grove, part Indian; Roy
Clapp, for bankruptcy too many times; William Snell, for living with a
woman not officially his wife . . . Alonzo Dunn, character and affiliations questioned."[25] But the pressure to grow the Klan and the opportunity for leaders and salesmen to enrich themselves often militated
against compliance with this reform.

Evans may have been naïve about management. Observing the ora-
torical skills of Indiana Klan leader David Stephenson, another young
man on the make, Evans made him the chief recruiter for seven states.
This turned out to be a major mistake. With a vast and open field for
profit and power, Stephenson became a rival to Evans, and his criminal
activity contributed to the Klan's decline. "I'm a nobody from nowhere,
really—but I've got the biggest brains," he boasted. "I'm going to be
the biggest man in the United States!" But Stephenson was a fraud
several times over. He claimed to be the millionaire son of a wealthy
businessman and to have earned a decoration for bravery in World War
I. In fact he was the son of a Texas sharecropper, his education at a

parochial school (!) ended with the eighth grade, and his stint with the army was as a recruiter in Iowa. He boasted of owning wholesale coal supply and auto accessory companies but in fact worked as a salesman for someone else's coal company. He married at least three women, drank heavily, got into fights, beat his wives, and attempted to rape several other women.

Stephenson was, however, a lively speaker. As a teenager in Oklahoma, he had been attracted by the famed Socialist Oscar Ameringer and got a job with the Socialist Party newspaper. He was drawn not to Socialist ideas but to Ameringer's style, which entailed selling his politics like a vaudeville pitchman. From him Stephenson learned how to work a crowd at Klan events.[26] An enterprising publicist, he turned the Indiana Klan newsletter, the *Fiery Cross*, into a newspaper and gathered nine hundred boys to sell it throughout the Midwest, claiming to reach three hundred thousand readers. He grew the Klan enormously; in southern Indiana, some 23 percent of native-born white men joined. He developed a mystique around his leadership by not allowing his subordinates to use his name, so the rank-and-file Klansmen knew him only as "the Old Man." In that position he too made himself millions and acquired a mansion in Atlanta, a summer home, and a luxurious yacht that he kept on Lake Erie.[27] But despite wealth and authority, Stephenson could not tame his out-of-control drinking and aggression, which would ultimately undermine the whole organization.

WHAT ALL THESE FOUNDERS SHARED was respectability; however much they exaggerated or lied, they passed as honorable citizens, and that was key to the Klan's success. It was not secret because it did not need to be. It remained legal and reputable. Local KKKs were often listed in city directories, "along with sewing clubs and agricultural societies," as sociologist Kathleen Blee put it. In Dinuba, California, the Klan recruited through an advertisement in the high school annual. In Kokomo, Indiana, the *Daily Tribune* announced Klan meetings in its front-page "What's Doing" column. The Johnson County, Indiana, fair designated a "Klan Day" during which all shops and offices were to close at noon. In some towns and cities, a significant proportion of residents were members or belonged to members' families.[28] Many spoke of their Klan membership with pride, and scholars who interviewed Klan members decades later found that most of them remained unashamed, because they did not consider it a "hate group."[29] The Klan's ordinariness, which arose in part from its "dog whistle" methods—that is, singing different tunes to different populations— and in part from sheer duplicity, maximized its influence. Some Klanspeople in some locations preferred to hide their membership, but none felt the need to hide their agreement with its agenda. That the Klan produced whites-only and Protestants-only sociability did not make it exceptional, because most Americans socialized in segregated spaces.

Some contemporary 1920s critics made the erroneous assumption that merely exposing the Klan would isolate and shrink it. That folly was demonstrated when in 1921 the *New York World* newspaper published a series of investigative reports on the KKK by a disaffected former Klansman, including an official list of its recruiters; the articles were syndicated and published simultaneously in newspapers throughout the country. The reporters and editors expected these revelations of KKK bigotry and vigilantism to put an end to its revival. Instead they generated a large increase in its membership,[30] signs of the anypublicity-is-good-publicity effect and of the welcome its ideas received.

Similarly, opponents generated congressional hearings about the Ku Klux Klan, conducted by the House Committee on Rules in 1921. This too grew the Klan. As its spokesman, Simmons presented the KKK as a benign fraternalist and nativist organization—nativism, aka anti-immigrationism, being completely respectable. The hearings concluded that no action was required.[31] As a journalist for *Collier's* wrote, "Congress, by failure to act, gave Simmons a chance to say that it had put its stamp of approval on the strange new order." When Simmons returned to Atlanta, "calls began pouring in from . . . all over America for the right to organize Klans." Simmons told a journalist that "we worked twenty-four hours a day trying to meet the demand."[32] In other words, testimony that liberals would find appalling appealed, by contrast, to many Americans.

Many contemporary scholars and critics, such as Frank Bohn, Clarence Darrow, Frank Tannenbaum, and William Allen White, branded the Ku Klux Klan an aberration, an outlier in the national political culture. In that understanding they shared, ironically, a key Klannish idea: that one and only one ideology was truly American. For most of these critics, that was liberal individualism. This premise led them to diagnose the Ku Klux Klan's rise as the inane hysteria of uneducated, lowbrow hicks, a "booboisie." In branding Klansmen as backward, uneducated, isolated from culture, provincial, insane, busybodies, believers in ghosts, gullible, shabby of mind, social deviants, and representative of the lower classes, critics were expressing a snobbish disdain often repeated in urban elite responses to populism. The liberal *New Republic* magazine echoed this disdain, even suggesting that people joined the Klan because of the monotony and boredom of small-town life.[33] (Klanspeople simply ricocheted that disdain, condemning the immoral vices and mixed cultures of the metropolis.) More accurately but equally disdainfully, the renowned southern historian Francis Butler Simkins called it "an authentic folk movement."[34]

Scholars also condemned the Klan as an example of the irrationality of the crowd, a theme developed in the 1960s by historian Richard Hofstadter.[35] He identified a "paranoid style" in American mass politics, which he identified with its reliance on conspiracy theories, as in the Klan's allegations of secretive Catholic and Jewish plots to take over the United States.

Popular writers also mocked Klanspeople's conformity. Novelist

Sinclair Lewis regularly made fun of the Klan type: George Babbitt, in his 1922 novel *Babbitt*, gave birth to a common noun that describes a close-minded, narrow-minded, conformist whose interests and ethics were confined to his business world: "Just as he was an Elk, a Booster, just as the priests of the Presbyterian Church determined his every religious belief . . . so did the large national advertisers fix the surface of his life, fix what he believed to be his individuality."[36] In his 1926 *Elmer Gantry*, Lewis specifically ridiculed the evangelical and racist beliefs of his hero.

Writing in 1967, historian Kenneth Jackson disproved the small-town-hick thesis by showing the Klan's great strength in the cities. Studying nine cities between 1915 and 1930, he showed that 50 percent of active Klanspeople were urbanites, and 32 percent lived in the country's larger cities: there were at least fifty thousand Klansmen in Chicago, thirty-eight thousand in Indianapolis, thirty-five thousand in Philadelphia, and the same number in Detroit, for example.[37] Others have since shown that in many states Klan per capita membership was larger in cities than in smaller places.

The condescending diagnoses of the Klan's popularity by its critics ignored how many other elites and intellectuals shared its worldview. The Klan's favorite term for the whites they approved of, "Nordic," probably came from Columbia- and Yale-educated lawyer Madison Grant, a distinguished exponent of "scientific" racism; his 1916 book *The Passing of the Great Race* raised an alarm about the new non-"Nordic" immigrants, such as Italians and Jews; he recommended requiring that these "unfavorable races be kept segregated in ghettos." Woodrow Wilson and many in his administration regularly voiced anti-Semitic opinions. American colleges and universities systematically applied quotas to Jewish applicants; as Jewish immigrants began to achieve academic success, Columbia's medical school reduced its proportion of Jewish students from 47 percent in 1920 to 6 percent in 1940.[38] Congressional debate on the immigration-restriction bills of the 1920s referenced the deplorable "fact" that 80 to 90 percent of the undesirables were Jews. As H. L. Mencken pointed out, "If the Klan is against the Jews, so are . . . three-quarters of the good clubs.[39]

Anti-Catholicism was not confined to the Klan either. A weekly newspaper from Missouri, the *Menace*, devoted specifically to anti-Catholicism, had a circulation of 1.5 million. Populist southern politician Tom Watson used "tested and proved" anti-Catholicism to win.[40] The Sons and Daughters of Washington (referring to George, not the location), various Protestant newspapers, immigration restrictionist groups and politicians—the list of Catholic-haters included many organizations, politicians, and media across the nation. The bigoted Hearst newspapers were then the largest media conglomerate in the world. Frank Bohn, a Klan opponent who published in the *American Journal of Sociology*, wrote of the "dangerous theory . . . that anyone over twenty-one . . . can vote intelligently" and lamented that "barbaric and totally illiterate negro slaves, directly after their emancipation, were permitted to vote and sit in the state legislatures" and that "millions of peasants . . . mostly illiterate and possessed of not the slightest background of political experience . . . have been invited to join us and hastily receive all the rights and privileges of citizenship."[41]

Klan race thought mirrored the principles of eugenics, accepted in the 1920s as state-of-the-art science. Resting on Lamarck's mistaken genetics, eugenical theory assumed that socially acquired characteristics could be inherited. From this pseudo-science it logically followed that those of northern European ancestry ruled because they were superior and deserved to rule. Leading eugenists such as Madison Grant and Harvard PhD Lothrop Stoddard led the campaign to encourage greater fertility among the "superior" class and to discourage fertility among the inferior class—and their definitions of these classes were identical to the Klan's. Many universities and colleges required students to study eugenics. Every biology textbook of the period included a chapter on eugenics. The National Education Association formed a eugenical practices committee.[42] Thirty states passed eugenical compulsory sterilization laws. In short, there was nothing aberrant in the Klan's racial hierarchy.

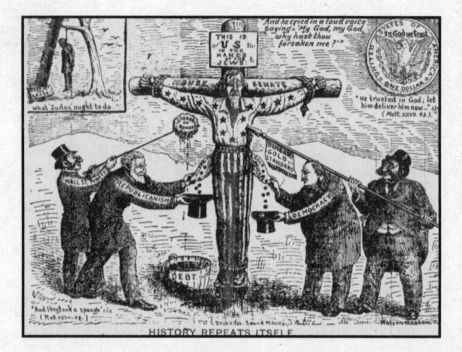

Cartoon from *Sound Money* magazine, 1896.

Chapter 2

ANCESTORS

THE KU KLUX KLAN OF THE 1920S HAD SIX ANCESTORS, each of them long embedded in American history. Each of them contributed one of the Klan's six main ideological components: racism, nativism, temperance, fraternalism, Christian evangelicalism, and populism.

The first parent, obviously, was the original Klan. This lineage was familial as well as organizational: Confederate General Nathan Bedford Forrest, Imperial Wizard of the first Klan, was the grandfather of Nathan Bedford Forrest II, Grand Dragon of the Georgia realm of the second Klan. That Simmons wanted to appropriate the Ku Klux Klan name for his new venture resulted from both lack of imagination and filial pride. He continued not only the Klan's name but also its alias, the Invisible Empire.[1]

The first Ku Klux Klan arose in 1866, just after the Civil War, but became most potent after the federal government abdicated its responsibility to guarantee the political citizenship of black men (not women) through the franchise and declined to create a basis for the economic survival of the freedpeople. Klansmen convinced themselves and their supporters that the abolition of slavery put the south into a crisis: freedpeople and "carpetbaggers" were running amok, assaulting white women, and threatening white power. To prevent disaster, the

Klan claimed, white men of courage had no choice but to defend their society. They did this through terrorist lynchings and beatings, strategically employed, suppressing black citizenship at the polls and in the courts, and reimposing black economic subjugation through sharecropping. This Klan used a veneer of secrecy to maintain the fiction that the perpetrators of racist violence were unknown. In fact, they were well known: their lynchings rested on widespread white consent and the open collusion of law-and-order officials. Klan secrecy served not to protect its members, who needed no protection, but to intensify its fear-inducing aura.

For the second Klan, by contrast, northern society, economy, and law created more constraints. Liberal tenets of the rule of law were stronger, so without maintaining a law-abiding legitimacy the Ku Klux Klan could not have spread so widely. Legitimacy did not make the 1920s Klan less reactionary or bigoted but did underlie its success.[2] These latter-day Klansmen practiced various secret rituals and paraded in masks but often proudly proclaimed their membership; the Klan ran candidates in elections, advertised openly, and sponsored popular events open to all. (When the state of Michigan prohibited wearing masks in public, the state's Klan membership actually increased.[3]) While the second Klan did little lynching, it did at times employ nonlethal and occasionally lethal terrorism, in which police forces were active participants.

The Klan's second parent was nativism, an anti-immigrant movement and state of mind. Its bequest provided its offspring a route to legitimacy. Nativism already had a long and respectable tradition in the United States, a tradition that encouraged the second Klan to broaden its enemies list beyond African Americans. Nativism's major organization had been the American Protective Association (APA), founded in 1887, which descended, in turn, from the "Know Nothings," an anti-immigrant political party begun in 1855.[4] The Daughters of the American Revolution similarly resented immigration and used language that the Klan would adopt—creating the category "pure Americans" to refer to those of undiluted Anglo-Saxon heritage.[5] Thus hostility to new immigrants was already seventy years old when the second Klan reinvigorated it. The APA prefigured many of the second Klan's principles: although denying that it was anti-Catholic, the APA denounced "Romanism" as inimical to patriotism—because Catholics obeyed the pope's teachings, they could not be truly republican. The APA took up the victim position, a stance characteristic of many conservative groups. It claimed that Catholics were not only plotting to take over the country but immigrating in order to effect a takeover. Its false claims— that 60 to 90 percent of government employees were illiterate Catholics, that the army and navy had already been "Romanized," that priests regularly desecrated the American flag—went unchallenged by many. APA members, like Klansmen later, had to swear that "I will do all in my power to retard and break down the power of the Pope . . . will not countenance the nomination . . . of a Roman Catholic for any office . . . [and] will not employ a Roman Catholic."[6] Nativist attitudes toward Jews were equally hostile but more complex, even contradictory. They branded Jews both congenitally stupid—eugenist Henry Goddard's "tests" allegedly showed that 60 percent of Jews were morons—and diabolically clever communists even as they were rapacious money-grubbers squeezing money out of virtuous Protestants. In both respects, the Klan and similar nativists saw Jews as a threat to American values.

Opposing immigration might seem a tricky posture in a country where none of the whites (or blacks) were indigenous, but these organizations focused specifically on the large-scale inmigration of Catholics, Orthodox Christians (sometimes called "Greek Catholics"), and Jews that had begun in the 1880s. The Klan argued not only for an end to the immigration of non-"Nordics" but also for deporting those already here. The date of their inmigration, their longevity in the United States, mattered not. The country should expel "certain types and races which will not in a hundred years of residence here be anything but a menace. They should be kept out—and put out."[7]

Today these claims might be read as religious prejudice, not racism. But at the time, religion, race, and nation were concepts loosely applied. For nativists, Protestantism was patriotism, and non-Protestants were disloyal. Replicating this fusion, Klan ideologues also denied that they were hostile to Catholics and insisted that if Catholics would practice their religion without their "Roman" hierarchy, the Klan would have no objections to their presence. Catholics were welcome to convert. By contrast, Jews and nonwhites—and many at the time still considered Jews nonwhite—were unredeemable, "hopeless," never able to participate in American citizenship.[8] In Klanspeak, "white" sometimes meant Protestant; an Oregon Klavern worked to defeat a Catholic running for Congress "in order to have three congressmen who are white men."[9]

A pair of anti-liquor organizations—the Women's Christian Temperance Union (WCTU) and the Anti-Saloon League (ASL)—also passed on their genes to the Klan. The larger association, the WCTU, called for prohibiting not only liquor but also tobacco, prostitution, immorality in entertainment, and Sunday store opening. Its temperance ideas were complex, imbued with some feminist impulses—fueled particularly by anger at the violence and deprivation that women and children suffered as a result of men's drinking. WCTU temperance rhetoric foregrounded stories of drunken men who were not only abusers but also nonsupporters, leaving their families in want by spending the household budget in saloons. Like earlier social-purity organizations, the WCTU offered a Victorian feminist analysis of prostitution, as the victimization of helpless women by male sexual predators. Its hostility to risqué imagery and entertainments reflected the assumption that any erotic material was injurious to women. Its anti-tobacco rhetoric expressed gendered resentment of male-only spaces, which reinforced men's conviction that they were born to rule—over both the country and their women and children.

Given its woman-centered principles, the WCTU might not seem akin to the Klan. But that kinship was mutual: the Women's Ku Klux Klan articulated similar women's rights claims, while the WCTU's racial and religious views mirrored those of the KKK. Both organizations identified immigrants and non-Protestants as the source of all the social vices. Both believed that Catholic immigrants had brought the scourge of alcohol into a culture that had previously been on a path to reject it. The temperance organizations made little distinction among different quantities and types of alcohol consumption. To them, Italian immigrants who drank wine (often watered wine) with their meals at home were no different from the Irish who drank ale and whiskey in pubs, and this blanket intolerance both reflected and strengthened anti-immigrant sentiment. So the anti-liquor groups looked askance both at big cities, with their commerce in alcohol and "loose morals," and at mining camps and factory towns, where male leisure led to drunkenness, brawls, prostitution, and rape. Hostility to cities also stemmed from the belief that immigrants and liquor brought political corruption.

The WCTU, the ASL, and the KKK also drew on the same constituencies—mainly evangelical Protestants who lived outside the big cities. Moreover, their memberships overlapped: many Klanswomen were also WCTU members, and many Klansmen were also members of the ASL.[10] As Clarence Darrow put it in 1924, "The father and mother of the Ku Klux is the Anti-Saloon League. I would not say every Anti-Saloon Leaguer is a Ku Kluxer, but every Ku Kluxer is an Anti-Saloon Leaguer."[11]

These three parents instilled a set of beliefs in their offspring. The Klan's fourth parent—the hundreds of fraternal societies in the United States—bestowed upon its child a mode of male bonding through brotherhood and ritual. Fraternal organizations have received little recognition in explaining Klan origins, no doubt because so many studies of the Klan focus on denouncing its outrages. By contrast, there seemed nothing outrageous about the fraternals. Many were mutual benefit societies, essentially insurance cooperatives providing for burials, medical expenses, and the support of widows. Their members contributed monthly or weekly payments and could receive help in crises—especially deaths, illnesses, or accidents. They provided a bit of security in the absence of a welfare state. Other fraternals were only clubs, creating conviviality, joviality, and economic opportunities. The largest were the Masons and the Odd Fellows, followed by the Knights of Pythias, the Ancient Order of United Workmen, the Knights of the Maccabees, and the Colored Masons. In 1897 some 5.4 million Americans belonged to fraternal orders, a number increasing to 10.2 million by 1926, with half a million children in affiliated youth groups. All provided opportunities for networking, a process even more important in this time before newspaper want-ads offered jobs. But above all the fraternals offered male friendship and entertainment in male-only spaces.[12] (Klanswomen also belonged to many sororal groups, but these were more often service and church groups.)

Overlap was particularly large between the KKK and the Masons, an order that had long been anti-Catholic. One Mason reported that "Klan-joining became contagious and ran epidemic" throughout the Masonic lodges in the 1920s.[13] In some locations, 60 percent or more of Klansmen were Masons.[14] Wherever the Klan was particularly strong, so were the Masons. The Klan ritual created by Simmons—its props, ceremonies, and ranks—drew heavily on Masonic rites. Klan recruiters typically began by using Masonic lodge membership lists. Not all Masons approved of the Klan, and some denounced it, but their protests could not overcome the widespread perception that the two organizations were comrades in arms.[15]

In fact, to many observers—and members—the Ku Klux Klan was just another such fraternal order; one Klan advertisement even called it "a Standard Fraternal Order."[16] A Wisconsin Klan recruiter called the Klan "a high, close, mystic, social, patriotic, benevolent association having a perfected lodge system."[17] Some recruiters invited men to meetings without naming the KKK.[18] Like the Klan, many fraternals employed arcane rituals—oaths, ordeals real or symbolic, initiation and installation rituals, and esoteric ceremonies. Like the Klan, they set out hierarchical ladders for members to climb, as in Scouting, but with fanciful, typically military titles—Field Marshal, Most Excellent Commander, Sublime Augustus, Dictator, Grand Knight, and Chancellor Commander. And almost all kept their rituals secret.[19] So Klan practices seemed ordinary to members of fraternal orders. In Indiana, the Klan appeared to some rural people merely an addition to their familiar Order of Patrons of Husbandry, known as the Grange. That organization, deeply rooted in midwestern America, already functioned as a center of sociability, with picnics, dances, and meetings that included Protestant worship. Maine fisherman Charlie York explained, "I never enjoyed any Lodge so much as I did the Klan at first. It had the principle of brotherly love for feller members and they was a high moral tone to it."[20]

In its exclusiveness the Klan was not particularly exceptional among fraternals. Almost all of them were religiously segregated: Catholics had the Knights of Columbus, among others; Jews had B'nai B'rith. Most were also ethnically delimited; different Slavic groups, for example, had separate fraternal organizations. "Since Catholics, Jews and Negroes all had their own secret orders," why shouldn't white Protestants do the same, a California Klansman argued.[21] Accused of excluding non-Anglo Saxons and non-Protestants from membership, the Imperial Wizard asked why it should be targeted when so many other groups limited membership similarly.[22] In some ways the northern KKK was more catholic (pun intended) than other fraternals, because it was open to a large majority of Protestant residents in its strongholds, regardless of their ethnicity, provided they were "Nordic." This meant that in places where Catholics, Jews, and people of color were few, Klan membership was open to almost everyone.

Christian evangelicalism was the fifth parent. Evangelicals never united into a single denomination but had been a major force in American Protestantism since the revivals of the early nineteenth century. The evangelical mission—to bring ever more people into born-again commitment—faced challenges by the 1920s, to the extent that some historians have argued that it was in crisis. Fundamentalism, the belief in the literal and inerrant accuracy of the Protestant Bible, was poaching members from the traditional evangelical groups, spreading particularly its denunciation of new science and social science. The "mainline" Protestant sects were also growing, drawing in congregants who tended to be more educated, more urban, and more liberal than the evangelicals. Clarence Darrow's humiliation of fundamentalist William Jennings Bryan in the Scopes "Monkey Trial" further threatened the prestige of evangelicals.[23] As often happens when closed worldviews are challenged, after the trial many evangelicals turned to more extreme creeds, such as premillenialism, the belief that Jesus would return bodily to gather in his saints, those whose rebirth had thoroughly cleansed them of sin. Accordingly, in this prediction, Jesus would then rule a world of peace for a thousand years, the final age of earthly history. These beliefs would appear in some local Klans, and as a whole the Klan could be said to represent an evangelical rebirth.

The Klan, in turn, strengthened the evangelical battle against sin. Defending Prohibition, one of the Klan's highest priorities, particularly attracted evangelicals, while the Klan fostered their anger at immodest entertainments (movies, dance halls, burlesque), advertising, and women's clothing, especially bathing suits. In doing so, the Klan also strengthened evangelical hostility to the groups they charged with purveying indecency: Negroes, Catholics, Jews.

"Populism," a label often applied to the Ku Klux Klan, points to another of its ancestors. But "populism" is a slippery term. In the 1890s "populism" was a left movement. Especially strong in the rural and small-town West and Midwest, the Populist Party elected eleven gov-

ernors and forty-five members of Congress. It expressed the economic
grievances of small grain and cotton farmers, coal miners, railroad
workers, and small businessmen against big finance and big business,
especially the railroads, whose policies were hurting them. These Populists shared a "producerist" ethic, which honored those who produced
goods or services while denigrating those who earned without producing, by merely managing, owning, lending money, or buying and selling.
But that ethic was malleable; as in many social movements, populists
were varied and inconsistent. The producerist ethic did not stop clerks,
merchants, or even "managers" such as school principals from supporting the party. Still, the Populists laid out specific proposals designed
to benefit working people, both agricultural and industrial. The Populist platform called for a progressive income tax, abolition of national
banks, direct election of senators, an eight-hour working day, and government regulation of railroads, telegraphs, and telephone services.
This populism not only spoke in the name of the common people but
also mobilized common people into political activism.[24]

Like most other broad movements, populism encompassed regional
variation and contradictory sympathies. Populists of the 1890s could
be found on both sides of labor conflicts, could be both bookish and
studious but also anti-intellectual, and could be racist or anti-racist.
In the South, leaders mobilized white support by exploiting and inten-
sifying racism. Congressman Tom Watson of Georgia, for example,
supported the whole Populist program; his most lasting victory was
institutionalizing rural free delivery of mail, a major boon to farmers. Yet he became a virulent racist when that became a way to win
elections.

A century later, "populism" has become a term applied to social
movements that express anger. By this definition any movement critical
of the status quo and evoking grassroots activism could be called populist, and the term thereby loses any specificity. The label is also applied
to movements that claim to speak for "the people," and in this sense it

can denote movements of both left and right. Hence the phrase "right-wing populism," used recently to delineate a movement more narrowly. Salvaging the term's usefulness, however, requires more precision. One common denominator in populism is its claim to be the authentic voice of "the people," and a manifestation of "the people's" will. That presumption has often led populists to deem their enemies inauthentic, to denounce not only their opinions but their entitlement to be considered honorable citizens—or even, in the case of the KKK, citizens at all. Thus populist rhetoric often asserts that the nation is being stolen by those who do not represent the people; that the people are being robbed of their birthright. It is that claim to a unique authenticity that often moves populism to the political right, because it evokes a mystical, doctrinal, ahistorical concept of "the people," a concept that often demands racial "purity."

These attitudes make some populists illiberal, uncomfortable with diverse opinions, and disinclined to protect dissenters. Among the many dangers of imagining the existence of one genuine nation is a call for the people to be undivided in their will. The second Klan trafficked in precisely that mystification of the nation. Its call for homogeneity provided the underlying ostinato in the Klan's song of patriotism. The Populist Party had encompassed political diversity, while the Klan formulated and imposed a singular set of beliefs. Even its perspective on immorality boiled down to a racialized Protestant intolerance of cultural difference. It is this conception that makes right-leaning populists so often hypernationalists, hostile to internationalism and cosmopolitanism.

Within the sacred nation, the KKK fumed, powerful but stealthy forces were injuring the majority and its values. But the KKK never enunciated an agenda that might have benefited working people or even small businessmen. Neither did it aim its fury at those responsible for injuring the people. For example, when the Klan praised Robert La Follette's Progressive Party in 1924, it was not because he called for public ownership of railroads but because of his isolationism, notably his opposition to US membership in the World Court.[25]

The Klan's enemies were not economic exploiters, unlike those of the Populist Party. While spouting a small-business ethic—honoring individual entrepreneurship as the basis for American greatness—it did not challenge economic policies that served big capital. Instead it blamed the country's woes on two overlapping categories of unpatriotic Americans: African American, Catholic, and Jewish minorities, but also big-city liberals, "a cosmopolitan intelligentsia devoted to foreign creeds and ethnic identities," whose culture was "without moral standards," that is, secular. When the Klan railed against big money, as it did very occasionally, it did so because it saw big money as Jewish.

Corrupt politicians arose, the Klan thought, from these enemy groups. It condemned corruption not among corporate or political leaders but only among small-time, big-city pols, and they were always identified as Catholics or Jews. (One major inconsistency marked this perspective: the Klan condemned the political class even as it worked to elect its own politicians.)

Many commentators think of populists as demagogues. If we define demagogues as rabble-rousers, leaders who exploit and build prejudice to elicit feverish rage while shutting down deliberation, it becomes clear that not all populist leaders were demagogues. Earlier progressive populists indeed spoke in honorific terms about salt-of-the-earth citizens and fulminated against economic and political barons, but also propounded structural criticisms and proposals for reform. The Ku Klux Klan, by contrast, used demagoguery as its exclusive approach—to recruitment, to persuading voters, to coercing elected representatives. Its leaders built fear through outrageous conspiracy allegations, fake news, and scapegoating. They whipped up intense rage. Passionate oratory, of course, marks many political campaigns, of all ideological persuasions. But the Klan used it exclusively to banish nonconformists and people of the "wrong" race and religion from Americanism. While the northern Klan carried out few lynchings or beatings, its propaganda constituted cultural, religious, racial, and political violence, and thereby legitimated physical violence in the eyes of angrier members.

In these ways the Ku Klux Klan created a populism focused on defending a privileged status—of race and religion—that it saw eroding. To categorize the Klan as "populist," then, requires modifiers that distinguish it. Its populist heredity is apparent, but so are its other five ancestors. And out of those the Klan created something new.

New but not, of course, completely original. The Klan had absorbed and remixed earlier influences, but its novelty never took it out of the American mainstream. In its prejudices it was, just as it claimed, "100% American." Never an aberration, the KKK may actually have enunciated values with which a majority of 1920s Americans agreed. But the Klannish spin whirled these ideas into greater intensity. The Klan argued that the nation itself was threatened. Then it declared itself a band of warriors determined to thwart that threat. In the military metaphors that filled Klan rhetoric, it had been directed by God— a Protestant God, of course—to lead an army of right-minded people to defeat the nation's internal enemies.

Anti-immigration cartoon.

(The Ohio State University Billy Ireland Cartoon Library & Museum)

Chapter 3

STRUCTURES OF FEELING

IN PROMOTING ITS IDEOLOGY, THE KLAN DID NOT only enunciate a set of principles, a faith, an ideology. It also fused its political and social ideas with an intense emotionality. This may well be an aspect of demagoguery, though it happens in many belief systems. To understand Klannish ideals we have to examine how Klanspeople felt. Like earlier nativists and racists, recruits entered the Klan because its ideas jibed with their own but then had their often inchoate attitudes organized into a particular "structure of feeling," to use Raymond Williams's concept.[1] To grasp this, we must rid ourselves of the notion that emotions are "innate" and instinctive; they can be learned as much as information can be, constructed as much as political positions can be. Sociologist Arlie Hochschild describes how groups develop shared emotions through "feeling rules";[2] the rules can be consciously and unconsciously taught, as for example when schoolchildren learn national pride through reciting the Pledge of Allegiance or singing an anthem, or when anti-abortion discourse "taught" women to feel guilty after abortions. To understand Klan assumptions and principles, then, we need to conceive of them as emotions as well as ideas.

The first Klan fought for a simple goal—to maintain white supremacy over African Americans—but its actions also intensified white fear of blacks. Although anti-black prejudice was not a major theme for the second Klan, it fostered those fears: "We believe in the supremacy of the white race, and that it is just and right the younger brothers should be taught to respect those lines of birth and color which the Creator in His superior wisdom has drawn."[3] At times Klan racism reflected white dependence on black labor: "By some scheme of Providence the Negro was created as a serf." At other times it apparently did not register this dependence and even argued for genocide, as when it debated the relative merits of reenslavement or extermination.[4] Despite this, Klan officers frequently insisted that the Klan did not preach hate but sought the "best interest" of black people—which meant keeping them in a servile place with few political and civil rights.

The Klan also built emotional abhorrence of "race mixing," an obsession built in part through titillating and sexually suggestive rhetoric. Classical Greek culture "receded as a result of absorption of the blood of colored races," and "Rome fell because she mixed her blood."[5] A Klan lecturer worked up a crowd by declaring that 113 mixed marriages were performed in Boston in the last year; "I'm sorry to say it was white women marrying black men. We must protect American womanhood." To which "a shuddering 'Yes, yes' went up from the crowd."[6] Local Klans showed and reshowed *Birth of a Nation* throughout the country (see figure 1) and used *Birth of a Nation*–type scare talk in speeches and publications: "The negro in whose blood flows the mad desire for race amalgamation is more dangerous than a maddened wild beast."[7]

Like many other racisms, the Klan's attitude toward African Americans exhibited a contradiction. On the one hand, it characterized African Americans as incapable of "understanding, sharing, or contributing to Americanism," let alone strategic action.[8] It frequently published "darky" jokes, and its speakers repeated them, with their demeaning renditions of allegedly ignorant African American speech and logic. Such a people, in the Klannish mind, could never operate in a modern society, let alone in a democracy. They were happy in their servility, uninterested in political participation. On the other hand, Klan propaganda some-times argued that African Americans were dangerous because they were organizing to challenge white supremacy, even going so far as to demand the vote—a view that betrayed an unconscious awareness that they were not unintelligent after all.[9]

But the second Klan became biggest in locations with very small black populations. Moreover, in spreading north and west, it faced a more diverse population. Not only were immigrants from eastern and southern Europe, the Mediterranean, and the Middle East arriving in large numbers through eastern ports; not only were Asians from China, Japan, and the Philippines coming into the West (despite offi-cial immigration bans); but in the western states there were also Mex-icans. (The Klan by and large ignored Native Americans, whom they probably regarded as noncitizens, safely controlled on reservations.) So white supremacy for the second Klan had to be defined more narrowly. Imperial Wizard Hiram Evans wrote that "the Negro is not the menace to Americanism in the same sense that the Jew or the Roman Catho-lic is a menace." Supremacy belonged only to native-born, Protestant whites, sometimes identified by the term "Nordic," sometimes "Anglo-Saxon," sometimes "right" or "true" or "100%" Americans. No Catho-lics, Jews, Orthodox Christians, or Muslims, and no people of color, could be truly American. A poem from Dexter, Maine, written by a fifteen-year-old Klan girl, expressed a Klan supporter's pride and plea-sure in this version of whiteness:

> There is an organization started called the K.K.K.,
> Members are joining by the thousands every day;
> Every true American surely ought to go,
> If they do not like it, they can just say so.
> But if you go once, you'll a member be,
> It's nice to be a 'white man,' you'll very soon agree. [10]

As Imperial Wizard Hiram Evans wrote, "The Ku Klux Klan of today is a new organization to meet a new problem."[11]

The Klan did not view Catholics and Jews as biologically inferior, in contrast to its anti-black racism, but charged them with specific offenses; these were neither minor nor victimless crimes but a form of treason, aimed at undermining the nation. The Klan saw itself as a public crier calling out an emergency, and as a civic movement responding to that emergency through cleansing the society of its filth. It was "divinely appointed to set the forces in operation to rescue Americanism and save our Protestant institutions from the designs of the Scarlet Mother," as anti-Catholics liked to call the Catholic Church.[12] In Klan theology, evangelical Protestantism was what the founding fathers had imagined and decreed—an entirely false and ahistorical rendering, of course, of their eighteenth-century religious creeds.

Another aspect of Klan Americanism was its suspicion of "elites." Central to this resentment lay a form of class analysis that enabled the Klan's claim to stand for the little men against the big men. This definition of elites differed from the more common usage in the mainstream press of the time, which typically defined elites as those with political and economic power. The Klan shared half of that definition, in its disgust with politicians (though Klansmen would soon join them); it represented "the people" against the pols. The Klan targeted neither large-scale economic power nor successful businessmen; in fact, it called for putting "big" men in office.[13] Its primary adversaries, those responsible for the erosion of American values and the American way of life, were not capitalists or men of significant wealth. Instead the elites it condemned were cosmopolitan, highbrow urbanites, who were often liberals. That stratum was eroding American morality, particularly its sexual morality. This anxiety was of course aimed at women, but not exclusively, as local chapters occasionally tried to discipline predatory and adulterous men. Klan theology also expressed nostalgia for an imagined, once-perfect America of farms and small towns. (The fact that the Klannish understanding of elites has reappeared in the political rhetoric of recent decades suggests that it has long formed a powerful stream of thought and feeling in the United States.)

As individual Klan writers and speakers elaborated their ideas imaginatively, one set of emotional tropes dominated: fear, humiliation, and victimization. "The Nordic American today is a stranger in . . . the land his fathers gave him . . . a most unwelcome stranger, one much spit upon, and one to whom even the right to have his own opinions and to work for his own interests is now denied with jeers and revilings."[14] Many social movements, even those that represent the privileged, thrive by positioning themselves as victims. Still, that the fears were unfounded did not mean they weren't genuinely felt. Friedrich Nietzsche recognized that this ressentiment, though rarely based on resentment of actual injuries, nevertheless created "a whole tremulous reality of subterranean revenge, inexhaustible and insatiable in its outbursts."[15] Klansfolk and their many sympathizers experienced their world, the America they imagined as traditionally unified and virtuous, as under attacks both open and surreptitious.

Klan discourse created "feeling rules" for its supporters. Raymond Williams's "structure of feeling" concept put the usually solid "structure" together with the usually airy "feeling" in order to characterize ways of thinking and apprehending the world that differ from formal political ideologies. He was making the point that culture is a material political force. True, Klan propaganda was also instrumental, using these anxieties as a recruitment strategy. But instrumentality and conviction were so fused that those who created the discourse probably could not tell them apart.

These alarms about the erosion of "true" Americanism flowed through stories of allegedly actual events. Because the threats were communicated through tales of distinct happenings, they were not easily susceptible to counterargument: a counterargument would have to deny what Klanspeople took to be facts, facts accepted because of their respect for those who told the stories. (After all, to challenge someone's anecdote or claim is more insulting than to offer a different perspective about a general claim. How does one prove the falsity of a concrete event that someone claims to have witnessed?) Suspicion of science—associated with elites and particularly with Jews, and inimical to faith—armored Klanspeople yet further against evidence. The Klan's multiple media—newspapers, pamphlets, sermons, radio stations—often limited its members' exposure to information that might have challenged their fears.[16] In some Klan-strong locations, members might never read or hear news from other sources.

Suspicion of science reflected a larger anti-intellectualism. That stance combined distrust of urban cosmopolitanism with reverence for faith. "We are a movement of the plain people, very weak in the matter of culture, intellectual support, and trained leadership," Imperial Wizard Hiram Evans declared proudly. "We are demanding . . . a return of power into the hands of the everyday, not highly cultured, not overly intellectualized, but entirely unspoiled and not de-Americanized, average citizen of the old stock."[17] The attitudes of urban, educated elites toward the Klan confirmed this populist resentment; they did look down their noses at people they took to be uneducated buffoons and made fun of the "old-time" values the Klan was determined to defend.

In response, the Klan used the criticisms leveled against it as more evidence of victimization. It claimed that its enemies constantly lied. *Middletown*, Robert and Helen Lynd's famous study of 1920s Muncie, Indiana, reported that "Klan feeling was fanned to white heat by constant insistence . . . that 'every method known to man has been used and is being used by the alien-minded and foreign influence to halt our growth.'"[18] The media hurled false accusations against the Klan, calling members "'tar-buckets, floggers, thieves, murderers,' etc., but never in a single instance have they been able to prove their accusations," wrote one Klan minister.[19]

Klan anti-Catholicism continued an old American tradition—historian Arthur Schlesinger Jr. called it the "deepest bias" in US history. Nineteenth-century nativists had been virulently anti-Catholic. Honored nineteenth-century figures such as Lyman Beecher (father of feminists Isabella Beecher Hooker and Catharine Beecher, and writer Harriet Beecher Stowe) urged excluding Catholics from western US settlements; some scholars have even blamed his rhetoric for stirring up episodes of anti-Catholic violence.[20]

The Klan's story about the Catholic threat focused similarly on the fact that the religion was global. Disloyal to America, Catholics functioned as underground warriors for their foreign masters. The pope was their one and only lord, so Catholics—also known as "crossbacks"—could never be loyal Americans. From his international headquarters, the Vatican, he sent out emissaries to do his mischief. The Vatican had minions everywhere, working full-time toward world domination. Klan speakers frequently implied that Catholics had a unique "lust" for public office, and that priests egged on their parishioners to that end.[21] Furthermore, that the pope and his flunkies commanded absolute allegiance demonstrated Catholics' authoritarianism, and consequent unfitness for democracy. The papal bull of 1894 forbidding Catholics to join secret orders exemplified this demand for total subservience. His priests and nuns brainwashed children through parochial schools, and the pope dictated what was taught there.

Klan leaders fought back with "black psywar." This is the name applied to a type of psychological warfare used by the United States during the Vietnam War, when it distributed material disguised as emanating from the National Liberation Front, also known as the Viet Cong. The Klan, along with earlier anti-Catholic groups, similarly invented, distorted, and used out of context material allegedly emanating from the Vatican. For example, "The Pope has received a detailed report of the elections in America, and has learned with great satisfaction of the successes attained by a number of Catholic candidates . . . we are trying to make the United States a Catholic country."[22] The pope had declared, in a rhyming allegation put out by the Klan,

> *"I've planned for this for many years, and I've started out to kill*
> *All who refuse to bow in submission to my will."*[23]

The Denver Klan forged a Catholic list that targeted eight hundred Protestants for economic ruin.[24] One might wonder whether the distributors of these items knew they were false. Probably not; as with many rumors, the source was obscure even to those who purveyed them. I think of this black psywar as similar to police planting evidence because they "know" that the suspects are guilty.

Some of the alleged Catholic plots were ferociously violent. For example, a counterfeit Knights of Columbus initiation pledge circulated by the Klan required a promise to "wage relentless war, secretly and openly, against all heretics, Protestants, and Masons . . . burn, waste, boil, flay, strangle and bury alive these infamous heretics; rip open the stomachs and wombs of their women and crash their infants' heads against the walls in order to annihilate their execrable race."[25] It is impossible to resist the suspicion that in attributing such violence to Catholics, Klanspeople's own suppressed impulses leaked out.

Despite attributing such violence to Catholics, Klan discourse typically gendered the Catholic Church female, referring to it as "the scarlet mother" or the "whore of Babylon" mentioned in the Book of Revelation. The gendering of Catholicism was filled with contradictions that similarly leaked Klanspeople's own anxieties. In charging that the pope demanded total allegiance, Klanspeople were feminizing Catholics, because blind obedience was antithetical to manly "independence." Yet in a different gendered twist, the Klan harped on Romanist crimes against women. Catholic masculinity was thus deformed, in failing to honor and respect women. Nuns were exhibit A. Alleged exposés by "escaped" nuns were already an old tradition of fake news—Maria Monk had published her escape story in an 1836 bestseller—and the Klan revived it. Convents were allegedly prisons, keeping women as slaves. "The crimes committed in Rome's sweatshops, where the girls have to toil under the eye of inhuman task-mistresses, are enough, if the truth were known, to cause the civilized world to revolt. The penalties meted out . . . are not far below the inquisitorial methods of the Dark Ages." A Muncie woman told Robert and Helen Lynd that when a nun was caught wearing rings, the sisters "just burned them off," leaving her with stubs for fingers.[26] Moreover, the nuns "were forbidden to write to their relatives and friends, and even when letters were allowed . . . they had to go through the hands of the censors and every word and phrase was eliminated that would give the slightest idea of discontent or ill treatment."[27] (The alleged censoring thus explained the lack of evidence for these claims.) In some convents "inmates" were "sentenced to lives of silence. Why should they be doomed to silence unless there is fear that through their conversation the iniquitous system may be exposed."[28] Klan talk deprived nuns of any agency of their own, an assumption that may have reflected some Klansmen's attitude toward their own women.

Worse, the nuns served as the sex slaves of priests. If "the first amendment gives a priest a right to run a harem in this country," a Bethel, Vermont, Klan supporter wrote to a newspaper, why did the government have the right to ban Mormon polygamy?[29] The Klan sponsored speaking tours by Helen Jackson, an "escaped" nun (and ex-convict), who peddled salacious tales of sadomasochistic and scatological practices by priests and female Catholic superiors. References to "moral leprosy," "vendors of filth," and secret doors to priests' bedrooms often figured among the charges.[30] One speaker even charged that nuns were forced to sleep with their excrement. These sensationalist reports increased newspaper circulation, and were intended to.[31]

Occasionally they were disproved: in Indiana a Klan attorney filed a writ of habeas corpus against a mother superior, to liberate a girl who had alleged abuse, only to have the girl tell authorities that she was homesick and had used the complaint—successfully—to get her passage back to Ireland paid for by the state.[32]

Even within the United States, the Catholic Church remained foreign. Not only was its Rome hierarchy "wholly Italian," but its US hierarchy also consisted mainly of foreigners. To make matters worse, it persisted in using foreign languages in its churches. The Klan called for prohibiting the American publication of newspapers or magazines not in English.[33] It denounced Catholic attempts to prevent intermarriage with Protestants by requiring that children be "bound in advance to Romanism,"[34] the assumption being that only by becoming Protestant could children be assimilated.

Centralization intensified the Catholic threat; while Protestants divided among countless sects, there was but one "Romish" Church. It had established fourteen US provinces, within which were one hundred dioceses ruled by "one hundred vassal kings of the Imperial Monarch, the Pope of Rome." Each king was an "omnipotent judge over his subjects." The twenty thousand priests constituted an army that collected taxes from their servile believers, sending a "steady stream of gold" to Rome to support its plan to acquire "world supremacy."[35] Thus Protestants needed a militant Protestant organization to resist, and the Klan arose for just this purpose.

The "Romish" drive for world domination was also responsible for wars. God had been warring with the antichrist since the time of creation, and he punished those who yielded to satanic temptation by raining war and destruction upon them. In the Klan's version of religious history, starting in the year 606 the popes had led Satan's campaign to enthrall the human race, producing yet further "divine retribution." "When America was discovered, the pope calmly announced that he would divide the new world into two parts, giving one part to the King of Spain and the other to the King of Portugal." The current pope, said the Klan, continues that campaign; the devil has never given up.[36]

JEWS WERE EQUALLY GUILTY of foreign allegiance, but to a different sort of master: a secular international cabal of financiers who planned to take over the American economy through its financial institutions—or even to establish "a government within our government."[37] These charges substituted a laic for a religious conspiracy, because, of course, Judaism had no central religious authority. The alleged conspiracy regurgitated the old libel that Jews were by nature swindlers loyal only to their tribe. The Jew was such a devious merchant that an "honest Gentile American cannot successfully compete with him."[38] (To the Klan "Gentile" meant Protestant.) The proof of the finance cabal's existence and purposes lay in the "Protocols of the Elders of Zion," but to the Klan it was outdated, because the Jews already controlled the nation's finances. (The Klan tried but failed to create its own banks so that its members could avoid using un-American ones.[39]) There was a populist charge to Klan anti-Semitism: Jews did not "produce" anything but functioned only as middlemen, buying and selling, and therefore contributed no economic value to the United States.[40] At the same time, allegations about Jews' alleged excessive love of money served to deflect attention from the Klan leaders' own profiteering, examined in the next chapter.

In one remarkable silence about the Jews, Klan discourse did not often employ the reverse side of classic anti-Semitism: that these dishonest merchant capitalists were also Communists. Those accusations would appear in American Nazi and fascist groups of the 1930s, but the 1920s Klan was notably disinterested in actual foreign issues. Moreover, the Klan was weaker in the cities where many Jewish socialists and Communists were found. On the other hand, recognizing that

Jews were often cosmopolitans confirmed the Klan conviction that they could not be patriots.

Conservative anti-Semitism has been categorized as anti-modernist, a revulsion toward modern artistic, commercial, and social culture, and the Klan shared those attitudes. It blamed Jews for women's immodest dress, makeup, and amusements through their control of department stores, garment manufacture, and the media—Hollywood above all. "The great Jewish syndicates, the rulers and promoters of the motion picture industry," were corrupting women and children. Attacks on "Jew Hollywood" were unrelenting: "Jew Movies urging sex vice" and "The poisonous flood of filthy Jewish suggestion, which has been paralyzing the moral sense of America's children" typified thousands of fear-mongering complaints. The Klan launched an attack on *The Pilgrim*, a 1923 silent film with a cameo appearance by Charlie Chaplin, on the grounds that his "burlesque" version of a hypocritical minister was an insult to Protestantism. (The Klan's reference to burlesque evokes, of course, the many Jews in the world of live performance and New York's risqué commercial culture.) Several states bowed to Klan pressure and banned the film. The *Imperial Night-Hawk* referred to Chaplin as a "vulgar" Jewish comedian.[41] (He was not Jewish but refused on principle to say so.)

As with attacks on Catholics, the Klan put out a great deal of fake news about Jews, its allegations safe from challenge because of the closed media world in which they circulated. Jews not only conspired to subvert decent women's morals, Klan publications alleged, but actually kidnapped women for their "white-slave dens." "What happens to the army of young girls who are lost every year? From 60,000 to 75,000 of them disappear annually. . . . The Jews get them and sell them as white slaves. They have a regular price list."[42] If this discourse had any effect, it might have been not only to cause women to fear Jews but also to confirm the imperative for women to stick close to home and avoid the public sphere.

Klan ideologues recognized that these Jewish campaigns worked because they sold. Jews "procured" young women "to enhance their own monetary interests. . . . The Jew knows what sort of motion picture will pay best."[43] In this understanding Klan spokespeople revealed a blind spot that has long characterized religious conservatism, blaming religious apostasy for subverting morality while discounting the influence of commercial economic motives.

But the Klan was never thoroughly anti-modernist. It fit what Jeffrey Herf, writing about Germany, called reactionary modernism: enthusiasm for modern technology combined with rejection of Enlightenment and liberal values.[44] Despite suspicion of science and what liberals call critical thinking, Klanspeople adored and exploited the technological products of science, as we will see below. The most offensive science was, of course, evolutionary theory, and anyone who defended it became a Klan target. "Investigation of attorney John Hodgin revealed the fact that he is an evolutionist . . . [who] believes that man and monkey are true kindred spirits. . . . He needs a little fixing over."[45] Evolution theory too was a Jewish project, promoted in order to undermine the glorious story of creation (an accusation that overlooks the fact that the biblical creation story came from the Jews). The Klan became the first national organization to deny evolution and to sponsor state laws against teaching it, on the grounds that it was not only anti-Christian but also part of a foreign and Jewish conspiracy.[46] When William Jennings Bryan died, just after the Scopes trial of 1925, the Klan threw him a large memorial service in Dayton, Ohio, where it burned a cross with the inscription "In memory of William Jennings Bryan, the greatest Klansman of our time." "We will take up the torch as it fell from [his] hand," the Grand Dragon of Ohio pledged, for "America cannot remain half Christian and half agnostic."[47] (Note the use of Lincoln's anti-slavery formulation.)

Jews, unlike Catholics, were irredeemable. Their dangerousness was of their essence. We see this in the Klan language, referring to Jewish "blood" or "race" in contrast with Catholic "faith." ("Blood" was of course the vernacular term for biology.) In viewing Jews as a "race"—a term then widely used indistinguishably from "ethnicity"—the Klan was in the mainstream. History had made Jewishness both an ethnicity and a religion, and well into the twentieth century, most Europeans considered the Jews both. Catholics could convert to Protestantism, but Jews would remain strangers to the nation even if they converted. They could not walk away from their faults, could not reject sin, because they were eugenically unassimilable. Hiram Evans announced that "they will never emerge for a real intermingling with America . . . not in a thousand years of continuous residence."[48] Biblically, the Jew was not only a Christ-killer but through the centuries proved himself "inflexible and unbreakable." One visceral Klan reinterpretation of Jonah and the whale made that clear: he emerged whole from the fish, not a bone in his body broken, because he was "indigestible," too hard even for the "powerful digestive machinery in the stomach of the monster."[49]

Another interpretation, in which historical characteristics are said to become biological traits—a standard eugenics move—argued that the Jews' history, their lack of a nation, made them congenitally incapable of virtue or patriotism. As the Imperial Wizard summed it up, the Jew could never be an ideal American because he was an ideal Jew.[50] There is some truth in his statement if we invert its value structure: many Jews, especially urban Jews, did share a cosmopolitan history and culture, a characteristic of considerable value in resisting ultra-nationalism. A corollary—that Jews "did nothing to wrest human rights from despotic power [while] the Cavalier, the Puritan, the Quaker and the English Catholic [i.e., Anglican], all Anglo-Saxon and all white, and all of Christian faith, had overthrown tyranny"—has less truth.[51] Jews numbered among the eighteenth-century American revolutionaries and were plentiful in nineteenth-century European struggles for republican governments.

Contradicting Jews' alleged inability to assimilate, they were also charged with a propensity for miscegenation. "The modern Jew" had "no code to restrain him in his dealings with Gentile women," to whom he was irresistibly attracted.[52] As a result of their lust for Gentiles, Jews were attracted to intermarriage. Jews lacked, the Klan explained, "that inborn feeling of supremacy toward the black races that is peculiar to the better born Americans."[53] Yet even if they did "miscegenate," thousands of years of persecution had made Jews "indelibly" unable to fit in.

Toward the end of the Klan's 1920s career, some of its leaders appeared to soften their attitude toward Jews. This may have resulted from the influence of Anglo-Israelism, a sect that first appeared in late-nineteenth-century England and is today found in the Christian Identity movement; it holds that Anglo-Saxons are the direct descendants of two of the "ten lost tribes of Israel" and that the Jews' claim to that descent is false. This argument rests on a nonstandard creation story: there were two creations—the first fashioned superior men of clay; the second, the accursed children of Ham, of mud. The mud people have no souls.[54] But the Anglo-Israelites often distinguished between the wealthier, more prestigious German Jews and the poorer Jewish immigrants from the eastern European pale of settlement. In 1926 Imperial Wizard Evans modified his earlier anti-Semitism in line with the Anglo-Israelite position: the true Hebrews, made of clay, were separated from true Americans only by religion and were thus assimilable—they had "shown a tendency to disintegrate and amalgamate." Eastern Jews, the mud people, were by contrast not "true Jews" at all "but only Judaized Mongols—Chazars. These, unlike the true Hebrew, show a divergence from the American type so great that there seems little hope of their assimilation."[55]

Oddly, Klan discourse placed the Catholics and Jews in cahoots. "The sons of Abraham have therefore become a strong ally to the papacy; they have nothing in common in religion, but they are one in their political propaganda against American institutions and principles."[56] "The press is largely controlled by the Roman Catholic priesthood and their Jewish advertisers."[57] That alliance appeared in Jewish support for Al Smith, the 1924 Catholic presidential candidate, whose closest adviser was the Jewish Belle Moskowitz. As the *American Standard* headlined in 1925: OCHS (JEW) WANTS SMITH (R.C.): OWNER OF NEW YORK TIMES WOULD GIVE WET PAPIST LIFE TENURE OF NEW YORK GOVERNORSHIP.[58] A Klan illustration entitled "The Men Who are Refusing to Bow to the Great Image," honoring Klansmen who turned their backs on the pope, shows Catholics and Jews side by side bowing and reaching out to him. (the Jew is identified by his large hooked nose; both the Catholic and Jewish men are bald, presumably another racial trait.)[59] The enemy attacked on many fronts, but its plots were connected through underground, invisible ligatures.

KLANNISH FEAR OF IMMIGRANTS was indistinguishable from these religious hostilities, for the bulk of the 1890–1920 immigrants were non-Protestant. That they were newcomers intensified fear and hostility, a reaction by no means confined to the Klan. "Strange shoddy has lately crept into the loom on which we weave our destiny. . . . Ominous statistics proclaim the persistent development of a parasite mass within our domain—our political system is clogged with foreign bodies." Moving from a weaving metaphor to one of illness, at a time when people were just learning germ theory, the author defined the problem as invasion. This particular screed appeared not in a Klan publication but in *McClure's Magazine*, a popular and mainstream monthly known for its Progressive Era muckraking, publishing Mark Twain, Lincoln Steffens, and Jack London, among other distinguished writers.[60] In a remarkable similarity to a discourse common decades later, Klan leader Evans charged that immigrants were stealing jobs from true Americans: "While the American can out-work the alien, the alien can so far under-live the American as to force him out of all competitive labor."[61]

Fear-inducing narratives like these usually take the form of conspiracy allegations, which strengthen the victim sensibility. If ordinary anecdotes or assertions are difficult to disprove, conspiracies can never be contravened, since they are secret, and all the more unprovable if they are accompanied by sham "facts." Brandolini's law, developed in the context of twenty-first-century social media, is equally applicable to 1920s Klan-speak: "The amount of energy needed to refute bullshit is an order of magnitude bigger than that needed to produce it."[62] Conspiracy theories are the opposite of institutional, economic, or social-historical analyses, which examine the long-term behavior of known institutions, as recorded in verifiable documents.[63] Explanations based on conspiracies appear most commonly among out-of-power groups, of course, and elites commonly disdain them, but that is partly because elites may see discreet decision-making by small groups as legitimate leadership.

In social movements, moreover, conspiracy theories that may be absurd and specious on their face nevertheless contain valid information about the motivations, grievances, insecurities, and even panics among their promoters, so they cannot be simply dismissed. Among Klan leaders, conspiracy theories also did a great deal of organizing work: they provided identifiable and unifying targets, supplying a bonding function that explanations based on historical analyses do not deliver.

The major function of Klan conspiracy talk was to instill fear. There were many things to be afraid of: Crime, for example, blamed on immigrants even though in the 1920s, as today, immigrants were less likely to commit crimes than the native-born. And that immigrants, and occasionally blacks, were stealing jobs from "true" Americans, that is, Anglo-Saxons. In fact there was little evidence of such theft of jobs, but mere allegations, often accompanied by fraudulent "data," nevertheless constructed anxiety. Many ministers participated in this construction of fear because it hotted up their sermons and very likely brought people into the churches.

The Klan tended to blame conspiracies for everything it disliked, even if it had to posit conspiracies including millions of people. Examples abound. A "class of cultured Negroes have organized societies to promote mixing of white and colored blood. The members of these societies are oath-bound to marry none but white women." Europe plotted to dump its criminals in the United States. Immigrants plotted to enter the country in order to "plunder, pillage, rape and murder" and thereby take over.[64]

In the case of anti-Catholicism, the existence of an individual leader—the pope—multiplied the conspiracy narratives. (See figure 4.) He was the butt of endless accusations. He had ordered the immigrants to come to the United States and told them exactly where to settle.[65] This "dago priest on the Tiber," as the Klan's *Fiery Cross* magazine liked to call him, had devised strategies to Catholicize the minds of American children through his schools and to seize control of police departments and local governments by infiltrating employees sworn to do papal bidding. The takeover had already begun. Imperial Wizard Hiram Evans asserted that "sixty-two percent of all our political positions, elected or appointed," and 90 percent of the police forces, were "occupied by Roman Catholics." A 1923 Klan candidate for governor of Maine charged that Irish Catholic women dominated the ranks of schoolteachers.[66] The pope was building a palace in Washington, DC, with a throne of pure gold, to prepare for the takeover that would occur once Al Smith was elected president.[67] In an alternative report, the pope had already arrived in person in Indiana, in disguise, to set up an alternate Vatican there.[68]

STORIES LIKE THESE WORKED ALSO because they were so rich in symbolic and emotional meanings. One overarching principle, purity, formed a core Klannish yearning.[69] The desire for purity involved not only a longing for innocence but also a fear of pollution. It functioned through a set of oppositions that brooked no nuances or qualifications: anything less than purity was pollution; anything less than godliness was ungodliness. This all-or-nothing form of thought intensified passions. The desire for purity was so emotional, even visceral, that it cries out for a psychoanalytic interpretation; but to the historian the fear seems less elemental than contingent, produced by an ocean of flamboyant, even garish rhetoric.

Purity was a capacious emotional structure, packed with overlapping meanings. They began with whiteness. White skin, or racial purity, entitled Klansfolk to pure white robes (although the Klan's simultaneous need for hierarchy led some of its leaders to wear robes of brilliant colors—purple and red, for example—to distinguish themselves from the rank and file, which contradicted the "scarlet" label they applied to the Catholic Church, since red was the color of sin).

Whiteness also signified the purity of Protestant religiosity. Klan discourse saw Catholicism as having deformed or polluted the purity of Jesus and his apostles through establishing a corrupt hierarchy; the Reformation cleansed the Church, but the Catholic hierarchy remained corrupt. If Jesus were still walking the earth, one Klan minister insisted, he'd be a Klansman.[70] Purity seemed to Klanspeople only available to white Gentiles; other religions could only masquerade as godly. Catholics and Jews were profane because they were controlled by unruly passions, lacking the discipline to resist temptation. Railing against the venality, self-indulgence, and licentiousness of the Church hierarchy, Klan leaders would later be revealed as hypocrites when their own sins and crimes became known.

Whiteness also signaled sexual chastity, that is, purity in the Victorian sense, confining sexual activity to marriage and attributing sexual "needs" only to men. But sexual purity also created its opposite, as for many anti-smut zealots: the Klan's stories of Catholic, black, and Jewish perversities formed a pornography that fused titillation with bigotry. These stories were sometimes smutty, sometimes scatological, sometimes veiled, whether about Jewish white-slave traders or Catholic abuse of nuns: "Language by both tongue and pen has been exhausted by those who have tried to give details of their lives in the convents."[71] One characteristic Klan illustration shows Catholic and Jewish men bowing to the pope, while another worshipper is a sinful woman, identified by her bobbed hair and low-cut shirtwaist.[72] (She was probably wearing makeup, too, but that does not show in the etching.)

Purity also required abstinence from alcohol. Pasting responsibility for violation of Prohibition onto Klan enemies was easy, because in Klannish imagining Catholics did the drinking and Jewish bootleggers supplied them.[73] In reality this map of sin was inexact, since many Protestants manufactured, wholesaled, retailed, and drank liquor, and the majority of Americans opposed Prohibition. Hypocrisy about drinking, once exposed, would add to the Klan's decline.

Purity meant homogeneity as well. Diversity seemed to Klanspeople a form of pollution, uncleanliness. Antagonism to diversity saturates Klan discourse, conveying a structure of feeling hostile to the very essence of big-city life and cosmopolitanism. The wish for societal endogamy, for conformity, was the aspect of the Klan value system that most expressed its romance with small-town life. Fear of heterogeneity underlay also its extreme nationalism and isolationism; Klanspeople saw little to admire in any foreign culture. Many Americans shared (and still share) this anxiety; nativists abhorred the "Babel of voices" that arose from the immigrant enclaves in big cities and industrial or mining towns.[74] These people looked and cooked differently, socialized with their own kind, spoke in foreign tongues. Such a hodgepodge led to chaos in the Klannish mind. Order required uniformity.

Purity also demanded a conservative gender system. Blaming Jews for subverting it followed logically, since they allegedly controlled commercial entertainment. But it was harder to attribute improper gender relations to Catholics because, except for their priests and nuns, their model for "right" gender relations, especially the proper place for women, was identical to that of conservative Protestants. So the Klan's gendered case against rank-and-file Catholics focused on men. Catholic men failed to protect and control their women and children, passively conceding to the Church the obedience women should owe to husband or father. Thus while obedience to the pope was itself a symptom of failed manliness, lack of authority over women compounded the weakness. These accusations were largely theoretical, and not conducive to specific allegations of conspiracies that the Klan favored. So its most common denunciations of Catholicism's sexual and gendered depravity focused on priests and nuns. Nuns upended the proper gender order, by agreeing to serve as slaves, even sex slaves, to priests and to do without motherhood. As for the priests, it went without saying that they were unmanly, accepting as they did a life ostensibly without sex, wives, or offspring—even as they indulged their perverse desires with nuns or with one another.

Klanswomen expressed their purity through their maternalist orientation, but in this the Klan differed hardly at all from hegemonic American beliefs. Motherhood was a woman's primary and highest calling, but she could also assert a social motherhood that took her into the public sphere. Women's roles in this maternalist imagination were multiple: they mothered their families, served the movement, and exerted influence on their men. This "republican motherhood," a modern translation of a discourse from the American revolutionary era, gave women political voice indirectly, through the male heads of families who represented them.[75] As one might expect, 1920s Klan leaders had once opposed woman suffrage, but never vehemently, and once it became law, they welcomed it, assuming that more WASP voters could only advance their cause. Like almost all contemporary observers, including feminists, Klanspeople assumed that women would use the vote in a uniquely womanly and motherly way, to uphold morals and to fortify men to resist sin.

This confidence that women were innately more nurturing, self-sacrificing, and moral than men would continue to characterize much of women's political activity for decades. Progressive-era women reformers of all ethnic and religious groups used maternalist premises, for example, to campaign for social welfare provision and against war. Klanswomen did not usually disagree with these priorities; unlike today's neo-conservatives, Klanspeople did not oppose government welfare programs and did not support a large military. They did, however, prioritize campaigns against sexual vice more than Progressive Era reformers and, of course, called for greater enforcement of Prohibition. Still, most Klanswomen's participation was behind-the-scenes support work, such as organizing and publicizing Klan events and providing food and entertainment.

As with gender, the Klan was entirely mainstream in its enthusiastic support of eugenics. Like many prestigious scholars and statesmen, it worried that people of "inferior stock" were reproducing at a higher rate than those of "superior" groups. President Theodore Roosevelt himself had made this danger, labeled "race suicide," into a national political alarm. That first generation of race-suicide alarmists blamed upscale women who were restricting childbirths or even forgoing marriage altogether. The Klan, by contrast, blamed only its racial and religious enemies.[76] One Klan tract provided numbers: 288,000,000 Catholics worldwide as compared to 161,000,000 Protestants. (That the rest of the world's population far outnumbered all the Christians evoked no comment.) True, the author admitted, in the United States Catholics constituted only 17 percent of the population, but members of the Knights of Columbus outnumbered members of the US Army by five to one.[77] The Klan even worried over the "enormous birth rate of the Negro population" that would "submerge" whites.[78] The accuracy or inaccuracy of these figures is beside the point; they functioned not to inform but to steer anxiety into Klan channels.

It is striking that the Klan never impugned women for low birth rates or urged "100% American" women to produce more children. Other conservatives of the time did denounce birth control, although it was not then a subject of particular concern to evangelicals. A group of New Jersey Klanswomen even invited Margaret Sanger to address them about birth control.[79] The Klan remained silent about the increasing availability of contraception and who was using it.

MY ATTEMPT TO MAKE ORDER within Klan emotion and ideology does not ultimately succeed, because Klan beliefs were riddled with contradiction. But the contradictions were themselves often effective mobilizers. Consider, for example, Klan rhetoric of strength and weakness. Both "right" Americans and their enemies were characterized sometimes as weak, other times as strong. Klanspeople were victims but also unvanquishable knights destined to overcome the forces of evil. African Americans were plotting to depose white rule but also incapable of conspiratorial strategies. Jews were servile and unmanly but had already taken over the economy and the media. Catholics were obsequious in their willingness to subordinate themselves but already controlled big-city politics and law enforcement. Inconsistencies like these worked to marshal both insecurity and confidence, a combination that drew recruits to the Klan.

Inconsistency also enabled the Klan to express grievances flexibly and in some instances to avoid deeper inquiry about the sources of those grievances. Jews functioned in Klan discourse to resolve contradictory attitudes toward capitalism and commercialism: by projecting lust for money onto "the Jew," Klansmen could adjudge their own profit-seeking as honorable, as we will see in the next chapter. Catholics' alleged authoritarianism suppressed questions about Klanspeople's own submissiveness to their unaccountable leaders. Similarly, the Klan worldview blocked inquiry into the actual causes of small entrepreneurs' and family farmers' declining fortunes. Blaming immigrants for "stealing" "American" jobs ignored employers' search for cheap labor. Blaming Jews and Catholics for introducing vice ignored the profit motive behind the entertainment and advertising industries' exploitation of sexual desire and the liquor industry's profits. This inconsistency and blindness served to make Klannish ideas fungible and capacious, adaptable to local contexts, and acceptable to those with great economic power.

KKK initiation ceremony near Richmond, Indiana, 1922.
(*Ball State University Archives & Special Collections*)

Chapter 4

RECRUITMENT, RITUAL, AND PROFIT

IN MANY RESPECTS THE KLAN MIGHT APPEAR ANTI-modernist, as in its romance about "old-time religion" and its campaign to "restore" "true Americanism." Yet in its organizing, it was not only modern but innovative. What made the Ku Klux Klan so wildly success-ful in the early 1920s was an aggressive, state-of-the-art sales approach to recruitment. One study labeled the Klan "a hybrid of a social club and a multi-level marketing firm."[1] Far from rejecting commercializa-tion and the technology it brought, such as radio, the Klan's system was entirely up-to-date, even pioneering, in its methods of selling. From its start, the second Klan used what might be called the social media of its time. These methods—a professional PR firm, financial incentives to recruit, advertisements in the mass media, and high-tech spectacu-lar pageants—produced phenomenal growth for several years. This was distinctly not a project of uneducated rubes.

Enlarging the Klan was the number one priority because Simmons, Clarke, and Tyler saw it as a business—not a social movement. Sim-mons literally owned the Klan, and when he was deposed, his succes-sors had to buy it from him. This is not to say that they didn't believe in the cause; as with all Klan leaders, it would be difficult to disentangle principle from profit motives, in part because they considered their profits honorably earned. They were champions of the business ethic, another respect in which the Klan was entirely mainstream.

Clarke and Tyler, following Simmons's original conception of his project, first sought to grow the new Klan by bringing in southern elites who could pay substantial dues, and they sent invitations to many upscale southern citizens. They apparently envisaged it as a private elite club with expensive entry fees. In one of many contradictory statements, they praised the first Klan in openly racial terms—"its valiant services in behalf of white supremacy insure it a place in the heart of every true American"—implying that the new club would be dedicated to the same cause. But they also described it as a "standard fraternal order." They promised that the new Klan would enlarge "the scope of its work" but also offered reassurance that it would retain "all of the protective features of the old Klan" and referred, ominously, to the "fourteen million people of the colored race" who were "organizing." Exploiting the anti-radical hysteria of the years after World War I, they also trumpeted the threat by "the Anarchist and Bolshevik forces . . . encroaching daily upon the basic principles of Americanism."[2]

Before long, receiving a tepid response, Clarke and Tyler realized the limits of this southern recruiting strategy and decided to take their project national. They divided the country into nine domains, each headed by a Grand Dragon (sometimes called a Grand Goblin); under these were head recruiters in each state or groups of states, called King Kleagles; and under each of them were local salesmen, or Kleagles.[3] (The Klan tried to make every possible label start with a *K*, typically followed by an *L*. A glossary of the most common Klan titles appears in appendix 1.) In essence they were setting up a decentralized system of franchises, in which local recruiters sent much of their revenue to the men above them and kept some themselves.

Kleagles, or recruiters, worked on commission: new members would pay an initiation fee, labeled a Klecktoken, of $10 (worth $122 in

2016). Of this, the individual salesman would keep $4; the remaining $6 would be forwarded up through higher officers, each one keeping a percentage, to the Atlanta head office. Veterans of the nineteenth-century Klan—obviously declining in numbers—were exempt from paying the Klecktoken. But all members paid dues, ranging from 8-1/3 to 15 cents a month, and Kleagles and higher officers took commissions from these as well. The Atlanta team also instituted a ladder that members could climb, the rungs called "degrees" as in Masonic groups: you started out at K-Uno, then could advance to K-Duo, K-Trio, and K-Quad; each degree required another initial payment and higher dues. Members joined chapters, known as Klaverns, and each chapter had to pay an Imperial Tax to the national headquarters and a Realm Tax to the region, the amount based on the intake of monthly dues.

With such financial incentives, it is not surprising that within a year, Clarke and Tyler had 1,100 active Kleagles in the field. And each new member could in theory become a Kleagle himself, thereby keeping 40 percent of the Klecktokens. Through amalgamating financial, patriotic, and racist interests, the Klan spread like a prairie fire.

Recruitment was everywhere the priority: in fact, in these first years, it seemed that the only thing the Klan did was recruit more Klansmen. National leaders instructed each local Klan group to "solve the problem of mobilization [which] means the procurement of qualified aliens."[4] An "alien," in Klanspeak, was anyone outside the organization; nonmembers were thus equated with foreigners. Members of the Klan were by contrast "citizens," and membership constituted "citizenship."

This was a pyramid scheme. Before long members began to bump against the ceiling imbedded in all pyramid schemes—that eventually the most recent joiners could not recover their expenditures, let alone earn. Resentment grew as a result, but it did not reflect opposition to the system. For rank-and-file Kleagles, as for the Klan's leaders, there was no conflict between the Klan's mission and their profits; on the contrary, the monetary incentive may have increased their commitment to Klan principles.

The Klan also profited from sales of goods. Clarke established and owned a company that manufactured Klan costumes for $4 each, later only $2 each, and sold them for $6.50.[5] Not coincidentally, the costumes were designed so that wives could not hand-sew them. The headgear and Klan insignia had to be just so, which made the members want the real, manufactured object. Klan leaders ran many side businesses as well—notably a recording company and a realty enterprise that bought lots in bulk and sold them singly. Klan-friendly merchants began marketing all sorts of other Klan-marked trinkets and memorabilia. A "Kluxer's Knifty Knife," a "real 100% knife for 100%% Americans," could be bought for $1.25. A member could buy a brooch for his wife: a "zircon-studded Fiery Cross." A larger cross that a man could wear on the watch chain he displayed across his chest cost $2.90. For only $5 you could get, allegedly, a 14-karat gold-filled ring with a 10-karat solid gold Klan emblem on a fiery red stone. Also for sale were phonograph records and player-piano rolls with Klan songs. (See figure 19.) Advertisements for this merchandise appeared in newspapers across the country and in flyers at large Klonvocations.[6] The Klan's for-profit life insurance plan claimed $3 million worth of policies in 1924—a dubious figure. It claimed to provide burial insurance as well, but this service never actually materialized.[7]

Accepting these numbers as approximately accurate, joining the Klan cost $23.30 for the first year (worth $318 in 2016)—a $10 initiation fee, $6.50 for the costume, annual dues of about $5, and a yearly $1.80 tax to the national headquarters. In addition members were dunned for insurance, contributions to political candidates, gifts to churches, and special projects, such as an $80,000 auditorium with four thousand seats in Fort Worth. According to one recent estimate, the Klan took in at least $25 million ($342 million in 2016 dollars) annually.[8] This is likely an exaggeration, since as much as one-third of the members were in arrears, never paid, or soon quit paying dues.[9] Still, even allowing for exaggeration, Klan profiteers did very well by soaking their members.

In 1922 Hiram Evans abolished the commission arrangement, although not all local Klans complied. Another road to profit remained, however—becoming a Klokard, lecturer, or Kleagle, recruiter. These positions brought in wages or fees per lecture or per recruit, often $25 a lecture ($342 in 2016). Accomplished speakers such as ministers could do well for themselves and their congregations, and many nonministers could draw big groups with sensationalist rhetoric.

Even enthusiasts began to notice that bringing in new members seemed to be the only Klan activity.[10] One reason was high turnover. A study of the Indiana Klan showed that few other than leaders stayed for long. In one town, of 1,067 listed as Klavern members, 61.5 percent had been suspended at least once for not paying dues.[11] Whether because of the relatively high costs, disillusionment with the profiteering, or the fact that the rituals lost their thrill, many rank-and-file members left. Moreover, since many joined due to social and economic pressure, or because they sought to be part of an in-group, they may have lacked a steadfast commitment to Klan principles. One Indiana man later recalled his thinking at the time: "Maybe you'd better belong to it, if you weren't a Catholic or a Jew or a black man. Maybe you'd best get in there. It got pretty prestigious just in that respect."[12]

Clarke and Tyler also employed a second strategy in growing the Klan: autonomy for the local Klaverns. This was shrewd. Decentralization attracted initiates by exploiting local grievances and/or by catering to local elites. A few symbolic operations were centralized: the Imperial Wizard and his Empress, who held their positions for life according to the Klan constitution, had absolute authority regarding rituals, codes, signs and countersigns, and robes and insignia, but not over local campaigns. A Klan Manual of Leadership insisted that "the first and most essential duty of every leader is to KNOW COMPLETELY the situation in which he is to act [and] what is wrong with the community. . . . The situation will be different in each."[13] Klaverns could focus on whatever enemy or alleged threat would work in their locality (for example, Catholics, sexual immorality, bootleggers). In some areas the Klan was, in the words of a contemporary, "a club thrust into the hand of the prohibition minority";[14] in others the Klan avoided the temperance issue. The Oak Creek, Illinois, Women's Ku Klux Klan focused almost exclusively on temperance and soft-pedaled nativism; five years' worth of meeting minutes revealed no reference to blacks or Jews (although its condemnations of films, dance halls, and other sinful entertainment represented lightly coded attacks on Jews.)[15] In Evansville, Indiana, a Klan-controlled municipal government actually appointed African Americans to city offices—though only because they functioned, allegedly, as "puppets directed by the Klan."[16] In Southern California, the Klan cooperated with the Irish-dominated Catholic Church in its struggle for ascendancy over Mexican American Catholics. In Maine and Massachusetts, Klan groups admitted foreign-born Protestants (in order to bring them into alliance against Catholics), and in many locations the Klan established an auxiliary, the Royal Riders of the Red Robe, to bring in the "right" foreign-born members.[17] The Klan was a chameleon, changing colors to blend into the environment.

Klan decentralization and finances combined to produce a somewhat feudal or tribal structure. In return for autonomous control over their fiefs, local leaders paid taxes, which we might call tribute, upward and recompensed themselves by taxing their vassals. So despite the formally autocratic power of the Imperial Wizard, officials beneath them could amass considerable financial and political power, which they could use to challenge the top leadership. Rivalry at the top then undermined Klan stability. Even when recruitment-by-commission was in theory abolished, rank-and-file resentment grew. Local Klansmen took offense at the lack of accountability regarding where their payments went.

These two organizational strategies—financial incentives and local autonomy—reinforced each other. Opportunities for earning meant that Klan leadership prioritized expanding the dues-paying membership. Accomplishing that meant allowing local Klaverns to set their own action agendas, which in turn made the Klan more attractive locally.

Another tactic, this one not entirely deliberate, helped build the Klan: like many other organizations, the Klan exaggerated its size, and doing so made it more desirable to potential recruits. Grand Dragon Stephenson claimed to have a quarter-million members in Indiana; a dubious boast because if true, it would have meant that members constituted more than 30 percent of the state's white male population. In 1924 the Klan claimed 10,000 members in one Indiana county, but a membership list found later showed that those who paid up numbered about 3,000, and the largest Klan event there drew about 2,000. A Klan organ announced a parade of 50,000 when about 2,700 showed up.[18] These exaggerations operated both as draws and as intimidation: people longed to be part of an ascendant movement and could be afraid not to be part of it, especially given its threatening rhetoric. Possibly more important than intimidation was the concern not to be left off of a bandwagon. The exaggerations were self-realizing. Creating the impression of huge size and unstoppable forward progress, the myth of the Klan as destiny contributed as much as any other tactic to the Ku Klux Klan's great temporary success. French philosopher George Sorel, another notorious anti-Semite, theorized how myth, as opposed to reason—or fact, I might add—built social movements. The core of the Klan myth lay in the notion that it represented the defense and manifestation of America's true character. Looking at the Klan's recruitment success from this angle resolves any apparent contradiction between the principled and self-interested motives of joiners. Its appeal lay precisely in the joining of principle with promise of success.

FOLLOWING A DECISION TO JOIN the Ku Klux Klan, the recruit entered a world of arcane ritual—secret rites, oaths, code words, and props. All contributed to the power of the Klan myth. Participation in this insider world not only solidified commitment, not only created a titillating enjoyment perhaps analogous to today's computer games, but also attracted newcomers who heard about Klan ritual. Contemporary observers saw that the aura of secrecy magnetized the Klan.[19] In fact, it benefited from both secrecy and lack of secrecy: it could publish openly, parade its distinguished members openly, invite the public to its grand pageants, but simultaneously offer enough cryptic knowledge to make members feel like performers in clandestine drama. Its esoteric ritual might seem anti-modernist if we accept it at face value. It is also possible, however, that many Klanspeople adopted a playful, even kitsch attitude toward the occult rituals in which they indulged. They were performers in pageants, much like those who engage in historic reenactments today.

In these rituals, the Klan outdid all the other fraternal orders— though only in intensity, since almost all the fraternals used elaborate rituals. Even Grange meetings, for example, involved "signs, passwords, regalia, and initiation ceremonies," and its members "progressed through several 'degrees,'" up to the seventh degree, which entitled members to participate in the "secret work" under the supervision of a "high priest."[20]

Ritual began with the costume. While the first Klan's robes served to hide members' identities and to frighten those it tried to intimidate, they were also the costumes of a performance, enjoyable in itself, as Elaine Frantz Parsons has argued.[21] Dressing up served the same functions for the second Klan, but in a more complex way. The costume heightened the intensity of ritual conducted, often, in the dark with faces unseen. It marked a privileged membership and an honorary brotherhood. Klan propaganda maintained that the costume not only symbolized purity but also abolished class and other invidious distinctions and thereby strengthened brotherhood. Some KKK practices make this claim seem suspect, however. Leaders often appeared in richly colored robes, for example; rules instructed that the office of Kligrapp, or administrative officer, "should be filled by a competent business executive," and that every Klavern must have a minister as Kludd (chaplain), thus following the principle that "big" men must be selected to office.[22]

The required costume consisted of four pieces: First, a full-length white robe with a red, white, and black insignia over the left breast. The insignias varied slightly, but all contained a cross (typically a Prussian cross) within a circle—sometimes called a crosswheel—with a diamond in the center, which occasionally contained a red mark in the shape of a drop of water (the blood-drop). Second, a sash tied around the waist. Third, a hat, called a helmet, lined with a stiffened material to create and stabilize its cone shape, with a regulation red tassel hanging from the top. And fourth, two "aprons" attached to the helmet. The back apron hung from the bottom of the hat to the shoulders; the front apron was attached to the front of the helmet with eye holes cut out. Child-size robes were also available, and one might imagine children's pride in wearing them.

Hiding identity through this costume expressed, physically and metaphorically, the secrecy that furthered the Klan's magnetism and prestige. To be entrusted with a secret is to receive a gift of high value, and the secret then represents that trust and requires that it not be violated.[23] After a new member was inducted, the veteran Klansmen were to raise their aprons so as to reveal their faces—thus learning the identity of one's brothers and sisters was itself a gift. (This gift not only consisted of welcome into a brother/sisterhood but also had economic value, as we will see in the Klan's economic warfare, discussed in chapter 9.)

The Klan's bible, created and copyrighted by Simmons, was the Kloran. The name's resemblance to Koran is probably not coincidental. Many Klan terms were orientalist or even Latin—the language of the Catholic mass—in origin: thus "Klaliff" from "caliph," "Kloncilium" from "concilium." Unlike the bible, however, the Kloran was a secret document; it had to be "rigidly guarded" and "MUST not be kept or carried where any person of the 'alien' world may chance to become acquainted with its secret contents."[24] The secrecy necessitated weighty oaths of initiation, accompanied by threats of punishment, "direful things," should a member breach this trust. The oaths may not have actually frightened an initiate, but they surely symbolized his absolute and theoretically unbreakable bonds with his brothers. Since these oaths were sworn in the midst of ritual, they took on added magnitude.

Every Klan event had to display four symbolic objects: an American flag, a sword, "Klan water," and the robes themselves. The flag, of course, stood for Americanism: red for blood, white for the purity of white womanhood, and blue for the skies of freedom. The sword symbolized the fierce fight necessary to protect Christianity and America. "Klan water," another source of profit, had to be purchased from the national headquarters, where it was made sacred, like holy water in some churches. With it a new member would be baptized, pledged to cleanliness in mind, spirit, and body; it also, somewhat heretically, made new members part of the body of the Klan. The robe was emblematic of purity.

Klan membership entailed learning a new vocabulary, symbolizing entry into a mythical universe, resembling perhaps that of a Wagnerian opera, access to which was a privilege awarded only to the anointed. Officers, beneath the Imperial Wizard, included three Great Klaliffs, the Great Klabee, the Great Kligrapp, the Great Kludd, and the Great Night-Hawk, together forming the Furies. Chapters were known as

Klaverns, each headed by an Exalted Cyclops. (The Cyclops, some-times spelled "Cuclops" or "Kuclops," was probably associated with the Illuminati, whose single all-seeing eye originally signaled opposition to obscurantism and superstition.) The twelve officers of a Klavern, or local chapter, each of whom had his own *K* title, formed the Ter-rors. The profusion of official posts allowed many members to hold offices, thereby increasing their investment in the organization. Days of the week, weeks of the month, and months of the year each had new names,[25] almost all of them intended to frighten.* Years were counted in Roman numerals and dated from the founding of the first Klan, so that AD 1922 became AK LVI. Different gatherings, meet-ings, and ceremonies had specific labels: for example, a Klonklave was a weekly meeting of a Klavern; a Klonverse was a monthly province meeting; a Klonversation was a "naturalization" ceremony, which was the Klan term for initiating an "alien" into the order; a Klonvokation was a national convention.[26]

Klansmen were also provided with secret acronyms, composed of the first letters of words in a phrase. Thus one might ask, Ayak? (Are you a Klansman?) To which one would answer, Akia. (A Klansman I am.) Cabark meant "constantly applied by all real Klansmen." Cygnar: Can you give number and realm? Itsub: In the secret unfailing bond. Miafa: My interests are for America. Particularly important was San-bog: Strangers are near, be on guard. Oddly, one key Klan motto was written in not-exactly-correct Latin: Non Silba sed Anthar, Not for Self but for Others. I rather doubt that Klanspeople were able to commit all this to memory; in fact, they frequently carried scripts or copies of the Kloran during ceremonies.

---

* The days of the week were Dark, Deadly, Dismal, Doleful, Desolate, Dreadful, and Desperate. The months began with Bloody and ended with Appalling, in one version; in another, from Dismal to Dying. Even the hours were renamed, from one o'clock, Fearful, through Startling, Awful, Woeful, and finally Appalling and Last. What fun it must have been to coin these names.

The words uttered in a meeting followed a script. The Exalted Cyclops calls out, "The Kladd of the Klan." That man, custodian of Klan paraphernalia, comes forward. The Exalted Cyclops says, "You will ascertain with care if all present are Klansmen worthy to sit in the Klavern during the deliberations of this Klonvocation." To which the Kladd must respond, "I have your orders, Sir." Whereupon the Kladd approaches each member, who must make a countersign and whisper the password directly into his ear. And so the script continues for many pages. Sociologist Kathleen Blee has pointed out that many Klan verbal rituals resembled Catholic catechisms.[27] As in Protestant services, however, members joined in singing hymns and patriotic songs, each at a prescribed moment.[28]

Klavern meetings proceeded with prescribed staging directions as well as scripts, and participation in these choreographed articulations of space contributed to the fun of performance.[29] Military metaphors abounded; for example, "The Klaliff (vice Cyclops) having been assigned the duty of directing the military machinery, he should appoint as his assistant a Lieutenant Colonel . . . [and] one Corporal to serve each eight Klansmen." Members took up assigned posts. Echoing the insignia on the robe, these involved circles, squares, and crosses. The official form of a Klavern was a square, within which was a circle, within which was another square, within which was an altar. The assembled Klansmen reproduced these shapes with their bodies, limited by their need to use rented or borrowed spaces. Four leading officers stand in the four corners of the square; three Klokanns stand against one wall; the Kligrapp (administrative officer) stands against the next wall clockwise from them; the Klarogo (guard of the inner room) is at the door to an inner den where, ideally, lockers store costumes and symbolic items; Klexters (outer guards) stand at the door leading to an outer room where candidates for naturalization are kept until called in for their interrogation and ceremony. The circle within the square, really four discontinuous arcs, is formed by standing Klansmen.

Props had to be displayed in a prescribed design. The Klokard (lecturer) drapes an American flag on the altar, and its stars must lie toward his left and on the opposite edge. He places a sword across the flag with its hilt toward the Exalted Cyclops.

Movement within meetings was minutely choreographed. In verifying the membership of each attendee the Kladd always moves counterclockwise. Once confirmed, they sit unless they have forgotten the password, in which case they remain standing until authorized by the Kligrapp. If Klansmen from other Klaverns are visiting, they come to the Exalted Cyclops's station, then turn to face the altar. The others all stand and give "tsog," the sign of God. Then the Exalted Cyclops gives two raps with his gavel and says, "My Terrors, you will take your respective stations." And so on.

The most elaborated event was naturalization, the induction of new members. (See figures 6–9, 22.) Its ritual was of supreme importance, because it marked the passage from "alien" to "citizen"; by underscoring the momentousness of joining, it helped produce the Klan's attractiveness. The ceremony's official design, like that of Klavern meetings, sculpted space symbolically, so as to "afford them [the candidates] a safe journey from the world of selfishness and fraternal alienation to the sacred altar of the empire of chivalry, industry, honor and love." After several scripted questions and answers verifying that the candidate is approved, the Night-Hawk (courier) delivers application petitions and Klecktoken payments to the Kligrapp, who then rises and hands the petitions to the Exalted Cyclops, who then instructs the Night-Hawk to inform the candidate as to the duties of Klansmen. The Night-Hawk goes to the door and, without leaving the inner room, repeats those words to the candidate. The Klokard then administers a Qualifying Interrogatory of ten questions to the candidate, reporting back that he has received the correct answers. The Kladd, or conductor, then lines up the candidates and, after further scripted, stilted dialogue, and whispering again the countersign through the door, brings them into the inner room. The lights are now turned down so that the space is nearly dark. The waiting Klansmen must be completely silent and immobile; the Kloran explicitly forbids smoking at this point. (Allowing for difficulties in memorizing all this, the Kloran specifies that officers are allowed to use flashlights to read their lines.) Then the Kladd leads the candidates through prescribed steps, counterclockwise around the altar. If there are enough candidates, he forms them into a "three-quarter hollow square" facing the altar. The Night-Hawk holds aloft a fiery cross at the corner of the altar just to the right of the Exalted Cyclops, exercising all the while "good military mannerisms." Several officers then line up on the missing fourth side of the square, to "complete the quadrate." The Exalted Cyclops holds up a vessel of "dedication fluid" (the purchased Klan water) and pours a few drops on each candidate's back, then on his own head, then tosses some drops upward, and finally moves his hand horizontally in a circle around each candidate's head. (These four locations symbolize body, mind, spirit, and life.)

At best, these ceremonies, held in darkness, with men anonymous behind their robes, must have been electrically charged, possibly even eerie and intimidating, as was their intent. For the initiate, the weirdness, the out-of-the-ordinariness, made a "naturalization" not just a club meeting but also a memorable drama that enhanced the value of belonging to the Klan. For veteran members, the drama confirmed their belonging. I suspect, however, that Klavern size and the spaces they could secure required improvisation or even abbreviation of the choreography and script.

Urbane twenty-first-century readers may find these rituals absurd and hokey, even puerile. Once immersed in this material, however, one begins to see them as participatory theater, a game of make-believe. Beyond their bonding effect, beyond confirming that membership in the Klan brought honor and prestige, they provided enjoyment. This was a time before movies were widespread, when radio was still new and theater not plentiful, when Americans spent their leisure time in participatory activities. They sang in church and at home, played pianos and guitars, gathered for card games and ball games and quilting sessions. These practices allowed potential members to understand the Klan not as a group in which you discussed books or politics, not as a meeting in which you listened to speakers (although lectures and traveling circuses remained popular diversions), but as a club. The make-believe quality of Klavern meetings made them folk theater, albeit not performed for an audience other than the participants. Not a creative folk theater, because the ritual was prescribed, but one in which an imaginary, possibly medieval, possibly "Oriental" society was imagined; much of the Kloran could be described as a new compilation of the folklore of emperors and knights—and "knights" was a favorite Klan word.

The pleasures of this ritual were, then, multiple: the participant was a member of a theatrical troupe, allowed a fantasy world alongside workaday life; he reaped the security and prestige of being an insider, enhanced by knowing that so many were excluded "aliens"; and, of course, he was nourished by a bonding that offered deliverance into a brotherhood as a respite from the loss of community that increasingly characterized modern life.

Entertainment at a Colorado KKK summer picnic.
(*Royal George Regional Museum & History Center*)

Chapter 5

SPECTACLES AND EVANGELICALS

KLAN RITUALS TOOK ON A DIFFERENT AND MORE capacious appeal when they were mass performances, staged for audiences. At the time, political parties held large, raucous gatherings to build and confirm electoral support. Protestant camp meetings were a popular attraction. But the Klan outdid these by far. It mounted extravagant productions that offered entertainment for all, and the fact that they also formed a recruitment strategy was of more than incidental value. They were profitable investments, recouping expenditures many times over by presenting the Klan as a booming, wealthy fraternity and thereby attracting new members—and new Klecktokens. If Klavern rituals strengthened small-scale bonding, these public events strengthened wholesale bonding, feeling oneself a part of groups of thousands. They were visible representations of Klan strength.

These monster events took place by the hundreds, and they were wildly popular. They brought the Ku Klux Klan to a large public, and, depending on the audience, could be attractive, intimidating, or both. Even those intimidated could be attracted, because these large gatherings featured amusements typically associated with county or state fairs. The Klantauquas, as some labeled them, point to one of the contradictions of Klan strategy: Klanspeople sometimes sought secrecy, largely because mystery made it more attractive, occasionally because members wanted deniability. But the Klan also sought publicity, not only for its cause but equally, if not more importantly, in order to grow. In this respect it differed from other fraternal orders, many of which preferred to remain closed, and selective in admitting new members. To the extent that the Klan resolved this contradiction, it did so by developing nonmember supporters. That tactic became increasingly important as the recruitment-by-commission system ended and the Klan began to emphasize electing candidates for public office. The big outdoor spectacles thus served many purposes: to attract voters, to project an image of the Klan as a benign fraternity, and to provide leisure activity that strengthened Klan solidarity.

None of these purposes prevented turning a profit. Sometimes there was a small admission charge, and rides and games might also bring in money: a Klonvocation in Iowa in 1925 took in $810.50 from entrance fees, plus $190 from tickets for rides, amounting to $13,950 in 2016 dollars.[1]

Typically staged in summer, often on Independence Day, and outdoors, these KKK pageants might last well into the night. Open to everyone, located in fairgrounds, public parks, and donated private fields, they were announced in newspapers, handbills, and posters tied to trees far enough in advance that word spread widely. Ministers promoted them in sermons. People from miles around anticipated them with excitement and attended in the thousands, sometimes the tens of thousands. One huge event in Racine was co-organized by Wisconsin, Illinois, Indiana, and Michigan Klans.[2]

The Klonvocations typically culminated in long parades, and anyone, including nonmembers, could walk with them, enjoying the bands and floats. One parade featured men carrying horizontally a thirty-foot-long American flag, into which people tossed money, followed by a motorcycle brigade, a thirty-piece band, a fife and drum corps, stilt walkers, and floats, one of which was a miniature schoolhouse surrounded by an oversized American flag. In evening parades through towns, the

Klan sometimes arranged to have streetlights turned off so as to make their burning crosses show more dramatically.[3]

Unlike Klavern meetings, these events were family affairs. They were carnivals but never carnivalesque, offering respectable entertainment and participatory activities for people of all ages: music, rides, ball games, races, contests with prizes, lots of food to sell or share, even hot-air balloon rides. Huge tag sales offered bargains. Physicians staffed first-aid stations. Concerts featured children and teenagers from the Klan's youth groups, and of course minstrel shows, when white performers sang and danced in blackface. Drum and bugle corps performed. Competitions included beauty contests and team sports; a Minnesota event featured a "fat man's race" for those over 225 pounds.[4] A Nebraska event featured a "water pageant" at which displays floated around the lake on pontoons.[5] Some of these happenings involved mass naturalizations—in one 1922 Chicago event, 4,650 initiates joined; in Dayton in 1923, 7,000; in Farmingdale, New Jersey, 1,700; in Oakland, California, 500.[6] (See figures 6 and 7.) No doubt these are exaggerated figures, but in any case there were masses of recruits. Klanspeople spent considerable labor and money on these events, but they were calculated investments.

The spectacles often featured daredevils. In a 1924 Indianapolis event, a Kokomo man leapt from a hundred-foot tower into a net.[7] They often featured airplanes, which says something about the resources that Klan leaders could command. (See figure 13.) Parachutists jumped from planes. "With the black sky as a background, a flaming red cross streaked across the heavens . . . when the aviator turned on a red electrically lighted cross on the bottom of its fuselage," one reporter wrote of a Klonvocation in Jackson, Michigan.[8] (The Klan's airplane stunts prefigured those of later air shows, particularly one made famous by the Italian fascist pilot Italo Balbo, who led a squadron of daredevil seaplanes from Rome to Chicago, arriving at the 1933 World's Fair, commemorating the city's founding in 1833, to a cheering crowd of

thousands.[9]) In Kansas City, Missouri, in 1923, the show was introduced by "a white-robed horseman on a white steed" standing atop a
hill as a plane covered by a huge fiery cross swooped low" over him.[10]
These performances were "calculated to inspire curiosity on the part
of those outside the Klan and make them want to be inside," as one
contemporary perceived.[11] This was superb entertainment, free to all
comers, like free circuses.

Events like these made some attendees think of the Klan as an innocent community group. Even members of the very groups despised by
the Klan frequently admitted to enjoying the spectacles, and no doubt
some risked mingling with the crowd, undetected if they were white.
The Klan's mystique, and its reputation for throwing these extrava-
ganzas, attracted many who did not join and perhaps had no intention
to join.

The culminating events at these mass occasions usually featured choreography for hundreds or even thousands of participants. (See figures 11
and 12.) In creating these compositions, the Klan was participating in a
form of political entertainment that became popular in both the USSR and
Nazi Germany in the 1930s: mass calisthenics and military parades. This
kind of spatial sculpture, patterns created with organized, unison-moving
bodies, became an international modernist political style. Although the
United States did not showcase many military parades at the time, choreography that used human bodies to create moving shapes could be seen in
the Busby Berkeley films. Attentive Klanspeople might have condemned
Busby Berkeley dance numbers for the immodest, provocative dress of the
female performers but might also approve of the choreographic collectiv-
ism, which they understood to signal power in unity.

The Klan's outdoor spectacles used lines of people to articulate the
space in large fields and, frequently, to define a "stage." Sometimes Klan
VIPs would enter in slowly driven open cars, followed by Klansmen on
horses. Rank-and-file Klansmen and Klanswomen would enter walking
in slow, coordinated processions, all in white robes, each carrying a torch.

They moved in unison so as to form shapes. The shapes delineated insiders and outsiders, but not necessarily in simple binaries. There might be outer rings or squares of Klansmen, within which were smaller shapes within which were groups of officers and podiums for speakers. If the event was a naturalization, the initiates were lined up so as to enter dramatically; in one case they formed a cross in the center of a circle of Klansmen; in others they knelt in rows. Klanswomen might form their own shapes inside or outside the Klansmen's perimeter. Farther outside, Klan family members clustered; "aliens" tended to stay back. For particularly dramatic effect, the Klansmen sometimes used their cars to define and sculpt the space. At a 1924 evening rally in Holton, Michigan, they arranged seven hundred cars (quite possibly an exaggerated number) in a circle with their lights focused on the center, producing what one journalist called a "picturesque diffusion of rays."[12] The lights distinguished inner from outer space, those illuminated from those in darkness.

Not all was frolicsome. Ministers almost always spoke and, like official Klan speakers, outlined the threats facing Americans. Frequently introduced by city or state officials, they emphasized local concerns— law and order, women's immodesty, high taxes, even "the insidious trend" of Protestant church involvement in the peace movement.[13] Elected officials often spoke at Klan happenings, a practice with multiple implications: they were lending legitimacy to the Klan, which in turn provided an audience for electioneering and communicated Klan approval of these politicians.

There were always evening cross-burnings, held when possible on hilltops to maximize their visibility. In an Oklahoma event, the fiery crosses were accompanied by "flares of natural gas" and a "powerful searchlight erected on a high tower."[14] These were not necessarily direct threats, as threats are usually understood today. The first Klan and the third Klan (that which re-formed to combat the civil rights movement) typically burned crosses on or next to the homes or gathering places of African Americans. These burnings delivered messages to those who violated the economic or political racial order, or even contemplated doing so, warnings of worse to come. In these large Klonvocations, the cross-burnings were instead awesome symbols—of the Klan as the army of the cross, and of an awakened and mobilized Protestantism. Many spectators saw them only as Fourth of July fireworks. They elicited the thrills and the magnetic attraction of fire. Klaverns competed to produce the largest crosses, some reported as fifty feet high.[15] If live fire was used they were wooden, wrapped with burlap, soaked with kerosene; but often they were electrical, studded with yellow or red light bulbs.

Still, even if the burning crosses did not target particular individuals or institutions, they functioned as generalized threats. They worked to create anxiety that not joining the Klan could leave one in a vulnerable position—deprived at least, discriminated against at worst—and in this way they encouraged membership. For those unable to join the Klan, members of despised groups, the burnings must have produced discomfort at a minimum. They reinforced, simultaneously, unbelonging and vulnerability.

ORGANIZED CLUBS AND ACTIVITIES for families added to the benefits of belonging. They fostered a community spirit that might otherwise have been inhibited by a closed fraternity. In fact, the Klan always presented both open and hidden faces: fetishizing secrecy in the Klaverns, yet organizing a range of participatory and wholesome projects indistinguishable from those run by a YMCA, a labor union, or even—on a smaller scale—the Communist and Socialist Parties. Klanspeople sponsored thousands of small clubs and outings, of astonishing variety: singing groups, bands, Bible study groups, gun and rifle clubs, fishing and boating expeditions, dances, camps for children, musical performances, drama clubs, and the ubiquitous tag sales. Many were sex-segregated, as was customary, although Klanswomen did most of the work involved in activities not specifically limited to adult men. A Klan family could spend all its leisure time immersed in Klan community and culture.

Klansmen organized sports teams wherever their communities were large enough. Teams were integrated into school and college competitions, as for example when the Patchogue, Long Island, New York high school basketball team celebrated its victory over the Ku Klux Klan basketball team from East Moriches. That sport, however, was rare among Klansfolk; baseball dominated. It was the American game and, of course, the white, Protestant, rural game, one that required access to large open spaces. Baseball represented the small-town, homogeneous society that the Klan idealized. Teams involved Klanspeople in competitions with "aliens," which stimulated publicity, which in turn drew in new Klan members.

Klansmen played baseball in three contexts. In large gatherings, Klansmen and boys mostly played against each other, nonmembers joining in occasionally. They played propaganda games against "aliens," and these were purposely designed to attract audiences and publicity; for instance, the Youngstown Klan team challenged the Knights of Columbus, and the Klan played Wichita's "crack colored team," the Monrovians (the Klan lost). Finally, in areas of Klan strength, it operated sandlot teams that played in recognized leagues, sometimes semipro teams. Indiana, a Klan stronghold, fielded a dozen such teams. These leagues might play in stadiums, and the newspaper coverage might list all team members— no secrecy here. In Los Angeles the Klan team played a three-game charity series against a B'nai B'rith team, and in 1927 in Washington, DC, the Klan played against the Hebrew All-Stars (whose team included Abe Povich, brother of sports journalist Shirley Povich). Newspaper coverage typically treated the Klan teams like all others, with no particular attention to Klan politics.[16]

Thus baseball functioned to normalize the Klan, so that it could appear as a benign club, akin to the Elks or, again, a labor union. More,

the KKK's love of baseball became another route to community clout—
even audacity. A Cincinnati minister, writing in 1924 "at the request of
Imperial Officials" of the KKK to August Hermann, commissioner of what
would become Major League Baseball, asked him to designate July 20,
when the Cincinnati Reds would play the New York Giants, as Klan Day.
To support the request, minister Orval W. Baylor pointed out that the KKK
had a hundred thousand members in the Cincinnati area.[17]

Normalization within communities sometimes resulted from stealth.
Recruiters frequently invited men into a new fraternal group, without naming it. In Windsor, Vermont, for example, at a public meeting,
the speaker first spoke in favor of "100% Americanism" and traditional
morality, but then asked all who were not white Protestants to leave
and only afterward began to condemn Negroes, Jews, and Catholics.
The Klan began its Madison, Wisconsin, career in that way: in 1921
the Kleagle advertised in Madison's main newspaper, "Wanted: Fraternal Organizers, men of ability between the ages of 25 and 40. Must
be 100% Americans. Masons Preferred." By 1922 the Madison Klan
was calling itself "the Loyal Businessmen's Society." On the University of Wisconsin campus it established a fraternity called Kappa Beta
Lambda, its initials standing for "Klansmen Be Loyal"; its members
hoped to "make the university a center for the Promotion of Christianity, Americanism, and Klansmenship."[18] But stealth was only a veneer,
or was soon dropped, because recruiters soon established an official
campus Ku Klux Klan society. This was a supra-fraternity, allegedly
including only the "most accomplished" members of the other fraternities. The 1921 Badger yearbook featured a group portrait of twenty-
nine members of the Ku Klux Klan "Honorary Junior Society."[19]

Klanspeople also celebrated community rites—christenings, weddings, and funerals—in Klan style. (See figure 21.) Sometimes nonmembers attended these ceremonies, and in those cases they again served
to legitimate the Klan and present it as nonthreatening. Klan ministers,
known as Kludds, conducted the ceremonies, surrounded by Klan offi-

cers and sacred symbols, in turn surrounded by Klanspeople in full regalia. Klan weddings might bring in attendees who were complete strangers to the marrying couples. Brides and grooms eagerly scheduled their rites through Klan auspices, because these events were more likely than private weddings to capture press coverage that showed off the bride's beauty and her gown to a large audience, and surrounded the couple with lavish decorations, pageantry—and gifts. Attendees were encouraged to understand these rites, and the gifts they brought, as fostering a new Klan family. Such a wedding magnified the blessedness of the bonds being promised, because bride and groom were marrying not only each other but also the Klan and through it Americanism, Protestant strength, the purity of married love, and the larger family of Klansfolk.

Ceremonies centered around babies were smaller, typically conducted by Klanswomen in their own meetings. In an Oak Park, Illinois, chapter, newborns were "dedicated to Klancraft" and received a silver baby spoon engraved with Klan insignia.[20] Some baptisms occasioned large public events. In Saginaw, Michigan, in July 1924, a "mammoth" picnic featured simultaneously twelve christenings and one wedding, accompanied by a band concert. Occasionally Klan ministers baptized adults who had experienced rebirth into the Klan.[21] The Women's Klan also sponsored "beautiful baby" competitions.

Klan funerals were more prescribed and more public than christenings or weddings. The Klan published a handbook on funerals, including a script and, as usual, instructions for the spatial choreography. The handbook prescribed specific hymns and texts for sermons or other testimonies. It detailed the required order of the funeral march, where each officer should be placed, and location of the burning cross(es). (Clearly the ministers who officiated had little autonomy.) The flower arrangements had to show the letters KKK, formed either with ribbons or with the flowers themselves. Messages to the deceased were to be placed in sealed envelopes and placed on the coffin. Funerals could be large spectacles, attended by strangers, and they often included parades. Businesses might be closed, street traffic diverted.[22] The language merged Christian with Klan theology: invitations announced that the member had passed "to the Klonklave on high"; once there, the departed ones had the pleasure of residing in a paradise populated only by white Protestants. Funerals sometimes "outed" people not previously known as Klan members and thereby increased, posthumously, the prestige of the deceased.[23]

THE KLAN'S RELIGIOUS RITES might suggest that it functioned as a Protestant denomination. Its scripts resembled Bible readings and prayer, and its meetings resembled church services. Many religions practice prescribed spatial design, in which movement patterns, along with props, take on symbolic meaning. But the Klan was not a denomination; it sought to incorporate existing Protestant churches, not replace them, and to put evangelism at their core. It was in many ways a pan-Protestant evangelical movement, that is, an attempt to unite evangelical Protestants across their separate denominations.[24] Klan bishop Alma White, of the Pillar of Fire denomination, described the rise of the second Klan as a second, twentieth-century Reformation. "The heroes of a new Reformation are here, robed in white, emblematic of the purity of the principles for which they stand . . . which our enemies are doing all in their power to destroy."[25] A Klan minister in Maine described it as "the rising of a Protestant people to take back what is their own."[26]

Evangelical, charismatic, and Pentecostal churches constituted the Klan's recruiting ground.[27] Many associate the Klan with fundamentalism,[28] but this was not universally accurate. Some of the hardest-line fundamentalists, such as the Church of the Nazarene and the Church of Christ, ignored the Klan, because their theology required that the faithful should not be involved in political or nonchurch organizations.[29] In some places the Klan also reached out to nonevangelical, mainline

Protestant churchgoers, and it had some success with German American Lutherans.[30] In general, however, the mainline denominations, such as Episcopal, Presbyterian, Methodist, and United Church of Christ, did not respond enthusiastically. In fact, Klan rhetoric sometimes denounced these liberal beliefs directly, charging that "modernist" theology was nearly as wrong as Catholicism.[31]

When recruiters came into a new region, they went first to Masons but next to ministers, promising to help them increase church attendance. An estimated forty thousand ministers joined, their congregations serving as "Klan sanctuaries and recruiting camps." Ministers frequently identified themselves as Klansmen during services. Of the Klan's thirty-nine Klokards, or traveling lecturers, twenty-six were ministers.[32] The Southern California Ku Klux Klan, for example, was organized by the Rev. Leon Myers. He arrived there in 1922 to take over the largest church in town and organized a "Men's Bible Class" that became Anaheim's Klavern. (The Ku Klux Klan touted Anaheim as the "model Klan city," aka "Klanaheim.")[33] Ministers who risked opposing the Klan could become vulnerable to retaliation. Klan officials sometimes asked friendly police to "investigate" allegations, in one case that the Rev. X's "sister married a reformed Jew . . . who was associated . . . in the work at this Negro school," or that X was head of an "Inter-Racial Committee, which is branch of Negro association in New York."[34] Shades of McCarthyism.

Once they assembled a small core group, Klansmen liked to "invade" a church service, bearing a cash contribution and praise for the piety of the congregation. This tactic, usually prearranged with the minister, not only bought good will but also served to obviate fears that the Klan intended to compete with or poach members away from the church. In fact, there was reason for those fears, since for some members, Klan meetings replaced Sunday church services.[35] For these "visitations," another Klan word for the practice, they would wear their hoods, or at least their robes, and march ostentatiously down the center aisle, typically at an agreed-upon moment in the service, so as to make the whole congregation aware of the donation. Kathleen Blee described an "invasion" into a Lynbrook, New York, church where forty Klansmen presented a silk American flag and a purse of gold, after which the Rev. Paul Hill thanked the Klan for its generosity.[36] (Klan donations to churches seem never to have been made privately.) Sums of $25 to $30 were common (the equivalent of $342 to $410 in 2016). When the minister approved, the Klansmen would lead hymn singing, reciting the Pledge of Allegiance, and prayer; they might even deliver a sermon of their own. One such included a Klan prayer:

> Oh God, give us men. . . . Men whom the lust of office does not kill, Men whom the spoils of office cannot buy. Men who possess opinions and a will, Men who have honor, Men who will not lie, Men who serve not for selfish booty, but real Men, courageous, who flinch not at duty, Men of dependable character, Men of strong sterling worth. The wrongs will be redressed, and right will rule the earth. God give us men. Oh God, for Thy glory and our good we humbly ask these things in the name of Him who taught us to serve and sacrifice the right.[37]

Ministers, often paid very little, struggling to keep their churches in repair, rarely refused to cooperate; those who did might be denounced as modernists or worse.[38] Ministerial support for the Klan led some opponents to charge that these preachers had been bought. Clearly ministers in some communities faced considerable pressure.

The Klan's mobilization of evangelical ministers foreshadowed— and probably helped generate—the entry of Christian Right preachers into conservative politics fifty years later. One of the first great radio and tent evangelists, Robert Shuler, based in Los Angeles, frequently lauded the Klan—"as sweet music as my ears have ever heard," he called Klan rhetoric—in his thunderous sermons denouncing threats to white supremacy. He called the KKK the only hope to save the city from liberals and black people and even joined Klansmen in vigilante actions against speakeasies.[39] Anticipating more recent Christian Right leaders, Shuler also became a significant force in Los Angeles politics; in 1929 he chose the winning candidate for mayor.[40] Evangelist Aimee Semple McPherson similarly endorsed the Klan in her tirades against Japanese Americans— she labeled them Satan's saboteurs—and depended on its support. In 1926, after she was charged with faking her own kidnapping, presumably to collect a ransom, rumors circulated that she had actually been off on a tryst with her lover. The Klan repaid her loyalty, defending her by smearing her prosecution as a Catholic plot, and she was acquitted.[41]

The Klan gave one of its largest donations—$1,568 (worth $22,500 in 2016)—to the Rev. Bob Jones, to help him establish his conservative whites-only Bob Jones University.[42] (The university grew out of Jones's distress after his friend William Jennings Bryan was so humiliated in the Scopes trial.) Jones campaigned for Alabama Grand Dragon Bibb Graves in his 1926 winning campaign for the governorship, and Graves delivered the keynote address at the groundbreaking that same year.[43] The school grew considerably during the civil rights struggles of the 1950s and 1960s, when pro-segregation White Citizens Council members sought to avoid integrated education. It would not enroll African Americans until 1971, and then only if they were married and would therefore not live in dorms, even as it tightened its rules against interracial dating. Noted Christian Right evangelists and politicians, including Billy Graham, Billy Kim, Tim LaHaye, Terry Haskins, and Asa Hutchinson, have been among its students.

The 1920s was not the first time that evangelical Protestantism wielded great political influence, but it may have been the first time that bigotry became a major theme among its preachers. That so many ministers and preachers endorsed the Ku Klux Klan and even declared membership in it underlines two important Klan characteristics: its assimilation to conservative Protestantism and its respectability within mainstream politics.

Klansmen ride, Tulsa, Oklahoma. (*Associated Press*)

Chapter 6

VIGILANTISM AND MANLINESS

THE NORTHERN KLAN WAS NOT PRIMARILY A VIOLENT group. But that depends on one's definition of violence. Take the Klan's terrifying 1925 attack on the family of Malcolm Little, the future Malcolm X. The family lived in Omaha, where Malcolm's father, Earl Little, was both a Baptist minister and an organizer for Garvey's "back to Africa" movement, the Universal Negro Improvement Association. (Had the perpetrators known anything about Garvey's impulse to persuade African Americans to leave the country, might they have supported him? Perhaps not: they no doubt sensed that any organizing among African Americans was dangerous to white supremacy.) Rev. Little had been threatened many times, but one incident drove the family out of Nebraska entirely. While Rev. Little was away, preaching in Milwaukee, a group of Klansmen on horseback arrived and ordered Malcolm's mother to bring out her husband. They proclaimed, in her account, that "the good Christian white people" would not stand for his "spreading trouble" among the "good Negroes" of Omaha. Mrs. Little, visibly pregnant with the future Malcolm, and alone with three small children, explained that her husband was not at home and tried to convince them to leave. Undeterred, they galloped several times around the house, carrying burning torches, whooping and yelling. They shattered all the windows. Had Earl Little been there, his wife thought, they would have lynched him. Their threat worked: soon after Malcolm was born a few months later, the family moved, first to Milwaukee, then to Lansing, Michigan. Attacks on the courageous reverend did not stop, however. In Lansing a group calling itself the "Black Legionnaires," determined to stop him from opening a store outside the black neighborhood, burned the Little home to the ground.[1]

The Omaha attack was not only terrifying but also terrorist, continuing the first Klan's strategy: its intention was not only to stop Rev. Little's activism but to warn other African Americans that they must not challenge white supremacy. Behind the attack, no doubt, was the Klansmen's confidence in their impunity. With some forty-five thousand fellow Klansmen in Nebraska, the attackers could be confident that juries would never convict them.

The attack on the Littles was typical of the northern Klan's vigilantism—usually stopping short of murder or physical assault, but nevertheless communicating a credible threat of violence to Klan enemies. The vast majority of Klanspeople never participated in this vigilantism, but some did, and their attacks were in many ways an unsurprising result of the Klan as an organization and a movement.

Like all fraternal orders, the Klan drew in members by offering the pleasures of male bonding. This was particularly attractive because those opportunities were shrinking, due to the transformation of the economy. In the rapidly corporatizing world of the 1920s, ever more men performed white-collar work, spending their days at jobs not previously considered manly. They worked not with hammers or drills but with paper and pen. New white-collar and service-sector workspaces increasingly included women, whose presence constrained homosocial male camaraderie. All this just as fraternal orders of the older sort were fading and women were transgressing gender and sexual norms. The Klan, as a fraternal order, offered compensation for these losses.

Klan rhetoric not only featured masculinist language, appealing to "real Men," but also employed feminine labels to shame enemies. "Remember when you come to lodge that this is not an old maid's convention," the minutes of an Oregon chapter read.[2] An Oregon Klan political candidate called an anti-Klan newspaper a "poor old female . . . busy feathering its nest," while a Klan minister spoke of his contempt for "mollycoddle Masons" and "softshell" preachers who urged ecumenism.[3] These quotations could be multiplied by the hundreds. At the University of Wisconsin, the Ku Klux Klan fraternity required pledges to parade around the capitol pushing baby carriages as part of their hazing.[4] Klan writings and lectures painted the Protestant Jesus as virile and aggressive, the vengeful Redeemer, in contrast to the gentler, empathic Jesus of the mainline, liberal churches.[5]

Klan speeches and publications harped on crime as evidence of the need to restore manliness. Urban crime rates were escalating—nationally, crime rose 24 percent in the early 1920s—but not escalating nearly as much as Klan talk suggested. Besides, much of the increase was in auto theft, hardly surprising since autos were rapidly increasing in numbers and typically had to be parked on the streets, where they were vulnerable.[6] Where African Americans were part of local populations, the Klan blamed them for the alleged increase in crime, no matter the actual statistics.[7] So did many non-Klan whites: rumors among Omaha whites blamed rapes and assaults on black men despite the fact that whites carried out most of them.[8]

Crime surged also because of Prohibition, which had criminalized previously legal bootlegging and saloonkeeping. For the Klan, making home brew or drinking alcoholic beverages was now criminal. Defense of Prohibition was universal among the Klan's diverse Klaverns, and arguably responsible for the fact that many relatively tolerant citizens shrugged off its racist rhetoric. One journalist called the Klan "the extreme militant wing of the temperance movement."[9] (See figure 5.)

The Klan projected its anti-Catholicism and anti-Semitism onto violations of Prohibition, presuming that those religions and demon rum were exactly coterminous: Catholics and Jews drank and purveyed alcohol. Its speeches and publications always tied Prohibition violations to "wrong" religions: "A certain Catholic priest named Father Grace was . . . convicted of illegally securing five barrels of whiskey from the United States warehouse by means of liquor permits to which he had forged the name of the Mother Superior of a Catholic Home for the Aged"; "a certain Jewish Rabbi in a Midwestern city was convicted of securing absurdly large quantities of liquor for sacramental purposes and selling it."[10] In Colorado the Klan tried to ban the use of "intoxicating beverages" in religious ceremonies, a move that targeted both Catholics and Jews.[11] Alliances between temperance advocates and the Klan happened in many places, as in Asbury Park, New Jersey, where the Civic-Church League joined the Klan to dry up New Jersey's resort towns.[12] As one Klan writer put it, "People used to say that the saloon was a recruitment agency for crime. But . . . some religions are recruiting agencies for crime, too."[13]

Unsurprisingly, plenty of Klanspeople drank. Oregon provides many examples of this hypocrisy: Klansman Ray Cook was arrested on a charge of violating Prohibition. Grand Dragon Fred Gifford allegedly treated new Klan initiates to alcoholic drinks. At one Klan event the food was so good "we forgot our crave for moonshine for the time being." One Klavern member was criticized for bailing out "bootleggers and Chinks." He was reminded, "You are living in America, now, not in a foreign country."[14] (Ultimately Klan drinking led to exposures of hypocrisy and contributed to its demise.)

Klan crime talk sounded a steady drumbeat announcing the collapse of law and order. In fact, the Klan became the leading law-and-order spokesgroup in the 1920s. Its crime talk functioned as a potent recruitment strategy, kindling fear and promising a satisfying moral superiority to potential members. Crime discourse also evoked resentment, typically shared by police, that criminals were going free through trivial, procedural legal loopholes. Law-and-order talk could thus authorize action outside the law.

Vigilantes occupied a central place in Klansmen's traditions and venerations. In their recruitment campaigns they frequently showed the virulently racist film *Birth of a Nation*, in which the protagonist, Klan Grand Dragon Ben Cameron, and his mounted followers saved "white womanhood" from the "savage lust" of black men. The film not only intensified latent racism but also stirred the imagination of Klansmen longing to be equally heroic.[15] Aware of the attractions of these heroes, Klan spokesmen talked a slippery and sometimes bluntly dishonest line about vigilantism. Hiram Evans tried to protect the Klan's respectability, in large part so as not to jeopardize its profitability. In order to scrub their reputation clean, Klan leaders not only denied that members ever broke the law but insisted that the accusations were calumnies spread by Klan opponents.[16] When Klansmen were seen, leaders typically claimed that the guilty ones were actually "aliens" who masqueraded in white robes in order to defame the Klan—"thugs parading under the guise of the Invisible Empire," as a Washington Klan minister put it. Moreover, leaders claimed that accusations were simply inventions of the allegedly Catholic-controlled press.[17]

Evans and his allies may have tried in earnest to keep Klansmen within the law. But they also understood that vigilantism attracted members, so their recruitment pitches frequently hinted at vigilante opportunities. (See figure 17.) One 1934 article wrote about "night-riding" that "these methods are the great attraction . . . that renders the greatest personal satisfaction."[18] Klan fraternalism sent the message that true manhood required action against the forces antagonistic to true Americanism. As William Reich wrote about Nazi street violence, it allowed "little men" to act "big."[19]

So the Klan's belligerent rhetoric encouraged vigilantism even without an explicit call for extralegal action. Simmons called for the "Klan army" to be drilled and equipped. "When the Knights of the Ku Klux Klan take their place upon the firing line to preserve and save the most sacred heritage of the white race," he declaimed at a 1922 Klonvocation, "something is going to crack in America."[20] Several contemporary critics pointed out that World War I veterans "never had quite enough excitement" from their war experience, since American participation was so brief. As Frank Bohn wrote in 1925, to "organize a thousand healthy, sturdy, adventure-loving young men, half of whom have just been mustered out of the army and navy; to fire their hearts with the thought that their beloved country was in imminent danger of destruction; and then expect them to be satiated by repeating the Klan ritual once a month and waiting for election day, surely that was expecting to pluck figs from thistles. . . . Such an outfit would quite likely look around for a way of saving the country described neither in the four gospels nor the federal Constitution."[21]

Given the enormous size of the 1920s Klan, it was no doubt true that only a small percentage of Klansmen participated in vigilantism. Bohn guessed that "probably nine-tenths of them . . . do nothing but repeat the ritual, pass pious resolutions, and go home."[22] But some did more, and if leaders tried to control them, their efforts were unsuccessful. The least violent vigilantism targeted saloons and roadhouses, gambling parlors, dance halls, and prostitution. Klansmen would raid these locations together with police officers or do so themselves and turn offenders over to the police. Or they might issue warnings, either verbally or through cross-burnings.[23] In New Jersey they burned a cross in a field owned by an Irish Catholic, and another at a corner in the main African American shopping district in Metuchen.[24] But they tended to go after local, small-time offenders rather than producers and distributors of liquor, who often had powerful supporters. In Indiana, Grand Dragon David Stephenson set up his "G-2" system, recruiting Klansmen to gather intelligence on violators—not only on "aliens" in their communities but also on other Klanspeople. (A Stephenson rival claimed that he had modeled his spy network on that of tsarist Russia.)[25] A Klan letter to a newspaper in the Ozarks threatened not only bootlegging but "parking automobiles along our highways . . . for what is believed to be immoral purposes."[26]

A smaller number of raids were large-scale: In Anaheim, California, for example, Klansmen launched raids on several locations in one evening, turning up and turning in, they claimed, fifty-two bootleggers. In a much publicized series of raids in Indianapolis, the Klan got 125 people arrested and convicted.[27] One Indiana sheriff worked with a civilian "booze squad" to arrest liquor scofflaws, and we can be sure that it included Klansmen. The violators then appeared before Klan-sympathizing judges—one a future Klaliff—who always convicted them.[28] In Oklahoma, and perhaps elsewhere too, Klan membership was automatically suspended for any man called for jury duty, so that he could deny it and not be excluded for bias.[29] Occasionally Klansmen threatened or even attacked women for immodest dress; vigilantism extended to behavior that was not illegal but, to the Klan, evidently immoral.

Violence varied by region and by the level of resistance to the Klan. In New England, the Midwest, and the Pacific Northwest, the Klan confined itself mainly to threats. Some were verbal: "If you are the mouthpiece of American labor in this locality," an Oregon Kleagle warned, "and do not endorse the above principles . . . then you would be a fit subject for a Vigilance Committee."[30] Or a threat to a Vermont journalist: Unless "certain newspaper reporters . . . stop attacking the Klan, they will be taught the same lesson that some editors in the south have learned."[31] Others were symbolic, as when Denver Klanspeople pasted placards announcing their meetings on the walls of synagogues and Catholic churches.[32] The Klan's "black psywar," distributing frightening material allegedly from Catholic sources, constituted a form of vigilantism.[33] Taken in the aggregate, it seems clear that these threats also constituted terrorism, aimed not only at particular individuals but at sending a message to whole communities of people—intimidating nonconforming groups into submission to Klan "law."

Other threats were physical. In Lewiston, Maine, the Klan set off a "dynamite bomb" to announce its presence.[34] Two Colorado Catholic businessmen received a letter from the Klan threatening them with "death or worse" if they did not leave town.[35] "Warning parties" might beat or humiliate a target. One repeated stunt involved capturing a man, telling him he would be hanged, hanging a noose from a tree and then around his neck to induce him to plead for his life, then releasing the terrified and humiliated prisoner. In Arkansas City, Kansas, Klansmen invaded "Darktown" and kidnapped a black man who, they claimed, stole suitcases from the train station, and hung him until he "confessed," then forced him to leave town forever.[36]

Three Oregon cases known as the "Oregon outrages" captured widespread press attention when night riders terrified their victims with such lynching threats. J. F. Hale, a piano salesman—white—was accused of illicit sexual affairs, and the would-be lynchers demanded that he break off the improper relationships. He may have been targeted also because he owed money that a Klansman was having trouble collecting. Sam Johnson, described as "part-Mexican," was accused of stealing chickens and being an "idler." Arthur Burr, an African American bootblack accused of bootlegging, received the worst treatment. Vigilantes abducted him and took him to the very crest of the Siskiyou Mountains, where they strung him up and let him down three times. Releasing him, they fired revolvers near his feet, demanding that he leave the area permanently, yelling, "Can you run, nigger?"[37] Though charges were brought against three groups of Klansmen, in each case juries acquitted the culprits, on the grounds that because the victims were morally bad, their vigilante punishment benefited the community.[38]

By contrast, Oklahoma, Indiana, Kansas, and southern Illinois—locations that were as much southern as northern—experienced a great deal of actual Klan violence: whippings, tar-and-featherings, and lynchings. In all four places, some degree of racial segregation was in place, and Klan violence helped keep it in place. In Oklahoma, Klan-provoked violence became so widespread—with a reported "one flog-ging for every night of the year"—that the governor placed parts of the state under martial law; Klan efforts got him impeached in 1923.[39] Oklahoma law officers sometimes handed suspects over to Klan whip-ping parties or even participated in the beatings. In Kansas, Klansmen abducted an anti-Klan mayor, tied him to a tree, and "laid thirty stripes on his bare back." In "Bloody Williamson," as one southern Illinois county became known, the local Klan and the Anti-Saloon League merged into the Williamson County Law Enforcement League, which soon became run by the Klan. Attacks on the operators of the wide-open bars produced lethal battles in 1924 and 1925, involving gunmen and the deployment of military forces, and ended by forcing the anti-Klan sheriff out of office. These armed skirmishes killed twenty people.[40]

The North was not entirely immune to Klan violence, however, and sporadic episodes transpired in many locations. In La Grande, Oregon, Klansmen were warned "that all K.C. [Knights of Columbus] carry a 32-automatic when they go out at night," surely an intimation that Klansmen might start fights.[41] Particularly dramatic was the protracted struggle between the Klan and the Catholic University of Dayton. Klanspeople burned crosses repeatedly on and around its campus, including one cross allegedly a hundred feet high. As crosses burned, several hundred Klansmen in dozens of cars would drive "in single file 'past the blazing emblem,' all the while issuing 'a volley of threats.'"[42] At one point the Klan set off twelve bombs throughout the campus; luckily, or perhaps deliberately, the bombings took place during Christ-mas vacation, and no one was hurt.[43] In Steubenville, Ohio, masked Klansmen attacked a meeting of the Sons of Italy and shot two men to death.[44] In Denver in 1922, Klan death threats and physical violence became so common that the *Denver Post* pronounced the situation "on the verge of civil war." The Catholic newspaper there reported that a Klan plan to burn Catholic churches was scotched only when the Grand Dragon pointed out that since the churches were insured, Catholics would just rebuild them.[45] In Inglewood, California, a city in Los Angeles County, Klansmen raided an alleged bootlegging operation run by Basque immigrants Fidel and Angela Elduayen. Two hundred Klansmen first blocked off the surrounding streets, then moved in; they tied up and beat the couple and destroyed their furniture. Presumably others came to the defense of the business, because Klansman police officer Medord Mosher was killed and two others wounded in the struggle. One hundred fifty subpoenas were issued, thirty-seven Klansmen indicted, all acquitted.[46]

Far western states saw many Klan assaults, notably against Mexican Americans and Asian Americans. In California's great agricultural valleys, the Klan murdered Mexican American farmworkers and tried to force the "wetbacks" out.[47] In 1927 and 1928 vigilantes forced all the Filipino farmworkers out of Wapato, Topenish, and Wenatchee in Washington state; this kind of violence continued into the 1930s, when they bombed and set fire to several Japanese-owned farms.[48]

Because vigilantes needed anonymity, they sometimes formed subgroups with different names. In Oklahoma, for example, the Klan created whipping squads, sometimes called Vigilance Committees or Citizens Committees. One such group was named, paradoxically, the Sanhedrin, after the ancient Jewish council of judges; its charge was "to take care of these little matters in our neighborhood."[49]

The KKK typically justified vigilantism by charging that the police were not doing their jobs. This was a tricky claim to make, because it might antagonize police officers, so Imperial Wizard Evans promoted another strategy: not ending vigilantism but legalizing it through official cooperation with lawmen. It was already the case that law officers were often Klan members. Uniformed law officers, who frequently paraded with Klansmen, often allowed Klan vigilantes to serve as formal or informal deputies. The Portland, Oregon, Klan announced that 150 members of the police department had become "citizens" of the KKK. Portland's mayor formed a hundred-man vigilante force to augment the police force: they received guns, badges, and the power to make arrests, but their names would remain secret—while the Klan would "advise him" in selecting them.[50] In Anaheim, California, a city government controlled by the Klan allowed on-duty police officers to patrol in Klan robes and symbols.[51] In Dayton, the Catholic university president did not bother to call the police because he knew they would not act against the Klan.[52] In Madison, Wisconsin, a former police chief recalled that "pretty near all" of his men were members. They joined other Klansmen to form the Klavaliers, which they described as a "military unit trained to fight crime, fires, floods, riots, and strikes"; its members, deputized under the police department, helped "clean up" the neighborhood known as Little Italy, arresting its "most noted characters." (The local WCTU expressed its approval.)[53]

True, sometimes the Klan did not initiate but only revivified vigilantism, or responded to previous violence with more violence. A Klan organizer came to Duluth, Minnesota, sensing fertile ground after three black circus workers were lynched by a white mob who believed, falsely, that the workers had raped a white girl.[54] Indiana had a particularly long tradition of legal vigilantism: an 1865 law allowed residents to form armed associations to "defend their communities." In the nineteenth and earlier twentieth centuries, these white groups had driven out the entire black population in one county; ambushed thirty African American miners; formed "Night Riders" who destroyed the barns, farm equipment, and crops of their enemies; and organized the infamous "White Caps" who roamed the state forcing "undesirables" off their farms.[55] In the 1920s, Klansmen resurrected the nineteenth-century Horse Thief Detective Association, which claimed forty thousand members in 1924; between 1922 and 1926, the peak of Klan influence, HTDA "constables" were appointed by the county commissioners. Ohio Klansmen also adopted Horse Thief Detective Association as their vigilante moniker; members made "contributions" to state policemen in return for deputy status.[56] In Oakland even federal agents incorporated a group of Klansmen into raids on Prohibition violators.[57] In short, Klan vigilante actions were often legal.

Targets of Klan aggression were not always passive or nonviolent themselves, and anti-Klan forces sometimes initiated violence, directed at cross-burnings and Klan parades. In 1923 in Bloomfield, New Jersey, a crowd tore the robes off some parading Klansmen; in Perth Amboy a mob of six thousand allegedly broke up a Klan meeting; in New Castle, Delaware, a thousand men forced the Klan off a field and destroyed the cross.[58] In response to the cross-burnings against the University of Dayton, its football coach recalled, "[I] called out all my big football players" and encouraged them to "take off after them" and "tear their shirts off" or "anything else."[59] In South Bend, Indiana, a "raucous band" of Notre Dame University students forced a Klan march to retreat, then threw potatoes through the windows of Klan headquarters.[60] In Maine, lumbermen responded to Klan threats by marching into Greenville to demonstrate their refusal to knuckle under.[61] In Auburn, Oregon, a fistfight during a Klan meeting—no doubt provoked by anti-Klan disrupters—required police to stop it.[62]

Anti-Klan violence sometimes became lethal, especially when its perpetrators were industrial workers. In Lilly, Pennsylvania, members of the United Mine Workers turned a fire hose on Klansmen, who responded by killing two union men.[63] A major battle took place in Carnegie, Pennsylvania: located near Pittsburgh, which had one of the largest Klans in the state, it was also home to miners of whom about half were Catholic or Orthodox. When twenty-five thousand Klansmen paraded in Carnegie in August 1923, no doubt choosing the location precisely because of its large population of non-Protestants, a road-block stopped them as they crossed a small bridge. Some two thousand protestors had gathered, and they ripped the electric KKK cross off the leading car, threw bricks and rocks, and shouted, "Get a rope, lynch them, kill them," according to the Klan newspaper. Then "from an alley near a Catholic church . . . Paddy McDermott, an Irish undertaker, . . . emptied the magazine of an automatic pistol into the ranks of the white clad Klansmen," killing Klansman Thomas R. Abbott. (Mrs. Abbott declared, said the Klan newspaper, that her husband's life "had been given to a noble and just cause.") Carnegie and Pittsburgh police arrested McDermott with a few other armed protestors, while the Klansmen "busied themselves in an attempt to find his murderer."[64] Thus in some cases the Klan could honestly complain of victimization.

Klan vigilantism sometimes expressly targeted labor unions, especially in cases where workers were not "Nordic." Klan leaders sometimes articulated a general antagonism toward industrial workers but at other times kept silent, perhaps because industrial workers put up the greatest resistance. In the Youngstown, Ohio, area, where the industrial workers were also largely immigrants and non-Protestants, a virtual army of working-class people successfully drove out the Klan.[65] The KKK particularly went after the radical Industrial Workers of the World (IWW, aka Wobblies), which had considerable strength in the Pacific Northwest and in logging and agriculture in other parts of the country. But in these battles, the Klan often won. It helped suppress the Agricultural Workers Organization, a union of wheat harvesters in Nebraska and an auxiliary of the IWW. It drove Wobblies out of several locations in the Pacific Northwest.[66] In Maine in 1923 the Klan threatened to force out IWW loggers, who were mainly Catholic Franco-Canadian Americans. Maine Klansmen were joined by expat Canadian Klansmen in attacking the labor unions through threats, cross-burnings, and bombings. Massing at a boardinghouse where many were staying, Klansmen threatened "to remove the Wobblies by force if they would not leave town voluntarily." When the workers would not budge, the Klan threw its support behind the lumber companies, who in turn persuaded the state to file conspiracy charges against the workers. The combination of criminal indictments, corporate blacklists, and community hostility brought victory to the Klan and helped set back unionization efforts for decades.[67] This episode was one of several that started with vigilantism and then brought in the law to achieve Klan goals.

Still, it was not uncommon for union workers to support the Klan, especially when they feared competition from immigrants. In southern Indiana, after the big 1919 coal strike, mine owners began importing eastern European immigrant workers. Some eight hundred native-born miners rallied to demand that the "undesirables" be driven out. The United Mine Workers union tried to maintain its nondiscriminatory policy, even threatening to expel any member who joined the Klan. But when a mine boss hired some Slavic workers, UMW members chased them out of town. As the foreign workers became more numerous, the Klan conducted a vitriolic propaganda campaign against them, on the grounds that they struck at "the heart-blood of the nation." On June 11, 1923, some thousand men, faces concealed, attacked immigrant workers, beating some of them badly, and in forty-eight hours had evicted 150 miners. As a result, native-born miners deserted the previously strong United Mine Workers and the Socialist Party—creating thereby a major shift in local politics.[68]

Very occasionally Klansmen supported labor struggles; these inconsistencies reflected both their ambivalent relation to corporate power and varying local sympathies. Klan rhetoric favored small over large business, and members at times backed union workers where they were "right," that is, native-born white Protestants. The powerful Oregon Klan supported the national railway workers strike of 1922, and in return many strikers joined the Klan. The La Grande, Oregon, Klavern voted to investigate four Klan strikebreakers, but its motive was also racist: the Klansmen were allegedly "teaching Negroes and Japs to take places of strikers."[69] When a Birmingham, Alabama, strike was broken by the owners, workers made the Klan their "underground union."[70] The Communist Party's southern newspaper, the *Southern Worker*, was printed by a shop co-owned by a Georgia Kleagle.[71] But the Klan more often allied with corporate owners, especially if workers were not "right," which was increasingly the case. In California, the Klan aligned itself with the big growers against the farmworkers, not only those of Mexican descent but also the perfectly "Nordic" "Okies."[72] In the 1930s the Klan openly aided the thugs used by the Associated Farmers and the California Citizens Association against farmworker unionization.

Vigilantism strengthened the Klan, even though it sometimes created enemies. Vigilante attacks not only cemented Klan solidarity but also strengthened Klansmen's pride. This pride came not only from good feelings about manliness but also from the conviction that they were performing responsibilities of democratic citizenship.[73] If democracy meant that the demos, the "people," should exercise majority rule through voting, why should not that principle apply also to meting out justice? This somewhat populist understanding should not be dismissed lightly. Critics of vigilantism need to bear in mind that its perpetrators believed themselves righteous and, in the Klan's case, obedient to the laws of God and country—to the true America, that is. Vigilantes moved from one manly position of protector—of women and the family—to another: protecting the American people. And while vigilantism was a manly art, we can be sure that many Klanswomen cheered it.[74] When Klanspeople believed social order to be threatened by untrustworthy populations, then true Americans had to act in defense to reinstate control.

Women's KKK funeral, Muncie, Indiana, 1923.
(*Ball State University Archives & Special Collections*)

Chapter 7

KKK Feminism

ALTHOUGH KLANSMEN OUTNUMBERED KLANSWOMEN
by six to one, at least half a million women (some claimed as many as
three million) joined the movement, and that doesn't count the many
who participated in its public events and supported its ideas. In fact,
women clamored to participate from the moment the second Klan reappeared. They contributed a new argument for the cause: that women's
emergence as active citizens would help purify the country. That claim
may well have emerged only after the woman suffrage amendment was
ratified, in 1920; before that, many Klanspeople of both sexes probably
had doubts about the righteousness of women entering politics. Nevertheless, the claim that women might bring "family values" back into
the nation's governance—a claim made at the time in movements of all
political hues—created a contradiction within conservative movements:
despite an ideological commitment to Victorian gender norms, including women's domesticity, many conservative women enjoyed participating in politics. In fact, some Klanswomen interpreted political activism
as a female responsibility. Then, once active, they often came to resent
men's attempts to control them and even challenged men's power. Thus
we meet a phenomenon that many progressive feminists found and still
find anomalous—the existence not only of conservative feminism but

even of bigoted feminism.[1] Readers who have not already done so must rid themselves of notions that women's politics are always kinder, gentler, and less racist than men's.

Women who became active in the Klan were continuing a populist tradition of the 1880s and 1890s. Even without voting rights, women had constituted a significant force in the Farmers Alliance and then in the Populist and Socialist Parties. Women activists spoke at meetings, edited newspapers, lobbied legislatures, published novels, wrote political tracts, ran for local offices, and got elected to leadership in the Alliance—in short, they engaged in every form of political activity allowed them. When the Populist Party emerged, women were increasingly shut out of official roles, not only because of their disenfranchisement but also because increasing Populist power made male leaders less open to sharing influence. (It was often the case that women had more space to lead in social movements than in formal political parties.) There were exceptions, though. Kansas feminist Mary Elizabeth Lease, to cite just one example, was a major Populist traveling speaker, in demand throughout the Midwest. She gave the opening address at the 1892 Kansas Populist convention and was an at-large delegate at the national convention. Many Populist women were also stalwarts of the Women's Christian Temperance Union. They brought these experiences into the Ku Klux Klan. They did not assume that politics was a male activity.

Moreover, women had won at least partial suffrage in 27 states and the Alaska Territory prior to the national amendment, and these states included those where the Klan was strong, such as Indiana, Iowa, Nebraska, and Oregon. But the 1920s political world into which Klanswomen entered was rapidly changing. After the Nineteenth Amendment was ratified, the most visible women's rights organizations waned in strength. As a result, the narrative of women's struggle for equality has often characterized the 1920s as a period of inaction or even retreat.[2] But that conclusion, while accurate with respect to electoral engagement, does not hold up with respect to social and cultural developments. For example, rates of women's college education mushroomed. Between 1910 and 1920 the number of women in college doubled, reaching almost three hundred thousand, or nearly half of all students in higher education. That increase continued during the Klan's heyday, growing by 84 percent over the 1920s. Similarly with women's employment: by 1920 women constituted 21 percent of all those employed outside their homes, a rate much higher among poor women and women of color, of course. Both changes—education and employment—drew more women into the public sphere; even those with husbands who could support a whole family were spending more time outside their homes. Progressive Era women activists had obtained a base for promoting women's and children's health and welfare in the US Children's Bureau. At the same time, divorce rates were growing, which meant that more women were not only leaving husbands but also fighting for child custody, always the right about which women cared most.

Meanwhile, commercial culture was responding to these changes. The stereotype of the new culture has been the flapper, but this was a small group compared to the millions captivated by new forms of leisure and social adventure, many of them entirely secular. Prohibition was flouted openly in big cities and discreetly in smaller locations. Advertising morphed from information about where particular commodities could be purchased to imagery that persuaded people that they needed new products. Nightclubs, records, and above all radios brought jazz out of Harlem into white communities. Radio broadcasting began in 1920; by 1930, 60 percent of Americans owned a radio, and as a result radically expanded the acquaintance of small-town and urban Americans with big-city culture. By 1927 fifty million Ford cars were on the roads—many with women drivers—offering greater mobility and privacy. Well into the 1960s, most young people had their first sexual experience in a car. For the young and unmarried, unchaperoned commercial leisure such as dance halls, soda fountains, and the movies—where couples could sit in the dark!—became a magnetic attraction. Images of beauty changed rapidly: women cut off and "bobbed" their hair (using, significantly, a male name to describe the new haircuts), and wore makeup, shorter skirts and brighter colors.

Together these cultural developments transformed social life and, of course, created a backlash. Conservatives railed at the decline of morals, and by this they meant mainly women's morals. Walter Lippmann's phrase "the acids of modernity" captured Klannish fears that the very ground of Protestant morality was being eroded.[3] The Klan blamed Jews and, to a lesser extent, Catholics for subverting what would later be called the gender order; nevertheless, Klanspeople fretted about immodesty precisely because this freer social and sexual culture appealed to Protestants as well. Because anxiety about immodesty focused on women, Klanswomen were both repelled and enticed by these developments, and this shows in the contradictions within their program and activism.

Klanswomen were often wives of Klansmen, but many joined on their own, and others led their husbands into the organization. In fact, some husbands resented their wives' Klan activities and absences from home, and some opponents taunted Klansmen with the charge that they were not man enough to keep their wives at home.[4] It seems likely, though, that Klanswomen often spent more hours on Klan work than did rank-and-file Klansmen because they had more disposable time.

Women did not always wait to get Klansmen's permission to join the movement but organized themselves independently through churches, clubs, sororities, and Klan picnics. Male leaders, alarmed by these initiatives outside their control, formed competing women's groups,[5] producing a variety of organizations with names such as Kamelias, Queens of the Golden Mask, and Ladies of the Invisible Empire. In 1923 Imperial Wizard Hiram Evans, seeing that women could not be kept out of the Klan movement, managed to merge these groups forcibly into the Women of the Ku Klux Klan (WKKK). Some preexisting women's groups resisted this merger, and then, after acceding, refused to accept a subordinate status. An Oregon group proclaimed that "the women's organization is an exact counterpart of the Klan itself, with no difference whatever except that of gender. They will use the same constitution, ritual, regalia and methods."[6] In another assertion of its independence the WKKK set up its headquarters in Little Rock, hundreds of miles from Atlanta, home of the Klan headquarters. By November 1923, the WKKK claimed chapters in all forty-eight states. In Indiana, the state of greatest Klan strength, where the population was 97 percent white and Protestant, the WKKK boasted of 250,000 members; if true (not likely), this would have meant that 32 percent of the state's native-born white Protestant women belonged.[7]

BRIEF PROFILES OF THREE WKKK LEADERS illustrate their combination of conservatism with assertiveness, a combination that many might find surprising. We have already met Elizabeth Tyler, cohead of the Klan's PR firm, who defied almost all the gender norms of the time and displayed a business acumen that might befit a CEO today. Her extraordinary career grew from both nativist and fraternal traditions. Born in 1881, married at fourteen, either abandoned or widowed at fifteen, she made several further brief marriages, becoming a multiple divorcée. In Atlanta in the 1910s she was a member of a sororal order, Daughters of America, an anti-immigration organization associated with the American Protective Association and many fraternal orders.[8] Tyler participated in the eugenics cause as a volunteer "hygiene" worker, managing publicity and organizing parades for a "Better Babies" campaign. Through that activity she met Edward Clarke. Together they sensed the profitable opportunities that could arise from professionalizing and commercializing their efforts and set up the Southern Publicity Association, selling their services to groups like the Red Cross and the Anti-Saloon League. In their first fifteen months of work for the Klan, they claimed to have netted upward of $200,000 ($2.7 million in 2016); this is probably an exaggeration, but they were doing well. Tyler personally owned and profited from the *Searchlight*, a Klan newspaper, and built herself a large Classical Revival house on fourteen acres in downtown Atlanta. It was she and Clarke who turned Colonel Simmons's feeble attempt to revive a southern organization into a mass national movement and a profitable business. When she turned her energies to creating an early women's division of the Klan, she took advantage of Simmons's temporary absence to put Clarke in titular control of the entire Invisible Empire.[9]

In 1919 their position became precarious when Atlanta police literally rousted them out of bed and arrested them for disorderly conduct; the "disorder" was the fact that they were sexual partners while married to other people. When the arrest was discovered two years later, newspaper coverage revealed not only the illicit sex but also that they had used false names and had been in possession of whiskey. The scandal was big news, covered even in the *New York Times* when the New Jersey Klan demanded firing Clarke and Tyler.[10] Learning of the arrest some Klansmen were doubly dismayed—by the alleged immorality but also by the discovery that a woman was a key organizer of the KKK. One vilified her, adding that her experience "in catering to [men's] appetites and vices had given her an insight into their frailties."[11]

Meanwhile, Klan opponents forced congressional hearings on the Klan in 1921. Fearing further exposure, since he was guilty of other improprieties, Clarke immediately announced his resignation. This made Tyler furious. She publicly denounced him, saying he was "weak-kneed and won't stand by his guns." She refused to resign.[12] She even survived an attempt on her life when unknown assailants shot up her home. The congressional report treated her with both respect and misogyny, as the éminence grise behind the Klan. Instead of backing down, she skillfully turned the negative publicity from the hearings into a successful membership drive that grew the Klan exponentially.[13]

Tyler was finally forced to resign by accusations, almost certainly true, of embezzling Klan money.[14] But she had been a gift to the national Klan. The organization might well have grown without this driven, bold, corrupt, and precociously entrepreneurial woman, but it would likely have been smaller.

While Tyler's audacity might seem surprising in a woman of the 1920s, the career of Daisy Douglas Barr undoes today's assumptions even more, because she was a Quaker. In the late twentieth century Quakers became associated with liberal theology, anti-racism, and other progressive attitudes. But a century ago the Friends church included plenty of racists and conservatives and was moving rapidly toward evangelicalism. Barr was by no means the only Quaker in the Klan; in the town of Richmond, Indiana, for example, some 7 percent of Klansmen were Quaker.[15]

A native Hoosier, Daisy Douglas Brushwiller was born in 1875 into a devout Quaker family. She was a prodigy: she was only four, she later said, when she first felt inspired to testify to her spiritual commitment, and at eight and again at twelve she felt "the personal call from God" to preach and spread the word. At sixteen—her autobiographical narrative placed these experiences, conveniently, every four years—she reportedly preached her first public sermon, after which she was "saved" at a United Brethren service conducted by a woman evangelist. ("Girl evangelists" were in vogue at the time.) At eighteen she married schoolteacher Thomas Barr, who joined the Klan at her urging and began leading tent revivals around the state. In 1910 she became pastor of the Muncie, Indiana, Quaker meeting. (Female ministers were uncommon in mainstream white Protestantism but by no means entirely absent.) Soon she too was preaching at revivals, causing many of her listeners to be "saved" and at least one sick man to be cured. She was prolific on paper as well as out loud, writing a great deal of poetry like this:

> I am clothed with wisdom's mantle . . .
> I am strong beyond my years;
> My hand typifies strength,
> And although untrained in cunning
> Its movements mark the quaking
> Of the enemies of my country.
> My eye, though covered, is all-seeing;*
> It penetrates the dark recesses of law violation,
> Treason, political corruption and injustice,
> Causing these cowardly culprits to bare their unholy faces . . .
> My feet are swift to carry the strength of my hand
> And the penetrations of my all-seeing eye.
> My nature is serious, righteous and just,
> And tempered with the love of Christ.
> My purpose is noble, far-reaching and age-lasting . . .
> I am the Spirit of Righteousness.
> They call me the Ku Klux Klan.
> I am more than the uncouth robe and hood
> With which I am clothed.
> YEA, I AM THE SOUL OF AMERICA.[16]

Daisy Barr thus fused religiosity and Klannishness with extraordinary confidence and without a touch of feminine meekness.

Like many other clubwomen of the time, Barr was a joiner, never limiting herself to a single affiliation. A woman of formidable energy, she also threw herself into an array of reform causes: president of the

* This is a reference to the "all-seeing eye" used by Masons as symbol of truth and power.

Indiana Humane Society, active in the campaign for Prohibition, creator of the Muncie YWCA (the Y's were then fierce temperance and revivalist organizations), and founder of a "refuge," the Friendly Inn, for former prostitutes. (Like many such reformers, she was baffled that the "fallen women" were not interested in being "rescued" by evangelicals.) When the Barrs moved to Indianapolis in 1917, Daisy became president of Indiana War Mothers. Soon after the woman suffrage amendment passed, she became the vice chair of the Republican State Committee, the first woman to hold such a position; the male co-chair joined the Klan, quite possibly, considering her charisma, at her urging. Meanwhile, her husband became Indiana's deputy state bank commissioner. This was a power couple.

Barr soon became Imperial Empress of a women's Klan affiliate, Queens of the Golden Mask. She wielded considerable bargaining power with Klansmen, a power enlarged when she established the "poison squad," a statewide women's network (of which more below). The squad practiced black psywar, spreading rumors, allegedly from Catholics or Jews, designed to make the alleged sources appear immoral and thus to build support for Klan political candidates. By 1923 she was head of the Indiana WKKK and a traveling speaker for the Klan itself. A whirlwind of energy, in July of that year she led a naturalization ceremony with two hundred women and claimed that one thousand would-be members were present but lacked the proper regalia required for admission. Three months later she led Indiana's most spectacular Klan parade yet. So influential was the Indiana WKKK under her leadership that she almost succeeded in moving its national headquarters to Indianapolis.

As WKKK spokeswoman, Barr frequently broadcast feminist messages. Her reform work had long been oriented toward women, and she campaigned to have a woman added to the Indianapolis police force—a typical Progressive Era cause, motivated by the belief that women were less corrupt and harder on moral offenses than men. She once publicly reprimanded a police officer for uncouth remarks. Her speeches honored woman suffrage and urged women to make active use of their new political citizenship. Her temperance arguments featured stories of drunken male brutality, as befitted a member of the WCTU. She hurled vitriol against gamblers, adulterers, and men who patronized prostitutes and despoiled young girls. She called on women to support female candidates, to step up and exert power in their churches.

Her affiliations arose, no doubt, from firm principle, but they were also lucrative. She contracted with the Klan to be chief WKKK recruiter for Indiana, Kentucky, West Virginia, Pennsylvania, Ohio, Michigan, New Jersey, and Minnesota. The agreement guaranteed her a dollar for each woman initiated and four dollars for each recruit within Indiana. Moreover, she became the conduit for puchases of robes, from which she likely received a percentage of sales.[17] (No wonder she refused to "naturalize" women who lacked the regalia.) But like Tyler, Barr was apparently not satisfied with these profits, and Klan leaders complained that she did not deliver the required sums to national headquarters. Numerous male Klan leaders did the same; the flow of money, combined with lack of accountability, presented irresistible temptations to corruption.

Klan feminism also appeared prominently in the work and words of the Rev. Alma Bridwell White. (See figure 20.) Although never an official of a Klan group, she was easily as influential as Barr in spreading its message. As evangelist, minister, and bishop, she founded the Pillar of Fire "holiness" congregations[18] and gained a national fame through multitudinous lectures and wrote thirty-five religious books and some two hundred hymns.[19] Her Pillar of Fire religious movement ultimately established fifty-two churches, not counting a few abroad, seven divinity schools, two radio stations, ten magazines and newsletters, and two colleges.[20] Like Tyler and Barr, she displayed extraordinary entrepreneurial skills, but her bigotry surpassed theirs and rivaled that of any Klansman in its intensity.

Born in 1862 in Kentucky, one of seven sisters, White was also a girl evangelist. She found rebirth at age sixteen at a Wesleyan Methodist revival where, she later wrote, "some were so convicted that they left the room and threw up their suppers, and staggered back into the house as pale as death."[21] She enrolled in Millersburg Female College, then at age nineteen traveled on her own to Montana and Utah, where she taught school—clearly an adventurous teenager. She married Kent White, a seminarian, and the couple started an unsanctioned Methodist Pentecostal church in Denver.[22] They soon broke with Pentacostalism and moved their church into the holiness movement, christening it Pillar of Fire. Already impatient with her husband, Alma White took over and soon became its recognized leader.

Defying protests from the Methodist hierarchy, White remained committed to arousing Pentecostal-style "enthusiastic" worship, with singing, shouting, dancing, and fits. *Time* magazine wrote that she generated "fundamentalist ecstasy and hallelujah-shouting."[23] Never particularly modest, she claimed the power to bring people to their knees, sobbing in an agony of contrition, or to "make them skip about the aisles, singing and shouting with joy."[24] As she described her method, she never prepared a sermon but chose a text and then waited for the "heavenly dynamite" to explode. Many Klan lecturers worked to induce a religious commitment among listeners, and many claimed biblical authorization for the Ku Klux Klan, but none as diligently as White. In writing and performing, she not only surpassed the fervor of Klan lecturers but even claimed that many biblical heroes were actually Klansmen. One of her many books, *The Klan in Prophecy*, reported that the KKK had been divinely ordained.

In 1907 one of the Whites' converts, a rich widow, gifted them a large farm property in central New Jersey. The Whites moved there, naming it Zarephath, after the biblical village where the prophet Elijah raised the son of a widow from the dead. In 1918 White arranged for the evangelist who had converted her to consecrate her as Pillar of Fire's bishop—the first woman bishop in the United States. She traveled the country speaking at revivals and camp meetings and established a mission in London, preaching against liquor and "present tendencies in women's dress."[25] Her stamina and ambition outdid even the most committed Klan speakers; she claimed to have crossed the Atlantic fifty-eight times and traveled fifty thousand miles in one year.[26]

Zarephath flourished and expanded. Alma White was part of a trend: the 1920s produced numerous female preachers, particularly Pentacostal preachers, many of whom could arouse zealous followers through their tent revivals. Even a few more mainstream religious groups, such as Reform Jews, Northern Baptists, and Presbyterians, were giving women larger roles, and the Methodist Episcopals decided in 1920 to allow women deacons. (African American churches had female ministers much earlier.) In starting a new church, Alma White was following the example of Mary Baker Eddy, founder of Christian Science, although she labeled Eddy satanic. White compared herself favorably to Aimee Semple McPherson, the most popular evangelist of the time, who advertised her ten-thousand-member congregation as the largest in the world. White emulated McPherson in establishing a radio station, WAWZ, the letters standing for Alma White Zarephath. (In 1961 Pillar of Fire established station WAKW in Cincinnati, the letters referring to her son, Arthur Kent White.)[27]

Pillar of Fire distinguished itself from other holiness groups through its explicit and intensive support of the Ku Klux Klan. White's writings and speeches focused on four pillars of Klan ideology: white supremacy, anti-Catholicism, anti-Semitism, and temperance. Perhaps because of her base in New Jersey, home of 117,000 African Americans in 1920, she emphasized racism against African Americans, while Klanspeople in locations with smaller black populations emphasized immigrants, Catholics, and Jews: "Social and political equality would plunge the world into an Inferno as black as the regions of night." Noah cursed Ham, the black man, she reported, and ordered that he must be the servant of Japheth. "Whatever wrong may have been perpetrated against the Negro race by bringing black men to this country . . . the argument will not hold that they should share equal social or political rights with the white men—the sons of Japheth." She advocated, therefore, repeal of the Fifteenth Amendment. "America is a white man's country and should be governed by white men. Yet the Klan is not anti-negro . . . [but] is eternally opposed to the mixing of the white and colored races. . . . God drew the color line and man should so let it remain."[28] "Red men" were equally doomed because God had given the land to the sons of Japheth.[29]

Her camp meetings and revivals began to feature cross-burnings and Klan lecturers. She published three books of praise for the Klan and a periodical devoted exclusively to the Klan, the *Good Citizen*, and offered positive appraisals of the Klan in her many other sermons, books, and hymnals.[30] The Klan funded her purchase of Westminster College (later renamed Belleview College) in Westminster, Colorado, a dilapidated former Presbyterian school; located high on a hill, it proved a perfect location for cross-burnings that were visible for miles. She established there another Christian radio station, KPOF, known as AM91: The Point of Faith. Three years later the Klan provided the funds to establish Alma White College in Zarephath, used frequently for Klan meetings and large spectacles. In 1926 the Klan joined White in establishing a 396-acre summer resort for its members in Zarephath.

Alma White anointed the Klan as the country's savior: "Now come the Knights of the Ku Klux Klan in this crucial hour to contend for the faith of our fathers. . . . There is no longer any excuse for those who, like Elisha's servant, have been blinded by the falsehoods propagated by the enemies of the Klan. . . . The Klan is a tree of God's own planting." She also situated the Klan in a historical patriotism: "Our heroes in the white robes are the perpetuators of the work so nobly begun by the colonists and the Revolutionary fathers." She supported the Klan's electoral activism: "They must name candidates who can be safely trusted, those who will not betray the public on questions of such vital importance as prohibition, restricted immigration, white supremacy and other issues." She also called for "the prevention of unwarranted strikes by foreign labor agitators."[31]

At the same time, White made no attempt to soft-pedal her feminism. She reprinted the 1848 "Declaration of Sentiments" from the famous Seneca Falls women's rights convention in one of her books. She condemned women's lack of legal rights vis-à-vis their husbands, calling for action against wife-beating and for women's right to their own property and legal domicile. (In many states a husband could still control his wife's property and require her to move with him anywhere he desired.) She called for sex equality in inheritance rights. Defying evangelical opposition to divorce, she argued for a woman's entitlement to divorce in case of infidelity or threat to her personal safety. She denounced the practice of granting child custody to men in divorce—important because the risk of losing children was by far the most important factor keeping women in abusive marriages. And she supported the Equal Rights Amendment, first proposed in 1923 (and, of course, still not ratified).[32]

This passionate feminism likely arose, in part, from her own ambition and a bitterness about the obstacles and insults she had encountered. But her brand of feminism also supported her religious bigotry. The Catholic Church rested on the subjugation of women, she charged. This accounted for its opposition to Prohibition: liquor was for Catholic men a tool for keeping women subordinated. Convents were "paper prisons" that served to keep women uneducated, in ignorance of cultural and political affairs; they continued the "Old Roman law which made women the chattels or the slaves of men." The church "hates any movement that tends to the uplifting and enlightenment of the tender sex."[33]

Each in her own way, Elizabeth Tyler, Daisy Barr, and Alma White rupture some commonsense expectations about the 1920s Klan and other conservative movements. Perhaps most striking was their entrepreneurship, which involved both ambition and skill, both principle and profit. In this respect, they probably differed from rank-and-file Klanswomen. Experienced at organizing large events, state-of-the-art in managing money, unafraid to attract publicity, they were thoroughly modern women. Nor did they disguise their work in sentimental, Victorian versions of femininity. Tyler's life itself challenged the sexual double standard; Barr and White, while properly married, rejected female domesticity. But their outlook on the world may not have differed so much from that of their followers and of hundreds of thousands, at least, of other Klanswomen. In this movement, as in liberal and leftist movements, women found themselves enjoying not only the sociability and prestige of club membership but also the opportunity to weigh in on political matters. The clubby solidarity of the WKKK, like that of the Klan itself, grew more attractive, more interesting, when it involved collective action.

Barr and White were also women's rights advocates, as was Tyler, implicitly, through her achievements. Their activism requires a more capacious understanding of feminism. Their combination of feminism and bigotry may be disturbing to today's feminists, but it is important to feminism's history. There is nothing about a generic commitment to sex equality that inevitably includes commitment to equalities across racial, ethnic, religious, or class lines. In fact, espousing sex equality and enacting female leadership have often been easier for conservative women, because their whole ideological package does not threaten those who benefit from other inequalities. (Leaders such as Margaret Thatcher and Sarah Palin may serve as illustrations.)

Barr's and White's fusion of religion and politics also suggests another way that Klanswomen fit into the American political tradition. That tradition may have been weakening among urban elites, but it remained strong in the Midwest and West and in smaller cities. Bringing religious passion to politics was not only an instrumental combination, though it was that. The women's mastery of public speaking, derived from church experience, not only benefited the Klan but also brought them personal rewards—fame, prosperity, and the pleasure of doing something so well and so highly valued. We should not assume that the late-twentieth-century rise of the Christian Right was unprecedented.

WHETHER INFLUENCED BY THESE THREE spokeswomen or by local campaigners, women's Klan groups sprang up across the nation. They often drew in women who were already members of other women's organizations, particularly elite societies. Some preexisting patriotic groups, such as the Dixie Protestant Women's Political League and the Grand League of Protestant Women, actually folded into the WKKK. The leader of the Colorado WKKK, Laurena Senter, was also the president of an array of Colorado women's clubs.[34] The first national WKKK leader, Lulu Markwell, was the former president of the Arkansas WCTU. An Indiana WKKK joined with the Colonial Dames to stage a pageant at which "Klanswomen dressed as Columbia, Uncle Sam, liberty and justice."[35]

There was particularly great overlap between the WKKK and the Daughters of the American Revolution (DAR), but their difference in priorities was significant. While the DAR was intensely racist toward African Americans, it did not agitate against Catholics or Jews; in fact, it acknowledged that some of them were eligible for membership, because they had ancestors who contributed to the American Revolution. And unlike the Klan, the 1920s DAR concentrated on reviling "subversives"—that is, liberals and radicals—continuing the postwar anticommunist hysteria. It created a blacklist of "seditious" organizations, ranging from labor unions to the Women's International League for Peace and Freedom.[36] It worked not only to protest "disloyal" speakers and deny them access to lecture halls but also threatened to expel any members who attended lectures by these "Liberals, Radicals, Socialists, Communists, and Anarchists," as the committee wrote.[37] True, the

Klan was isolationist and opposed US membership in the League of Nations, expressing views that were strong precisely in the midwestern, plains, southern, and western states where it flourished. But it identified its enemies by race, religion and place of birth rather than ideology. For example, its anti-Semitism did not much identify Jews with radicalism. That the WKKK avoided ideological and foreign policy concerns may also reflect the dominant assumption that women should not be concerned with international relations, a sign that it accepted some and challenged other aspects of the conventional gender order.

The first groups to appear called themselves Klan auxiliaries. They announced themselves boldly: Elizabeth Tyler announced that "we plan that all women who join us shall have equal rights with that of the men."[38] Many male leaders rejected this claim, because it implied a sex-integrated Klan. To admit women represented a major sacrifice to many Klansmen who valued their entitlement to a unique men's club and the male camaraderie they so enjoyed. But the evidence suggests that Tyler's claim was correct. In Maine, the Klan head explained, "women came to me in groups . . . and requested that a *branch* [my emphasis] for women be started." They then worked out plans for "such an auxiliary."[39] The Oregon chapter, for example, began as the Ladies of the Invisible Empire (LOTIE), organized through an ad in the Klan newspaper, the *Western American*—a typical way to reach recruits. And LOTIE's Supreme Grand Council included four male Klan leaders, who filed the articles of incorporation for the women's group.

But even the Klansmen most resistant to allowing women the use of the KKK name reversed themselves when they recognized their material interest: by making the women's organization official, the Klan could seize a significant share of women's Klecktokens (priced initially at five dollars but later raised to ten) and other payments. At least one Indiana WKKK Klavern had to send 66 percent of its revenue to Klan headquarters.[40] In Pennsylvania another dollar per woman member went to the state Klan, and this practice may also have prevailed elsewhere. Anti-

Klan journalists pointed out that women's groups were "profitable enterprises" for the Klan.[41] Unsurprisingly, there was rebellion. For example,
the Maine WKKK no sooner formed than it challenged the Maine King
Kleagle's demand for half of its dues; the challenge contributed to a
coup that forced his resignation.[42] Because the women's Klaverns were
often quite flush—the Arkansas WKKK took in $322,000 in 1925, for
example—conflicts over money soon weakened male-female unity in
the Klan.[43]

Official Klan publications typically communicated conservative,
even Victorian messages about what women should do: "God intended
that every man should possess insofar as possible, his own home and
rule his own household"; or "We pity the man who permits the loss of
manhood through fear of wife."[44] The most important female virtue
was chastity, and it was men's duty to protect and enforce that virtue.
Klansmen imagined "their" women as supporting the men, who would
monopolize the serious work. Typical of male expectations was a comment that the women "are going to play an important role in regard to
upholding the morals of our young women. Let us give them our full
support . . . and see that they grow in grace and numbers."[45] A Klan
newspaper assigned women to conventional, traditional domesticity:

> The charm of the home depends upon the woman, because the
> Woman is the Home. It matters not so much about the size of
> the roof nor the elegance nor plainness of the furnishings be-
> neath, as about the woman who dwells therein. If . . . each night
> sees her a better housekeeper, a better seamstress, a better cook,
> a better wife, a better mother, a better woman—which means a
> better citizen.[46]

WKKKers not only rejected that definition of their work but soon
rejected even the label "auxiliary" and began to identify as full-fledged
Klanspeople, full partners in the Invisible Empire.

Many of these new Klanswomen, already a part of the world of sororal orders, joined in search of female bonding. Writer Rebecca McClanahan recalled that her grandmother, envious that her husband had been admitted to the Improved Order of Red Men—which, of course, did not admit American Indians—yearned to be accepted by its little sister, the Order of Pocahontas, as she was "tired of being a paleface." She longed for connections to other women. Though Klanswomen did not typically engage in physical violence, the psychological violence of being excluded from a prestigious group could be painful indeed. Those admitted, McClanahan's grandmother knew, indulged in titillating rituals: initiates were "tied to a stake and then rescued by a warrior or warrioress, were given access to secret signs and passwords. . . . A complicated right-hand gesture signified, 'Who are you?' A left-hand response signified, 'A friend.'"[47] It was not only men who enjoyed these performances.

So the WKKK unified its many locals through rituals similar to men's, but just different enough to exhibit some creativity. (See figure 22.) It used the Klan's secret symbols, acronyms, gestures, and new names for days of the week and months, but created its own constitution, ritual books, and manifestos, including a women's Kloran. New initiates received congratulations for their womanly sacrifice and their decision to join the "delectable" Invisible Empire. They established their own internal judicial system, arguing that women could discipline and punish each other more effectively than men could. Crimes subject to WKKK discipline included disrespecting or disgracing women's honor, miscegenation, profanity, and failure to follow the rules of the constitution. The women's ritual used water differently than the men's: replicating a christening, they wet their fingers, then touched shoulders, foreheads, and the air, signifying body, mind, and spirit. The women's Kloran explained that the copper penny, used in many of their rituals, served as a reminder to keep church and state separate. The hourglass, another WKKK ritual object, symbolized women's patriotism: "So long as the sands of time run through the American hourglass, whenever Patriotism calls, we Women of the Ku Klux Klan will respond."[48]

The women's robes were similar, but they offered a discriminatory choice: an ordinary "Klan cloth" robe was five dollars, but you could order a satin robe for twenty-five. Men, of course, did not wear satin, a feminine fabric, but the availability of upscale regalia may have signaled something more: that women's interest in attractive clothing led to greater class differentiation within the movement, in contrast to the much-touted simulation of leveling among the men.

The WKKK adopted a heroine first exalted by an earlier Klan women's group, the Kamelia: Joan of Arc—yes, that Catholic heroine—as "Joan, the Militant Kamelia."[49] It did not seem to bother Klanswomen that they apparently could not find a Protestant heroine to honor in the same way, but the appropriation of Joan signals their desire to identify with someone powerful; her warlike militance did not seem to them unladylike. They identified with St. Joan because they, like her, were responding to the voice of God and defending their country against "foreign" invaders. There is a long tradition of ambitious and eloquent women defending their right to public leadership on the grounds that God called upon them. American feminists Maria Stewart and Angelina Grimké, leading spokeswomen for the campaign against slavery, used that justification for their public speaking. Its continued use in the 1920s suggests that some Klanswomen felt some anxiety about women's public activism. But they would not surrender. A Kamelia pamphlet about Joan of Arc insisted that Klanswomen's voices must "challenge and command."[50] Oregon Klanswomen created their own Joan image and used it on their publications: a woman dressed in Klan robes, riding a charging horse similarly robed, carrying a sword, the initials LOTIE (Ladies of the Invisible Empire) emblazoned on her headscarf.[51]

For the majority of Klanswomen, organizing social events and pageants was their biggest contribution to the cause. These events required massive amounts of labor, much of it done by women: finding a site, generating publicity, arranging for parking, preparing or ordering food and drink, designing and executing decorations, advertising, mimeographing programs, keeping children occupied and well behaved, ushering visiting dignitaries in and out, collecting items for tag sales and bake sales, handling the inevitable logistical breakdowns. Like churchwomen and clubwomen everywhere, they were party planners. This work was doubly traditional: an extension of their personal domestic labor and a service to Klansmen. (Indeed, one of the WKKK's most prominent lecturers was pressed into service as a secretary for a male Klan speaker.[52]) Without these hours of labor the Klan could not have become such a mass movement. At the same time, this work brought women together, and that togetherness both strengthened the Klan and, at times, challenged its male hierarchy.

Still, some Klanswomen enunciated ideas that did not comport with conventional domesticity. It may be an indication of women's influence that once the suffrage amendment passed, the whole northern Klan supported it enthusiastically—though, of course, only for white women. Support for woman suffrage also reflected the Klan's opportunism in their desire for white women's votes to counteract "alien" votes. Whatever the motives, WKKK members strenuously encouraged women's political participation, and understood that maintaining that right required vigilance. One recruitment leaflet declared that men should no longer hold "exclusive dominion" in the world of politics and chastised women for their political passivity.[53]

Klanswomen similarly supported women's employment and even called for women's economic independence. "Women's economic freedom, which has slumbered for ages, awakes."[54] Oregon Klanswomen urged members to patronize female proprietors.[55] Local studies report that about 20 percent of WKKK members were employed, and Kathleen Blee thought this an underestimate.[56] In one Klavern, 25 percent of the members were schoolteachers and one-third held middle-class jobs.[57] Surprisingly, and rather opportunistically, Oregon Klanswomen condemned the Meier & Frank department store for paying "slave wages" to the women and girls it employed; they knew, of course, that Meier & Frank was Jewish-owned.[58] The WKKK Imperial Commander's insistence that wives should be called "helpmeets" rather than "helpmates" suggests that many husbands could not single-handedly support their families.[59] Major Kleagle Leah H. Bell of Indiana told an audience of eight thousand that "the mothers of America" should "begin campaigning for an eight-hour workday."[60] Larger groups paid salaries to their staffers: Denver's WKKK Kligrapp (secretary) earned $150 per year ($4,387 in 2016), and at least one Indiana Klavern also paid salaries[61]—indicating that not enough volunteer labor was available, that some members needed the money, that women expected to be paid, or all of the above.

To a lesser extent the WKKK expressed opinions about national issues, supporting child welfare provisions. A 1926 Klonvocation called for uniform marriage statutes across the states so as to regularize domestic law in women's favor. As Blee pointed out, Klanswomen saw anti-miscegenation laws differently from Klansmen, as defense against white men who betrayed white women by consorting with women of color.[62] Oregon Klanswomen expressed outrage that you could, they claimed, get a divorce by mail in that state, and demanded that men be made to pay child support.[63]

In one small but much-cited indication of WKKK feminism, in 1926 the Silver Lake, New Jersey, Klavern invited Margaret Sanger to speak about birth control. A former Socialist Party member and feminist, and a nurse who had seen firsthand the economic and health costs of large families, she was the most prominent national leader in the campaign to legalize contraception. Sanger's background, anathema to Klan values, included cosmopolitanism, avant-garde arts, radical politics, even free love. Conservatives vilified her. Moreover, she had defied laws against obscenity—birth control was still legally obscene at the time—served some time in jail, and fled to Europe to escape further prosecutions. But by the mid-1920s she had brought the birth control movement into alliance with eugenics. She announced that her Birth Control League "was ready to unite with the eugenics movement whenever the eugenists were able to present a definite program of standards for parenthood on a eugenic basis," according to the *New York Times*.[64] Sanger was by no means a bigot. She accepted some eugenical categories, such as "feeble-minded," but never the Klan's racial and religious hierarchy. (She herself was of Catholic descent, although her father was a freethinker.) She did, however, see eugenists as allies in her campaign for reproduction control, and in that connection her interests coincided with those of the Klan. Sanger agreed to speak to the Klanswomen, although with considerable unease because she disliked the Klan's racism. They received her enthusiastically, and she reported receiving a dozen further speaking invitations from the WKKK.[65]

The fact that Sanger crossed paths with the WKKK says little about her politics; her policy was to speak to any group that would have her. Inviting her says rather more about the New Jersey Klanswomen. Because open endorsement of birth control was still a radical act at the time, and Sanger herself was controversial, inviting her suggests that these Klanswomen may have been interested in reproduction control. Notably, the WKKK never joined in the "race suicide" rhetoric that denounced upscale white women who limited births. The invitation also suggests Klanswomen's autonomy from the male leadership. Although we cannot assume that this New Jersey Klavern, located near Philadelphia, typified the WKKK, nevertheless birth control was then often in the news, and it seems likely that the power to control when and how often to be pregnant would have stirred many Klanswomen's interest.

Some Klanswomen even challenged one of the Klan's core premises—secrecy. All the Klan groups waffled on this principle, sometimes benefiting from the mystique of concealment, at other times from their public presence. Klanswomen, however, directly contested one kind of secrecy, that within marriage. They argued in the terms of modern, even companionate marriage that good spouses should have no secrets from each other. And they tied this complaint onto demands for economic equality. One woman complained to a Klan newspaper, "I help earn that money. I have a right to know where it goes. Yet my husband says he dares not tell me."[66]

Still, other evidence shows WKKK conformity to established gender rules. Women's sections in the Klan publication the *Kluxer* featured housewifely advice. "Style Tips" in one issue prescribed a dress code: no satin (despite the availability of satin robes), no fur; not too much rouge; never apply makeup in public; be attractive but conservatively so. The "Kook's Kitchen Kabinet" column provided recipes. Amid warnings of threats to America, the Klanswoman could find "answers to everyday questions like 'In making quick breads, how much baking powder is needed for each cup of flour?' or . . . 'What would you suggest as a nice plate lunch for home recruitment meeting?'"[67] But the magazine encouraged women's activism on matters regarding the campaign to keep Protestant prayer and "100% American" teachers in the schools. It emphasized that women could be both activists for the cause and exemplary housewives, even though "we are women and hence are not expected to be interested in certain problems of community welfare to the same extent that men should be interested."[68]

Women's Klaverns emphasized charitable work—raising money for orphanages, schools, and individual needy families or, occasionally, their members. They gave small amounts of cash, assembled gift baskets of food, and announced the names of sick members who needed visits. Southern Klans' charitable expenditures derived not only from pity but also from political strategy: $100 to the widow of a Richmond, Virginia, policeman killed by a criminal; $1,000 to the University of Virginia endowment; $100 to enable Confederate veterans to travel to a reunion.[69] The WKKK in eastern Oregon announced that it had sent fifty-four Christmas packages to "our disabled veterans."[70] Nevertheless, WKKK monetary contributions were, on the whole, negligible. Blee computed that one Klavern, by no means atypical, directed 0.7 percent of its expenditures to charity and concluded that boasts of charitable work were largely fund-raising propaganda. Moreover, much of the WKKK's giving amounted to placing Protestant Bibles in public schools. Few of the WKKK's or KKK's larger projects—orphanage, school, university—ever materialized.[71]

Family and charity remained Klanswomen's dominant conception of women's duties and contributions. The exceptions, their more modern and individual-rights assertions, may simply indicate different orientations among the various chapters. But they also point to a contradiction long embedded in feminist principles: some feminisms challenge the gender order and the practice of identifying women primarily or even exclusively as mothers and wives; others, equally feminist, accept that gender order and promote women's rights within it. (The latter perspective has been called both maternalist and essentialist, because it rests on the assumption that women are naturally nurturing and self-sacrificing, the key qualities associated with motherhood.) Both types see women as victimized by male dominance, but in different ways. Klan feminists belonged to the latter stream. Not all Klanswomen were feminists by any means, but those who were argued that women's responsibility for raising children and protecting morals required political activism to change laws and social customs. Some Klanswomen called their charitable activism "social work," a label then meaning reform work, in a usage common among progressive women reformers up through the 1930s.

Women often led in the youth divisions of the Klan. They visited churches to recruit young people and to persuade parents of their duty to see that their children were imbued with the "right" values. The national Klan, possibly responding to women's pressure, established the Junior Ku Klux Klan, for boys only, in 1923, and gave it a publication of its own, the *Junior Klansmen Weekly*. An adult Klavern was to supervise each Junior chapter. Soon more youth groups sprang up, and by 1924 fifteen states had chapters. The membership fee was only three dollars. The WKKK created the Tri-K Klub for girls, with its own robes, rituals, codes, and symbols. Its "katechism" (the Klan loved turning *C* words into *K* words) resembled that of the Scouts—"loyalty, obedience, selflessness, and Christian patriotism." Girls sang a Klan song to the tune of "Auld Lang Syne:"

> *Beneath this flag that waves above*
> *This cross that lights our way*
> *You'll always find a sister's love*
> *In the heart of each Tri-K.*[72]

Like Scouting, Klan youth groups emphasized sports competitions for boys and crafts for girls. Both sexes could serve as flag bearers and could play in drum and bugle corps. Girls specialized in singing and rhythmic chanting. One festival advertised "kute girls, katchy songs, and kunning costumes." Both Klansmen and Klanswomen adopted a maternalist line regarding the importance of bringing in girls: they would become the mothers who would produce the next generation of Klanspeople. They were to be taught not only true Americanism but also domestic skills and womanly chastity, and teenage girls could compete in beauty and popularity contests to become "Miss 100% America."[73]

Still, northern Klanswomen often campaigned differently than their male comrades. They placed a higher priority on disciplining immorality than their brothers did—another priority shared with progressive women. They bragged of this orientation: with a female Klan in action "many of the moral uplift problems of the present could be solved," one statement claimed.[74] Some of them succeeded in persuading towns and counties to ban or censor not only liquor but also dance halls, films, books, magazines, and Sunday store openings. Classics like *The Great Gatsby, Ulysses,* Dreiser's *American Tragedy,* Radclyffe Hall's *The Well of Loneliness* (a British novel about lesbians), Oscar Wilde's *The Importance of Being Earnest,* any of the "pulp" publications, anything by D. H. Lawrence or Upton Sinclair, even Voltaire's *Candide* could not pass Klanswomen's test. They abhorred interracial marriage, of course, for keeping families "pure" was squarely their responsibility. But they gave this cause a feminist twist, arguing that interracial sex and marriage were examples of male lust and its destructive impact on family life.

Klanswomen were usually unsuccessful, however, in getting Klansmen to bear down on immorality that victimized women. The limits of women's power in the Klan show in how rarely northern Klansmen acted in support of abused Klanswomen. As a Wisconsin Klan leader said, "Sometimes women would want us to go against their husbands for drinking or running around with other women. We refused to do that."[75] The leader of an Oregon Klavern warned, "If you married Klansmen insist on going out with another man's wife be awful sure she doesn't belong to a Klansman. You may have an occasion to meet that gentleman in the Klavern and I am sure it would be a very embarrassing position"—in other words, he was concerned more with protecting his Klavern than with upholding morals.[76] Nancy MacLean found that southern Klansmen sometimes punished men for abuse, nonsupport, and/or infidelity,[77] but there is little evidence of this in the North. Perhaps northern men were less abusive. More likely, northern Klanswomen were more embarrassed to admit their victimization, or were reluctant to undercut their premise that only immigrants, Catholics, and blacks were abusive. The northern Klan also manifested greater deference to the state—at least on issues involving complaints against men considered otherwise respectable. For example, consider this excerpt from minutes of the La Grande, Oregon, Klavern: "For the third time it has been reported that E. J. Schilling, who resides at . . . , has three children by his first wife who are being neglected most shamefully and several Klansmen have advised that we take this matter up. . . . I found that his particular case should come under the jurisdiction of the county health nurse."[78]

The La Grande Klavern's reference to a county health nurse—a position created by Oregon's Progressive Era women reformers—suggests a counterintuitive aspect of Ku Klux Klan principles. It was by no means eager to preempt state functions and sometimes sought to encourage them. It urged police to act more aggressively, and its vigilantes were quite willing to be supervised by the police, providing they operated from a Klannish perspective. (In this respect, the northern Klan was not so different from the southern, where police or sheriff collusion was involved in most lynchings.) Moreover, the northern Klan was no enemy of government welfare provision. "Taxes," one pamphlet argued, "should be looked upon by the taxpayer as the most important bequest he can make to his own children and to humanity."[79] In this respect the Klan's agenda resembled some aspects of women's progressivism. Woman suffrage added to its optimism that, rather than shrink the state, it could reform state activity so as to align it with Klan values. Moreover, in 1932 Klanspeople generally supported Franklin Delano Roosevelt's candidacy, despite his anti-Prohibition stance; this support may reflect the Klan's traditional—though not consistent—alignment with the Democratic Party, but it might also reflect Klanspeople's support for emergency relief. It was only later that they attacked FDR with anti-Semitic labels, calling him "Rosenvelt" and the like.[80] These flexible principles also showed in the sharp decline of anti-Catholic rhetoric in the 1930s.

In much of their agenda, and in the contradictions they expressed regarding women's place in the polity, Klanswomen were indistinguishable from many other clubwomen, including Catholics, Jews, and African Americans. Women's Klaverns seemed to spend more energy arranging social occasions for themselves than did the men's. They organized teas, parties, and card games, and sometimes joint socials with nearby Klaverns. They held receptions for visiting WKKK and

Klan VIPs. And of course they did much of the work for the larger Klan events. One such Indiana event involved camping out in the woods for three days[81]—one can only imagine how much women's work went into those arrangements.

Still, politics and political education remained a part of WKKK activity. While accepting that they were "not expected to be interested in certain problems of community welfare to the same extent that men should be interested," as one WKKK local put it, deferring to gender hierarchy, they nevertheless aimed to "assist all Protestant women in the study of practical politics . . . to scrutinize with impartiality the platforms of political parties."[82]

Klanswomen were probably divided in their attitude toward participation in conventional politics, which they considered corrupted by immigrant non-Protestants, but united in condemnation of the rebellion against Victorian standards of modesty that was steadily gaining strength. They feared what they saw as libertine behavior and unchaste media though they rarely acknowledged that they arose from commercial enterprises. They were thoroughly, consistently unhappy with unchaste dress, with improper leisure activity, music, and movies, and with sexual and artistic radicalism. In this perspective, despite the fact that the Klan flourished in many cities, its women members considered big-city life destructive. It was undermining the multifaceted purity that was core to Klan ideology.

Where the WKKK differed most radically was not in its bigotry— for many organizations shared in that—but in how the members acted on it. Vigilante violence, of course, remained always men's work in their world. Still, in promoting the hatreds and fears that gave rise to it, they bear moral, if not legal, responsibility along with the men. Moreover, in the political and economic warfare waged against "aliens," Klanswomen participated equally with Klansmen.

KKK members and Royal Riders of the Red Robe, a Klan auxiliary, welcomed by a minister, Portland, Oregon. (*Oregon Historical Society*)

Chapter 8

OREGON AND THE
ATTACK ON
PAROCHIAL SCHOOLS

STARTING IN THE MID-NINETEENTH CENTURY, AND
extending through the mid-twentieth century, Oregon was arguably the
most racist place outside the southern states, possibly even of all the
states. Its legislature tried to keep it all white, excluding people of color
with a host of discriminatory laws. So when the Klan arrived in 1921, its
agenda fit comfortably into the state's tradition. When I tell people that
Oregon was a stronghold of the Klan, they express surprise, even shock,
because of the state's current reputation as liberal. But that is because
they don't understand its history or demography. Neither did I, although
I grew up there. The fact that Portland is my hometown influenced my
decision to focus on the Oregon Klan as a case study, but the Oregon
case offers other advantages, too. The Klan gained particularly formidable power there, especially in Portland; Oregon shared with Indiana the
distinction of having the highest per capita Klan membership. Moreover, the Oregon Klan's muscle led it more actively into electoral politics
than most other state Klans. And the Oregon case provides insight into
the Klan's class composition and trajectory.

Klan recruiters probably understood Oregon's potential. Like Indiana, its population of approximately eight hundred thousand in 1920 was

overwhelmingly Protestant and white, and 87 percent native-born; of the foreign-born, half were US citizens. Its approximately 2,400 African Americans constituted 0.3 percent, its Catholics 8 percent, and its Jews 0.1 percent of the population, and this demography was both cause and effect of its history of bigotry. In 1844 the Oregon Territory banned slavery but at the same time required all African Americans to leave. In 1857, in the process of achieving statehood, it put two pieces of a future constitution to a referendum vote, and the same contradiction emerged: 75 percent of voters favored rejecting slavery, but 89 percent voted for excluding people of color. Meanwhile, the state offered 650- to 1,300-acre plots of land free—to white settlers. Prevented by federal law from expelling existing black residents, its constitution banned any further blacks from entering, living, voting, or owning property in Oregon (the only state to do this), to be enforced by lashings for violators. In 1862, forced to vacate the previous ban, it levied a $5 (worth $120 in 2016) annual tax on African Americans, Chinese, Hawaiians, and multiracial people who persisted in living there. The Chinese were specifically denied state citizenship. (In 1893 La Grande, Oregon, whites burned that city's Chinatown to the ground.) Oregon refused to ratify the enfranchisement of black men by the Fourteenth and Fifteenth Amendments; it only did so—and this may come as another surprise—in 1959 and 1973, respectively. In 1906 the Oregon Supreme Court ruled that the prevalent racial segregation of public facilities was constitutional. Interracial marriage was prohibited until 1951.[1] So except for the fact that its targets were new, Catholics in particular, the Klan could be said to be merely reviving old causes.

World War I had created a boom market for Oregon's key products: lumber, paper, grain, and ships. As global commerce grew, so did the Port of Portland. Although 110 miles from the Pacific, it sits at the confluence of the mighty Columbia and the Willamette Rivers, which produced a valuable deep-water port. Although the 1912 federal Rivers and Harbors Act transferred authority to the Port of Portland Commission, the port was then so important nationally that the US Army

Corps of Engineers maintained it. Then a 1920s postwar recession reduced demand for Oregon products, notably lumber, just as Portland experienced a taste of the "Roaring Twenties"—dance halls, speakeasies, movies, flapper fashion. This upsurge in visible "sin" naturally produced an opposition, including an evangelical revival, which in turn built a demand for action to suppress it. The combination of economic and cultural factors and a rich vein of possible recruits contributed to the Klan's high-velocity Oregon success.

The Klan also had a ready-made organizational base in Oregon. The Federation of Patriotic Societies (FoPS) arose in 1916 to fight Catholicism and to prevent Catholics from holding public office. Akin to the American Protective Association, it was headed by a virulently racist Presbyterian minister from South Africa. Very secretive—the *Oregon Voter* wrote that "the names of neither delegates nor participating bodies have so far been disclosed"—FoPS served as the political arm of seventeen fraternals, including the Knights of Pythias, the Odd Fellows, the Scottish Rite Masons, and the Loyal Orange Order from Northern Ireland. It pressured politicians to declare their religious allegiances, thus making Protestantism a public political qualification. By 1922 FoPS would become, for all political purposes, a Klan appendage, with the Exalted Cyclops as its president.[2]

The film *Birth of a Nation* further tilled the soil for the Klan in Oregon, as it did everywhere the second Klan arose. Playing in Portland theaters first in 1915, and again in 1918 and 1922, the last showing under Klan auspices, it drew huge audiences despite the unusually high admission price of two dollars. Protests on behalf of the approximately 1,500 African Americans in Portland persuaded the mayor to draft an emergency ordinance to ban it, but the city council would not go along. Yet this very mayor joined the Klan just a few years later, posing for a formal photograph with Klansmen and the chief of police—an indication of the Klan's power to change minds, or to intimidate.[3]

The Klan arrived in Oregon in 1921, when recruiter Luther Ivan

Powell arrived from California. Simultaneously, in a contested school board election, explicitly anti-Catholic candidates beat out the slate endorsed by all three major Portland newspapers. As is so often the case when examining 1920s religious prejudice, it is hard to know how much of the vote was anti-Catholic and how much a revolt against elite political insiders.[4] In any case, Klan recruiter Powell received an enthusiastic welcome. He began to gather joiners through a series of moves that were by then standard procedures for the Klan: after rounding up some Masons and other fraternal members, recruiters would arrange a public lecture by an "escaped nun"—in this case Sister Lucretia (Elizabeth Schoffen); distribute anti-Catholic pamphlets, slipped into cars and under doors; put on a lecture by a fire-and-brimstone evangelist; and persuade some ministers to endorse the Klan in sermons.[5]

Powell quickly established Klaverns in Oregon's six largest towns and soon boasted of fourteen thousand members, about 2 percent of the state's population. He claimed a thousand members in Portland within three months, and nine thousand before long; Portlanders eventually constituted 64 percent of the state's Klansmen. Crosses burning on Portland's Mt. Tabor and Mt. Scott were visible for miles.[6] Nearly every community with a population of one thousand or more had a Klavern.[7] The small town of Auburn in eastern Oregon reported being "flooded with application blanks" in one week.[8] By 1923 the state Klan professed to have fifty-eight Klaverns and as many as fifty thousand members, not including members of the WKKK or the youth groups. (These figures seem to be typical Klan exaggerations, but on the other hand they do not include the many nonmembers who supported the Klan agenda.)

Further roiling Oregon's traditional political alignments and contributing to Klan growth was a series of strikes in 1922, by longshoremen and railroad workers, both vital to the state economy. The IWW's relative strength in the Pacific Northwest probably explains why the Oregon Klan emphasized anti-Communism more than in other regions. Portland's mayor and the mainstream press warned of the "overthrow of law and order, the ruin of industry, and the Russianizing of the world."[9]

Recruiter Powell soon ceded leadership to Fred Gifford, who became Exalted Cyclops of the Portland Klan. (Powell later went on to lead a paramilitary group, the Khaki Shirts of America, which identified itself as the vanguard of US fascists; he would also join William Dudley Pelley's fascist Silver Shirt Legion in 1933.[10]) An engineer, Gifford began as a telegraph operator for the Southern Pacific Railroad, then became president of an Electrical Workers union local (though after a few years he became known as one of three "$1,000 Scabs" who had betrayed striking workers), then a supervisor for the railroad, then Bell Telephone's manager in charge of construction and maintenance for Oregon and Washington, then Northwestern Electric's chief of transmission.

This is the profile of an ambitious man as well as an employment biography typical of a Klan leader, moving from skilled working class to management. He was also a prominent Mason. He became a statewide power broker, able to grant or withhold support to politicians or lobbying groups eager for Klan support, and there were many such groups, including even the Oregon Automobile Association. The supposedly objective *Oregon Voter* weekly described his style:

> He is the type of man who knows how to keep himself in the background, while inducing activity on the part of other men by the rewards of publicity and public office. Briefly, he combines the attributes of the old-time political boss with a self-sacrificing spirit of devotion to a cause.[11]

By 1923 he was the leading Klansman of the West and a member of Hiram Evans's close circle. His office door said only "Frederick L. Gifford," and in the anteroom candidates for office and Klan workers waited to see the Exalted Cyclops. He "is naturally an exceedingly busy man, and has to conserve his time. The job of running an entire state is a big one," the *Voter* pointed out.[12] His powers extended into the national political theater: Portland mayor George Baker appeared at a Klan banquet in support of Gifford's plan to run for US Senate.[13]

A third Oregon Klan figure, this one less disciplined and more explosive, was Lem Dever, editor of the Klan's Oregon newspaper, the *Western American*. Having worked for the federal government's American Committee on Public Information, a World War I propaganda agency, he became a publicity expert and practitioner of black psywar. (He was responsible for the false oath attributed to the Knights of Columbus, mentioned in chapter 3.) To some extent he represented the pro-worker side of the Klan, promising in his paper that he would not accept advertising from open-shop (that is, anti-union) businesses and pledging his support for the AFL. At the same time, he was one of the few Klan leaders to promote anti-Communism, which he fused with racism, writing in the paper that "he had personal knowledge" of Lenin's plans "to lead the colored hordes of the world in battle against America."[14] The *Western American* was stocked on newsstands, and Dever promoted it with a sales contest that offered a Reo touring car valued at $1,895 as the prize. He defamed the major Oregon newspapers as "pope-bossed, Jew-kept."[15] He used his paper to terrorize individuals, as when he defamed a Greek American for late rent payments and rejoiced when the man fled town. After a few years a feud with Gifford led Dever to quit and denounce the Klan, but not to reject its ideology or methods.[16]

Two other Oregon KKK leaders, both ministers, stood out for their oratory. Reuben H. Sawyer was a representative of Anglo-Israelism; formerly a European evangelist for that sect, he founded a lively Anglo-Israelite church in Portland. This orientation made Sawyer one of the few Oregon Klansmen to prioritize anti-Semitism. His rhetoric was unusually foul: "The Klan is opposed to all groups and races which are not white. . . . It is repugnant to a true American to be bossed by a sheenie. And in some parts of America the Kikes are so thick that a white man can hardly find room to walk."[17] From 1921 to 1924,

Figure 1. Salt Lake City showing of *Birth of a Nation*.
(*Utah Historical Society, Shipler Commercial Photographers Collection*)

(*above*) Figure 2. William J. Simmons, initiator
of the second Ku Klux Klan.
(*Library of Congress Prints and Photographs
Division, Washington, DC [LC-USZ62-104018]*)

(*left*) Figure 3. H. W. Evans, Imperial Wizard, at
the mass Klan march in Washington, DC, 1924.
(*Library of Congress Prints and Photographs
Division, Washington, DC [LC-USZ62-61303]*)

THE DEFENDER OF THE 18TH AMENDMENT

(*above left*) Figure 4. Klan cartoon from Jeremiah J. Crowley's *The Pope: Chief of White Slavers, High Priest of Intrigue*. The accompanying text reads, in part, "Romanism is a Monster . . . the arm of subversion crushing the American flag, crushing the credulous dupe . . . greed grasping public moneys . . . tyranny destroying freedom of conscience."

(*above right*) Figure 5. Klan cartoon defending Prohibition.

(*below*) Figure 6. Klan mass "naturalization," 1922.
(*Library of Congress Prints and Photographs Division, Washington, DC [LC-F82-7717]*)

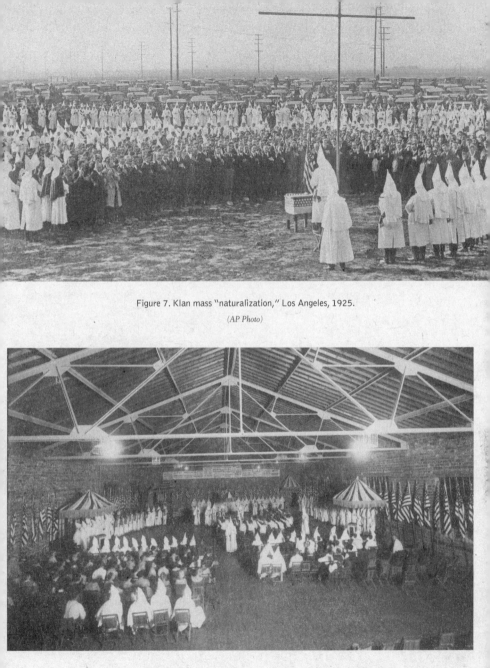

Figure 7. Klan mass "naturalization," Los Angeles, 1925.

(AP Photo)

Figure 8. Klan "naturalization," Moorhead, Minnesota.

(Clay County Historical & Cultural Society)

(above) Figure 9. Klan "naturalization,"
Anderson, Indiana.
(Ball State University Archives &
Special Collections)

(right) Figure 10. Cars on their way
to a Klan mass picnic.
(Courtesy of Western Heritage Center,
Billings, Montana)

(below) Figure 11. Klan choreography.
(Library of Congress Prints
and Photographs
Division, Washington, DC
[LC-USZ62-28024])

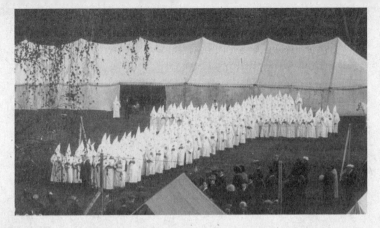

(above) Figure 12. Klan choreography.
(Library of Congress Prints and Photographs
Division, Washington, DC [LC-USZ62-77228])

(left) Figure 13. Klan leaders with their
airplane, 1922.
(Library of Congress Prints and Photographs
Division, Washington, DC [LC-F82-7420])

(below) Figure 14. Klan parade,
Madison, Wisconsin, 1924.
(Wisconsin Historical Society, WHS-1902)

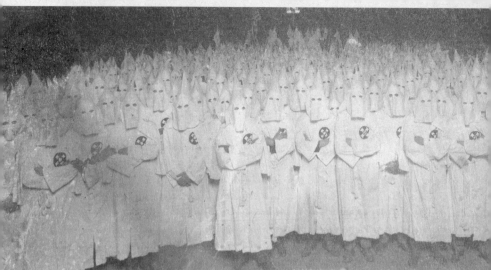

MUNCIE, IND. AUG. 25, 1922.

(above) Figure 15. Klan paraders, Muncie, Indiana, 1922. *(Ball State University Archives & Special Collections)*

(right) Figure 16. Formal Klan portrait, Racine, Wisconsin, 1924. *(Wisconsin Historical Society, WHS-38517)*

(below) Figure 17. Klan vigilantes. *(Ball State University Archives & Special Collections)*

"SWIFT"
DEL. ENGRAVING CO.

Figure 18. 1923 tobacco label for Klansman Tobacco,
All-American Cigar Co., Dallas, Texas.
(Everett Historical / Shutterstock)

(above) Figure 19. Recording from Klan
Music Company, Indianapolis.
(Courtesy Jeff Porter of AtlantaRelics)

(left) Figure 20. Alma Bridwell White,
Pillar of Fire bishop.

Figure 21. Klan christening.
(*Library of Congress Prints and Photographs Division,*
Washington, DC [LC-USZ62-23996])

Figure 22. Women's KKK "naturalization," Long Island, New York, 1924.
(*Library of Congress Prints and Photographs Division, Washington, DC [LC-USZ62-36658])*

he devoted himself to Klan work.[18] (We will meet him again as titular head of Oregon's female Klan group.) Then there was James R.
Johnson, another evangelical, even more rabid in his anti-Catholicism
and anti-Semitism. His speeches literally called for murder: "There is
only one way . . . to convert a Catholic priest. . . . Kill the son of a gun."
Fellow Klansman Lem Dever called Johnson "the best show in town,"
a reminder that in these days before television and talk radio, angry
lectures were a big draw.[19]

The Oregon Klan's most effective legislator was Kaspar K. Kubli (in
a linguistic coincidence, this was his real name), an Oregon native of
Swiss parentage; his initials brought him an exemption from Klan dues.
His father had first tried gold mining but then found better earnings,
as did many failed miners, as a merchant and freight hauler, so Kubli
worked in the family business and later opened a stationery supplies
company. Elected to the Portland City Council in 1904, then to the
state legislature in 1916, he became the Klan's representative as Speaker
of the House. Even before the Klan arrived in Oregon, he had won
passage of an act providing for mandatory sterilization of the "feeble-
minded" and "sexual perverts" (that is, gay men), supported excluding
women from juries and using injunctions to suppress strikes, and wrote
the state criminal syndicalism statute, which allowed prosecuting not
only dissenters but also anyone who rented space to dissenting groups.[20]

Anti-Japanese sentiment also helped build the Klan. Japanese immigrants began arriving after the federal government banned Chinese
immigration in 1881, and thousands worked on constructing railroad
spurs for logging companies. By 1907 Japanese immigrants constituted
40 percent of railway workers, while in Portland and other towns they
ran rooming houses and restaurants and worked in canneries. Taking
farm labor jobs, they also bought or rented land to farm independently.
Expert cultivators, they were soon outproducing and outselling many
white farmers, whose resentment built the Klan's rural support. Near
Portland, Japanese truck farmers flourished, in part because they oper-

ated through a cooperative; their productivity generated white claims that the Japanese would drive out "American" farmers. In the Hood River valley, where anti-Japanese sentiment was particularly strong, an anti-alien organization had arisen before the Klan arrived, and it was soon joined in defaming the Japanese by the American Legion. In central Oregon, where a California developer, the Portland-Deschutes Land Company, had hired Japanese workers, protests forced it to fire them.[21]

Out of Oregon's 1920 population of about eight hundred thousand, people of Japanese origin numbered only five thousand (0.006 percent); although they were mostly rural, fewer than 2 percent owned land, totaling less than three thousand acres (0.008 percent of the land).[22] But it does not require actual economic competition among ethnic groups to generate anger at alleged economic threats. Moreover, anti-Japanese sentiment grew also among the urban population. The Klan escalated this fear of "the Mongolian races." Even the anti-Klan governor, Ben Olcott, told the legislature that "Mongolian and Malay . . . cannot amalgamate and we cannot and must not submit to the peaceful penetration of the Japanese and other Mongolian races."[23] The increasing international prestige of Japan also contributed. Oregon nativists saw the Japanese as the "threatening vanguard of a rising nation intent on . . . subverting communities." In the 1920s in Oregon, "race relations" meant Japanese-white relations.[24]

In 1923, at the peak of Klan ascendancy, the state legislature passed an alien land act, barring immigrants from owning or renting land, with exactly one negative vote. (In nearby Washington State, the legislation even prohibited American-born citizens of Japanese origin, the *nisei*, from renting land on behalf of their parents; the Yakima Indians, theoretically exempt from state legislation, had been renting land to Japanese farmers for decades, but the secretary of the interior ruled that they must obey the prohibition.) Oregon also banned immigrants from operating hospitality businesses, so as to make it harder for the Japanese to find places to stay. Then it imposed a literacy test that left the right to vote in the hands of local registrars whatever their bias. Even a strongly anti-Klan candidate of 1922 favored denying land ownership or control rights to "Orientals."[25]

In southern Oregon and California, the Klan also targeted Mexican Americans, as well as Mexican nationals who came north to work in agriculture. Hiram Evans dangled an anti-Communist line to hook grower support: "Thousands of Mexicans, many of them Communist, are waiting a chance to cross the Rio Grande."[26] Many of these migrant farmworkers found that they had to vary their following-the-crops routes to avoid Klan attacks. By the 1920s, West Coast agriculture depended on a labor force of Mexican origin, so the interests of large corporate growers clashed to some extent with those of the Klan, and one farmworker recalled that growers had to patrol their fields to protect their field hands because "their crops were worthless without Mexicans." Still, Klan attacks probably made farmworkers less militant in their protests, so growers may well have appreciated the Klan's intimidating influence.

Klannish nativism was ever flexible, as was its ability to respond to local conditions. In Oregon, Klan efforts were almost exclusively anti-Catholic, mentioning Jews only occasionally. In the San Diego region, some Catholics even joined: members of the Catholic War Veterans and Knights of Columbus were known to be Klansmen.[27] And just as the Klan bent its agenda to fit local conditions, so did the Catholic Church. In Southern California, many white Catholics supported the Klan. Mexican anthropologist Ernesto Galarza reported that the Irish American clergy "had no sympathy for Mexicans who were seen as an endangerment to traditional American values. They often ignored the Klan's abuses toward Hispanics."[28] In Oregon, as in Maine, the Klan established an affiliate for immigrant white Protestants, the Riders of the Red Robe.

Astoria, a coastal Oregon city, home of the world's largest salmon cannery, provides an example of how local conditions complicated Klan activities. Astoria's Finnish workers became a somewhat liminal group in the Klan's universe. Finns were the largest immigrant group in Astoria, pulled in by the fishing and salmon industries there. As a group they were doubly divided: first, between Protestants and Catholics (plus some Orthodox); second, between those who supported Prohibition, and those who did not, including a substantial group of socialists. The latter group, probably a majority, refused to give up their taverns. The Klan was also divided between "moderates" and the extremists led by Lem Dever. The latter group responded aggressively. It organized a campaign that forced out the Catholic president of the Chamber of Commerce, the Finnish foremen in the salmon cannery, and all the Catholics on the school board. When the local newspaper protested, Dever threatened its editor and offered to buy the paper for the Klan. He even threatened the sheriff: "If you do not take immediate steps to clean out the so-called Whistle Inn . . . this organization will take prompt and drastic action." Receiving no satisfactory response, fifty Klansmen raided the tavern and managed to get the owners of the building prosecuted and the sheriff recalled. When in 1922 Klansmen of the Dever faction won a majority in a local election, electing the mayor and city commissioners, other Klansmen publicly denounced the Dever group for "wire-pulling," that is, rigging the election.[29] This intra-Klan conflict was not unusual, although it arose more often around personal animosities and accusations of corruption, as we will see.

Portland dominated the Oregon Klan both absolutely and proportionately. The five-thousand-seat public auditorium filled time after time for Klan rallies. At one lecture by Rev. Sawyer, the more than fifteen hundred who could not get in "surged" angrily through the center city; eighty-three policemen and fourteen deputy sheriffs were required to control them. Hysterical speeches by "escaped" nuns and priests could be assured of thrilled audiences.[30] The Portland police department became entirely KKKized: it established the Portland Police Vigilantes, a hundred-man group appointed by Gifford and commissioned as police deputies, while a nine-man Black Patrol used violence with total impunity; in 1923, it rounded up suspected IWW members and drove them out of the city.[31]

WHILE OREGON'S RACIAL resentments seethed, and while local Klaverns continued to agitate about local issues, a single campaign soon became the Klan's Oregon priority: getting rid of Catholic schools through a constitutional amendment. This was also a top item on the national Klan agenda, and similar bills were proposed in California, Michigan, Oklahoma, Texas, Washington, and Alberta, Canada. Promoters of a ban on Catholic schools saw Oregon as a test case, and hoped it would lead the way, because of its demography and history. Advocates admitted that there was no "immediate and particular danger" from Catholic or Jewish immigrants in Oregon, "but in the East the number of foreign-born and indifferent [sic] people is so overwhelming that such a bill as this one could never be put through." Oregon would "set the example for the rest of the country," argued supporters. They drew on Oregonians' nostalgic romance with the common schools of "pioneer" days; a key pamphlet, "The Old Cedar School," made the one-room schoolhouse a winning symbol.[32]

The Klan charged that the pope was using parochial schools in his plot to take over America. The Klan did not initiate this conspiracy theory; nineteenth-century nativists did. Even Lyman Beecher, once the country's most revered evangelical, had made this charge in 1835.[33] Standard textbooks, the Klan alleged, "were loaded with Catholicism. The Pope was dictating what was being taught to the children."[34] Thus in its campaign against Catholic schools, the Klan could claim to be fighting a defensive, not offensive, battle[35]—positioning Protestant Anglo-Saxons as victims.

But the Klan also argued that public schools needed improvement. Imperial Wizard Evans cited the results of the World War I draft, in which 24 percent of young men were found to be illiterate.[36] Presumably this resulted from Catholic subversion of public education. Anti-Catholicism thus made Klansfolk into ardent supporters of public education. Like Progressives, they called for more spending on the schools; unlike later conservatives, the Klan did not make cutting taxes or "small government" part of its agenda. It also called for a federal department of education, another agenda item shared with progressive reformers. This was not an original idea. The Sterling-Towner bill of 1919 had first called for creating such a department, raising educational standards, and providing federal funding for schools. That bill also aligned with Klan views that schools should promote "Americanization," then the liberal version of anti-immigrant policy. The national Klan also supported increased spending on public schools, higher pay for teachers, and literacy programs; when Sterling-Towner was reintroduced (as the Towner-Sterling and then Sterling-Reed bills) in 1921 and 1924, the Klan supported it. Ironically, conservative opponents of these proposals, aligned against the Klan on this issue, called the bills "a bagful of bolshevism."[37]

Amending the state constitution to make public schooling compulsory required a referendum. Progressive Era reforms had provided for referendums, initiatives, and recalls in many states; their primary motive was to counter the power of wealthy corporations, especially railroads, that controlled many western states in the 1890s. Oregon was one of the first states to allow these citizen initiatives, in 1902. (Others included South Dakota, Utah, Arizona, Colorado, Nevada, Montana, Washington, Michigan, Kansas, Louisiana, and Oklahoma.) Starting in 1894, Oregon's remarkable radical leader William U'Ren created a coalition of farmer, labor, and women's groups campaigning for these direct-democracy provisions. Stymied at first by the political machine that controlled the legislature, he got himself elected a state representative and from that position organized a revolt against the leadership, by exploiting faction fights within the Republican Party. His coalition got a direct-democracy amendment approved, appropriately, by direct vote; it won overwhelmingly, 62,024 to 5,668.[38] The anti-Catholic school bill that triumphed twenty years later thus signals the complex political meaning of these citizen initiatives: aimed at empowering citizens against political machines, they often provided mechanisms for making illiberal and intolerant law.

The Klan set to work gathering signatures to create a referendum to amend the state constitution so as to require all children to attend public schools and only public schools. Using a new strategy, the Oregon Klan established a front group, the Good Government League, which united other "patriotic" societies, including the Knights of Pythias, the Odd Fellows, the Scottish Rite Masons, the National League for the Protection of American Institutions, and the umbrella Federation of Patriotic Societies.[39] When the initiative went to the polls in 1922, the Scottish Rite Masons was its named sponsor, having already mounted a national campaign against Catholic and "Bolshevist" influence in the public schools, but it was widely assumed to be a Klan initiative.[40]

The Klan's Oregon strategy deemphasized the negative side of the amendment—prohibition of Catholic schools—and emphasized instead its positive content. It argued that strengthening Americanism—that is, patriotism—required educating all children in the same public schools. It emphasized the importance of unity—that is, conformity—in what children learned. Moreover, since Oregonians tended to revere the "pioneers" who had brought Euro-Americans to the state, the Klan presented its schools initiative as furthering "the interest of those whose forefathers established the nation."[41] In an attempt to make the proposed amendment constitutional, the authors wrote it to ban all private schools, not just Catholic ones. Through these strategies, the Klan probably drew in supporters who might have opposed outright discrimination against Catholics.

Some Klan propaganda for the "schools bill," as it came to be called, promoted it on egalitarian grounds, condemning private schools as sites where the rich removed their children from ordinary folk. One statement declared that "we do not believe in snobbery and are just as much opposed to private schools of the so-called 'select' kind as we are to denominational private schools." Advocates characterized opponents of the bill as "millionaires."[42] This argument resonated with Oregon's strong populist traditions, including progressive populist ideas, and drew on resentment of elites. Henry George's single-tax plan elicited considerable support in Oregon; U'Ren was an advocate. (George, a radical nineteenth-century political economist, had proposed a single tax on land holdings, assuming that landownership was the base source of wealth.) But Portland, the center of support for the Klan and the schools referendum, had very few secular private schools; and in Oregon as a whole, more than 60 percent of privately schooled children were in Catholic schools. The prejudice behind the proposed amendment was nevertheless clear to all. One Catholic who saw the "Little Red Schoolhouse" float in a Klan parade (described in the opening depiction of a Klan rally) as a ten-year-old understood it perfectly: "It was a body blow."[43]

The Klan was silent as to whether public school attendance should result in conversions to Protestantism, though this was the hope. In campaigns against Catholic schools, Klan leaders frequently spoke in defense of the separation of church and state, but in fact they were simultaneously promoting Protestant religious content in public schools. "One of our purposes is to try to get the Bible back into the schools," Rev. Sawyer announced."[44] Countless Klan political cartoons showed Catholics throwing Bibles out of schools.

The schools campaigns also showed that Klan bigotry was differentiated, especially between anti-black and anti-Catholic agendas: the Klan wanted Catholic children in public schools, while it was determined to keep African American children out. Klan biogtry swerved between contradictory premises: that immigrants of, say, Italian, Irish, or Finnish descent could be educated to become good Americans with Protestant values (an environmental premise), while people of color, notably African Americans and Japanese Americans, were of biologically inferior stock (the eugenical, hereditarian premise) and could never become "100%."

Meanwhile, the referendum on the schools amendment coincided with the 1922 state election.[45] Called by many Oregonians "the Klan election," it was high drama.[46] The Republican candidate for the governorship, incumbent Ben W. Olcott, refused to support the schools amendment, less from opposition to its content than because he felt it would strengthen the Klan, which he considered divisive. The Democrat, Walter M. Pierce, was an ardent Klan ally, and Exalted Cyclops Gifford campaigned and raised money for him. Olcott called the Klan a dangerous force, insidious, fanatic, aiming to "usurp the reins of government."[47] Pierce used, by contrast, a stealth strategy: rather than praising the Klan, he praised the schools bill, insisting that he was not anti-Catholic but pro-American. Still, he emphasized his Protestant lineage repeatedly: "Every one of my ancestors has been a Protestant for 300 years."[48] His platform was contradictory, as he campaigned for cutting taxes despite the fact that abolishing private schools would require higher taxes to support the public schools. Appealing to the lower middle class and to farmers, he called for a progressive income tax to reduce the burden of property taxes on smallholders.[49] Astute advisers encouraged him to tailor his message to women—"better tell no religious jokes now that women are voting"—and indeed there was a record turnout of women voters.[50] Despite the subterfuge of the Pierce campaign, everyone knew that the contest, called the "bitterest and closest political campaign in Oregon's history," was between Klan supporters and opponents.

At the same time, economic interests influenced the campaign. Portland's "big three" Klansmen all worked for utilities businesses—

Northwestern Electric employed Gifford; Pacific Telephone and Telegraph employed both Ole Quinn, Gifford's right-hand man, and W. C. Elford, secretary of the Federation of Patriotic Societies—and these enterprises supported and helped fund Pierce.[51] They were fighting off a demand for public power and communications. The *Portland Telegram*, opposing the schools bill, charged that the Klan represented "the capitalization of religious prejudice and racial animosity by public service corporations as the means of sidetracking the public mind from economic issues. With the people foolishly fighting over religion and fanning the fires of fanaticism, they have forgotten all about the agitation against 8 cent street car fares, high telephone and other service rates and reduced wage scales, that before the advent of the Klan threatened the profits of big business."[52]

Klan candidate Pierce won the governorship handily, carrying twenty-eight of Oregon's thirty-six counties. Among Senate candidates, twelve of the thirteen endorsed by the Klan won. The Klan gained a near majority in the House, where Klansman Kubli was already the Speaker, and a strong minority in the Senate.[53] The Klan delegation's unity made it the dominant power in both houses, however. Once in office, Pierce began rewarding his supporters, Klansmen prominent among them. A Klansman from Medford, appointed to a judgeship by Pierce, oversaw the acquittal of the vigilantes in the "Oregon outrages" (discussed in chapter 6). An anti-Klan newspaper editor charged that Pierce introduced the spoils system into Oregon. Before long, his corruption became so gross that his supporters deserted him; when they circulated a recall petition, rumors spread that Klanspeople initiated it as retribution, because Pierce had not appointed enough Klansmen to government jobs.[54]

Unsurprisingly, the schools amendment, shepherded by Speaker of the House Kubli, also won, but less overwhelmingly—by a 12,000-vote majority out of 210,000 votes cast. Portland gave the amendment its biggest per capita support, with the largest majorities in precincts inhabited by middle-class and skilled working-class voters. These were also the voters who had been most supportive of Prohibition, the single tax, and a ban on vaccinations. As elsewhere, the economic top and bottom were less enthusiastic about banning Catholic schools.[55]

Opponents of the schools amendment resorted to the courts, of course, and won. A federal district court ruled in early 1924 that the amendment violated the US Constitution and, perhaps more weightily, that the amendment deprived "parents of their rights, private school teachers of their livelihood and private schools of their property" without due process.[56] (In other words, the decision rested on property rights rather than civil liberties principles.) Governor Pierce immediately announced an appeal to the US Supreme Court. "The people [will] not stand for any half-dozen judges telling them that an overwhelming majority cannot make their own law," one newspaper editorialized. "We cannot understand why foreign minorities in America are ever listened to by our courts." Former US senator George Chamberlain argued for Oregon at the Supreme Court, primarily on a states' rights basis, but lost. In a unanimous decision the court found that the state violated the constitution, specifically the Fourteenth Amendment (which Oregon had not ratified), but also unduly interfered with parents' rights.[57]

While the amendment made its way through the courts, however, the state legislature moved to install further "Americanism" statutes. It enacted a requirement to teach the state constitution in every school, and to forbid wearing religious dress in the schools and to expel teachers who did so (some twenty nuns taught in the Oregon public schools). Prefiguring twenty-first-century battles over textbooks between historians and conservative politicians, the legislature also passed bills requiring the exclusive use of textbooks that "adequately stress the services rendered by the men who achieved our national independence, who established our form of constitutional government," and disallowing any textbook that "speaks slightingly of the founders of the republic . . . or which belittles or undervalues their work."[58] The legislature eliminated the Columbus Day holiday because of its Catholic associations.[59] After the Scopes trial, Oregon leaders, ever pragmatic, changed their strategy to campaign to have creationism taught alongside evolution.[60]

The Klan also conducted a campaign to get non-Protestant teachers fired, a drive that soon extended to all government workers. A Klansman in La Grande volunteered to "talk to our school board" to make sure the school clerk was a "100% American." The Klan complained that urban machine politicians were refusing to give jobs to white Protestants. "Former city manager Kratz had displeased Grand Dragon Gifford by refusing to cooperate with patronage appointments," a Klavern member reported. Government jobs were plums, and for every Catholic fired, presumably a Protestant would be hired, so Klanspeople stood to gain materially from this campaign. It is impossible to know how many non-Protestants lost jobs to Klan efforts, but we have a few examples: for one, the Klan-led anti-Catholic frenzy resulted in attacks on faculty "Romanists" at the University of Oregon.[61]

After defeat in the courts, figuring that prohibiting Catholic schools was no longer viable anywhere in the country, the Klan switched to promoting less wholesale bills in many other state legislatures, focusing on curricular requirements and control of teaching staff. These proposals aimed to require loyalty oaths of teachers; ban teachers from wearing religious clothing; mandate hiring only teachers trained in public schools; make a uniform textbook compulsory for parochial as well as public schools; set up a textbook commission to scrutinize all texts and license acceptable ones; require reading from the Protestant Bible each day, without comment; require schools to give pupils released time for religious study, and set aside one evening a week on which schools and churches would coordinate religious education; and require colleges and universities to grant credit for religious study in authorized churches.[62]

OREGON KLANSWOMEN organized themselves very early in the Klan's career. The WKKK recruited a thousand Portland women in one month, it reported in 1922; that this figure exactly matched Gifford's claim about male Klan recruits suggests a bit of competitiveness. Their enthusiasm for the work led them into a conflict with their male masters so intense that it actually produced a minor physical fight, which brought them legendary local fame. The fight drew public notice, interpreted either as the response of overexcited but endearing women or as the resistance of feisty women defending their autonomy. In actuality it arose from a serious grievance against male domination.

Portland women formed a Klan chapter, the Ladies of the Invisible Empire, known as LOTIE. They also created a youth group, the Junior Citizen's Club, and a front group for recruitment purposes, the Camaretta Club, dedicated to organizing benefit balls for local charities.[63] National Klan leaders denied that LOTIE was a Klan auxiliary, but its Oregon articles of incorporation listed four Klansmen as officers.[64] With its choice of Joan of Arc as a symbol, LOTIE apparently seemed too militant or insufficiently ladylike to some Klannish women, and as a result a rival group arose, the Americanization of Public Schools Committee, composed of wives and sisters of Klansmen. Making clear that it did not aspire to full membership in Klandom, this group declared that it had no constitution, by-laws, or ritual, while LOTIE adopted a full array of Klannish practices. Hostility between the two groups grew so public that the Oregon Klan paper called on them repeatedly to make up. There was so little difference in the groups' programs— they both supported the schools bill, the alien land and labor laws, and patriotic exercises in the schools—that their competition must have resulted from personal animosities and jealousies and/or from differing views about the degree of independence from male leaders they wished to achieve.[65]

At the same time, rivalries among national Klan leaders led to proxy battles using the various female auxiliaries[66]—fighting, as it were, over the bodies, and dues, of women. Hiram Evans wanted all the women's groups merged into the WKKK so as to achieve better control from the top. What emerged was a multifront battle among men who considered LOTIE as a property, much as the Klan itself was incorporated as a business.[67] Three Oregonians claimed it: Exalted Cyclops Gifford, one of the incorporators of LOTIE, wanted to install his wife, Mae Gifford, as head of the WKKK. Rush Davis, another of the incorporators, declared himself "Archbishop" of the Portland LOTIE and wanted his wife to run it; he also offered to sell it to the highest bidder.[68] Finally, Rev. Sawyer, the Anglo-Israelite preacher, increasingly on the outs with the Klan's leadership, sought to lead LOTIE as an independent organization rather than a Klan auxiliary.

None of these men consulted with the LOTIE women about their desires. But Oregon LOTIE's "Mother Counselor," Maybelle Jette, and her group determined to protect their autonomy—as well as their money, their agenda, and their headquarters in a major downtown Portland office building. A resultant confrontation became a story told with pride among Portland's Klanswomen, perhaps embellished, resembling a western film of the period. It began when Rush Davis invaded a LOTIE meeting, proclaimed himself the group's "royal master," and demanded that the women hand over their charter. When they would not do so, he sent a heavy who called himself "the Rattler" to intimidate them: "a picturesque gun-thrower from eastern Oregon, wearing a ten gallon hat . . . and carrying a six-shooter as long as a boot jack." He tried to block the door to prevent Mother Counselor Jette from entering the weekly meeting. Her "honor guard" dared him to lay a finger on her. "He rattled, and they laughed." So the cowboy withdrew.

Then Davis himself came back, forcing his way in while the women were engaged in prayer, thereby doubling their outrage. He reached "the platform, where the Mother Counselor sat enthroned, surrounded by her Guard of Honor, amidst all the panoply and ritualism of that Order. In an impudent, loud and threatening manner Davis demanded the Charter . . . be surrendered instantly to him. The Ladies calmly regarded him . . . as a rare and interesting bug." He lost his temper and grabbed the "dainty Mother Counselor by the arm and savagely twisted it, causing her to writhe in pain." Whereupon another lady, "a small but muscular lady of the Honor Guard . . . , raised on high a heavy umbrella which she carried in her hand (do I need to say that it rains a lot in Portland?) and deliberately struck him a powerful blow on the head. . . . Other ladies . . . swarmed upon him, pummeling, pounding and hammering. Several kicked him, where it hurts the most. (!) They raised welts on his body, bumps on his head, pulled his hair, scratched his face, bloodied his nose, blackened his eyes, and gave him a thorough and unmerciful whipping." As he fled, the Mother Counselor "led in singing of 'The Star Spangled Banner.'"

The women regaled the editor of the *Western American* with this story, and it seems likely that—in their outrage, joy, and a bit of smugness—they exaggerated a bit. We know that the editor, Lem Dever (the perfect name for a cowboy western), knew how to dramatize a good story. Still, the women's relish in describing their resistance suggests pride in their autonomy. Headlining LADIES HANDLE MAN WITHOUT POLICE AND IN DEMPSEY MANNER,* the *Western American* capitalized on the showdown: "Help!, Help!, Help!, yelped a certain ill conditioned citizen . . . when he undertook to be insolent to a group of Portland ladies. . . . It was the kick landing with deadly and unerring accuracy and in the tenderest spot, that cause[d] the ogler . . . to howl." Although the LOTIEs ultimately lost and were forcibly merged into the WKKK, in publicizing their story they had humiliated the Klan leaders.

The Klan VIPs, in turn, treated these women diplomatically—certainly a sign of grudging respect. Not only did they make no attempt

---

* A reference to boxer Jack Dempsey.

to punish Jette, but she remained Portland's WKKK Exalted Cyclops. Perhaps in an attempt to soothe, Gifford declared that "the women's organization is an exact counterpart of the Klan itself, with no difference whatever except that of gender." Still, some LOTIEs apparently refused to join the WKKK.[69] Rush Davis was forced to sign an agreement, as "owner" of LOTIE, giving up all rights to it. His wife became treasurer of the WKKK, no doubt in exchange for that concession. Gifford's wife received a bigger prize, becoming Imperial Commander of the Western States WKKK. Saving face, the Klan hierarchy insisted that a little family tiff had been inflated beyond the truth.

Unfortunately we have no information about the backgrounds of the LOTIEs or other Oregon Klannish women. But the little we know about Mother Counselor Maybelle Jette may shed some light on these Klans-women of the Northwest. Jette was already on her second husband, and she would have two more before her death at some point in the 1960s—hardly a conventional woman's biography. The Klan newspaper identified her as Oregon's youngest grandmother, at age thirty-three, and when her baby grandson visited LOTIE headquarters he "smiled and Kooed . . . a real Hundred Percenter." She had a particular interest in a WCTU children's home in Corvallis and pledged that LOTIE would contribute $5,000 to it.[70] She later worked as a newspaper columnist, using an alias, wrote poems, and painted landscapes.[71]

Even if no other power struggles involving Klanswomen reached this level of conflict, it seems likely that other such power struggles existed. They illustrate the contradictions involved in conservative women's activism. The umbrella-wielding, kicking LOTIEs, we must remember, would probably have enunciated conventional views about a woman's domestic and maternal destiny, even as they resisted men's right to govern them.

Because the Klan rapidly declined in size and popularity after 1925, what might have become of any women's drive for organizational independence is a matter open only to speculation. Equally unknown is whether Klanswomen would have modified Klan ideology and activity in any way. Still, conservative movements have generated many women leaders since then, and their programs have not differed notably from men's. Their determination operates within a contradictory set of premises: that women should be equally respected in public political activity even as domestic labor and motherhood should remain women's primary orientation.[72]

There was a stream of feminism in the women's Klan groups, discernible in the writings and speeches of leaders and in some of the activities of the rank and file. Klanswomen's family values differed little if at all from those of most non-Klan women, but because they were clubwomen, they enunciated the women's rights they wanted in writing and speaking. If we had minutes from WKKK meetings we might see more. But Klan feminists differed radically from the progressive feminist activists of the time. Klanswomen's priority remained the restoration of Anglo-Saxon Protestant control of American society, economy, and government, and the accompanying disempowerment of those the Klan called "aliens." True, many Klanswomen sought autonomy for their clubs. But even the woman suffrage supporters among them exercised their voting power in the service of Klan values and Klan candidates, all male.

KKK poster denouncing Catholic Al Smith, a candidate for
the Democratic presidential nomination, 1924.

Chapter 9

POLITICAL AND
ECONOMIC WARFARE

THE 1920S KU KLUX KLAN FUNCTIONED BOTH INSIDE
and outside the electoral system. In places it assumed some of the roles
of American political parties—influencing nominations, getting out the
vote for its candidates, and lobbying officeholders. It operated a political
machine that was remarkably effective for a short period of time. At
the same time, its members and their supporters used social-movement
techniques, such as rallies, cross-burnings, public pageants, vigilantism,
and an economic boycott of "wrong" enterprises, all of which strengthened its electoral clout. Like many social movements, it built alliances
with influential groups outside electoral politics, such as police forces
and churches. With remarkable fluidity, Klan activity varied by place and
opportunity, sometimes pouring energy into elections, sometimes into
propaganda that communicated its size and determination. Sometimes
the two tactics came together; this would show in the 1924 Democratic
Party convention.

The synergy between electoral and nonelectoral strategies is often
missed. Many scholars have conceived them as alternatives rather than
complements, and the distinction between them has often been blurred,
as when some electoral campaigns elicited large-scale participation. The
Klan did both, and its short-term success arose from this dual strategy,

even if it was unarticulated. In fact, it owed much of its considerable electoral success to nonelectoral activities that signaled its mass following. Many a candidate sought Klan support not because of principled agreement with its beliefs but out of fear of retribution. Still, basic to both electoral and social-movement strategy was the Klan's legitimacy and, in many locations, respectability.

The Klan made war via elections. No one has been able to count all the Klan candidates elected to state and local offices, and the exercise would probably not be worthwhile in any case because so many nonmembers shared Klan ideology. We can, however, note the members elected to high offices: sixteen senators, scores of congressmen (the Klan claimed seventy-five), and eleven governors, pretty much equally divided between Democrats and Republicans.

The Klan also exaggerated its political power; one of its lecturers claimed that twenty-six governors and 62 percent of Congress were Klansmen. It also took credit for reelecting Calvin Coolidge in 1924. "The New York Times conceded the fact," Klan leader Alma White wrote, "that the Ku Klux Klan won where it was an issue in the election."[1] Its political clout rested not only on numbers but also on the powerful positions occupied by its supporting politicians. Notably, Klan member Albert Johnson of Washington served as chair of the House Immigration Committee and led the drive for immigration restriction, the Klan's major national priority. (He had publicly bragged about his participation in a 1907 mass vigilante action that drove the entire South Asian population out of Bellingham, Washington.[2]) He surely knew that the Klan's main publication, the Imperial Night-Hawk, suggested in 1923 that the Imperial Wizard appoint "an Imperial Immigration and Naturalization Commission to outline a program" of restriction.[3] Other pro-Klan legislators led on other issues. Hatton Sumners, member of Congress for thirty-four years, led the House Judiciary Committee, where he smothered attempts to pass an anti-lynching bill. Congressman William Upshaw, an evangelist called the "Billy Sunday of Congress," leader in the Anti-Saloon League, and member of the board of trustees for Bob Jones University, served four terms (1919–27); in 1932, he ran for president on the Prohibition Party ticket. In Indiana between 1924 and 1926, eleven of the thirteen men elected to the US House of Representatives were Klan members, as were the majority of Texas and Colorado congressmen. Supreme Court Justices Hugo Black and Edward Douglass White were Klansmen. (Black was "naturalized" into the Klan, along with fifteen hundred recruits, in a monster event, but resigned later in his career.[4]) The Klan claimed President Harding as a member, and President Truman joined when he thought it was "just" a patriotic group (he quit when he learned that he would have to break off his friendships with Catholics).[5]

These examples do not include Klan-friendly politicians, who served the cause by deflecting attacks on the Klan—again vividly demonstrated in the 1924 Democratic convention. With their support, the Klan was able to thwart numerous attempts by its opponents to put together majorities that would support anti-Klan resolutions. Neither major political party and none of the presidents in this period—Wilson, Harding, Coolidge, and Hoover—could be persuaded to condemn the Ku Klux Klan.[6]

Klansmen and Klan supporters won elections through a national strategy referred to as "the Decade" and in Indiana as the "Military Machine." Laying the groundwork for this plan, Klan leaders developed an analysis of their chances in every state, producing in 1923 a chart assessing all US senators as to their Klan-friendliness (see appendix 2); this was no amateur, let alone country bumpkin, operation. Each county in Indiana was labeled a Klanton, headed by an Exalted Cyclops; each congressional district became a Province, headed by a Great Titan who did the work of a district political party chairman. The "Field Regulations" of this apparatus required constructing a list with the name, address, and vocation of every "alien" of voting age. Stephenson bragged that this network enabled him to instruct his subordinates with a single phone call.

He had plenty of cash to award to cooperative politicians. He loaned Ed Jackson his Cadillac for campaigning around the state, and later told grand jury investigators that he had spent at least $73,000 (worth over a million today) to get Jackson elected governor.[7]

The Decade's get-out-the-vote plan called on every Klan member to recruit ten people who would promise to vote for Klan candidates, and it worked. The Indiana machine was particularly methodical; in other locations electoral campaigns varied with the energy level of particular Klaverns. In La Grande, Oregon, for example, "twenty stalwart Americans placed under every door in this town a straight American ticket."[8] Klanspeople were proud of their successes. Klansman G. W. Price reported from Los Angeles that "we succeeded in having Friend Richardson nominated for Governor . . . [and] elected Chas. G. Johnson State Treasurer. . . . In Fresno we defeated Gearheart K.C. [Knights of Columbus, indicating a Catholic] . . . and elected . . . Judge Frederick Houser who presided at our trial."[9] Many candidates dog-whistled; that is, they adjusted their appeals strategically, avoiding religion-based attacks where they might hurt, focusing on cleaning up immorality when that would help. But some spoke in plain English. In the Oakland Auditorium a Klan speaker in 1922 announced that "the election of Richardson is imperative if we are to remove the Jews, Catholics and Negroes from public life in California." Richardson won with an overwhelming majority.[10]

THE KU KLUX KLAN TURNED the 1924 Democratic Party national convention into high drama and gained invaluable nationwide publicity for several weeks.[11] The proceedings, at Madison Square Garden in New York City, were as hotly contested as the Garden's sports events, and much longer. Unlike the uneventful Republican convention that of course renominated incumbent president Coolidge,[12] the

Democrats were divided, not only among candidates for the nomination but most intensely between pro- and anti-Klan factions. That Democratic convention came to be known as "the Klanbake," signifying both the intensity of animosities among delegates on the floor and the record-breaking heat outside. As historian David Burner wrote, "The deadlock that developed might as well have been between the Pope and the Imperial Wizard."[13]

The Ku Klux Klan was the protagonist in this drama. It was outraged because the New York delegation had the temerity to nominate New York governor Al Smith, a Catholic, for the presidential ticket. Before the convention he appeared to be the strongest candidate, but he was anathema to the Klan. Not only a Catholic, not only an opponent of Prohibition, he also aggressively denounced the Klan's candidate, William Gibbs McAdoo, former secretary of the treasury. A darling of evangelicals because he was an uncompromising Prohibitionist, McAdoo even supported the ban on alcohol at the convention. But he also commanded the loyalty of many working-class and populist voters because earlier in his career he had supported workmen's compensation for workplace accidents, unemployment insurance, the eight-hour workday, and a minimum wage. McAdoo's stances on these efforts also point to the commonalities between the Klan and the Progressives of the pre–World War I era on social welfare issues. But anti-Catholic fervor dominated all other Klan motives at the 1924 convention. It contributed mightily to Al Smith's defeat, not only then, but again in 1928 when he succeeded in winning the nomination but lost to Herbert Hoover.

In its campaign against Al Smith, the Klan made sure not to rely only on its dependable convention delegates. It mobilized hundreds of Protestant pastors across the country to sermonize against him, exerting indirect pressure on the delegates. It peddled stories to newspapers across the country, smearing Al Smith by associating him with New York's crime, political corruption, defiance of Prohibition, and general sinfulness. On Independence Day the Klan organized a mass rally for McAdoo, attended by twenty thousand, just across the Hudson River in Long Branch, New Jersey. There it burned not only crosses but also effigies of Smith. Attendees could contribute a nickel for the privilege of throwing baseballs at a portrait of Smith. Constructed as a typical Klan pageant, featuring several weddings and baptisms, it was also designed to pressure convention delegates. Because the convention continued for more than two weeks, this monster event featured prominently in newspapers; it provides a vivid example of joining social-movement with political strategies.

The party had chosen New York City as the convention site—a site used by Democrats for the first time since 1868—because it was doing so well there: in 1922, thirteen incumbent Republican congressmen lost their seats to Democrats, who were on average more sympathetic to the Klan. This victory had encouraged the Klan to go all out for the popular McAdoo. As H. L. Mencken wrote, "There may not be enough kluxers in the convention to nominate McAdoo, but there are probably enough to beat any anti-klan candidate so far heard of, and they are all on their tiptoes today, their hands clutching their artillery nervously and their eyes apop for dynamite bombs and Jesuit spies. . . . One sits through long sessions wishing heartily that all the delegates and alternates were dead and in hell—and then suddenly there comes a show so gaudy and hilarious, so melodramatic and obscene, unimaginably exhilarating and preposterous that one lives a gorgeous year in an hour."[14] After Franklin Roosevelt, in one of his first appearances after contracting polio, nominated Smith, New York's Tammany Hall political machine raised a ruckus, "armed with drums, tubas, trumpets and a bunch of ear-piercing electric fire sirens that were so loud that people scooted out of the hall with their fingers in their ears."[15]

If there was any doubt about the centrality of the Klan to convention deliberations and votes, that doubt was erased when a southern delegate introduced a resolution to add a condemnation of the Klan into the party platform. That delegate was Forney Johnston, a banker, former steel company head, and former governor of Alabama. This move demonstrated a strain of upper-class disapproval of the Klan, but it also reinforced the Klan's claim to represent the "common people." The resolution also demonstrated to any delegates who still considered the Klan a southern phenomenon that it commanded major northern support. (Nevertheless, even southern conservatives who despised the Klan could not bring themselves to vote for Al Smith; in all the many ballots he never received more than one vote from a southern delegation. The votes also showed that within the North, the Klan was strongest in the West: in all the many ballots, Smith never got more than twenty votes from states west of the Mississippi River.)

Forney Johnston's resolution took Klan delegates by surprise, and they reacted furiously. Not only was the convention divided about the amendment, but state delegations were also internally divided between pro- and anti-Klan members. Soon delegates were pushing and shoving on the floor of the convention. The governors of Kentucky and Colorado reportedly got into fistfights as they struggled to keep their state banners out of the hands of anti-Klan delegates. While those on the Klan's side shouted, "Mac, Mac, McAdoo," their adversaries shouted, "Ku, Ku, McAdoo." The final vote on the anti-Klan resolution could hardly have been closer: 542.15 in favor, 546.15 against. (Some state delegations split their votes, hence the fractions.) The results suggested not only how many supported the Klan but also how many feared antagonizing it.

Meanwhile, an impasse developed between the two major candidates, because nomination required a two-thirds majority. The deadlock continued ballot after ballot, and state delegations began deserting their original choice to support "favorite son" compromise candidates. None of these could bring together the required two-thirds. The convention continued through an absurd 103 ballots with sixty different candidates over sixteen days. Ultimately the episode was a Klan victory: it blocked Al Smith and grew its reputation as a national political force.[16] The victor, John W. Davis—first a congressman from West Virginia, then solicitor general, then ambassador to the UK—was in many ways a typical southern Democrat: he had opposed woman suffrage, child labor laws, and anti-lynching legislation but also, opportunistically, opposed Prohibition. In this convention, however, his politics hardly mattered. He was a dark horse, his nomination the product of delegate exhaustion, convention stalemate, and the fact that he did not evoke strong negatives.

Still, although the convention made the Klan a national power, it was in states and cities that the Klan amassed its greatest dominance. American federalism created both challenges and opportunities for the Klan: obstacles to national power but also openings for state and municipal power. For a few years it wielded determining political influence in several states—electing governors in Indiana, Oklahoma, Oregon, Colorado, and Texas. Klan Republicans swept to victory in Nebraska in 1926.[17] (Klan candidates ran mostly as Democrats but occasionally as Republicans.) For ten years, 1922 to 1932, the majority of all Oregon's elected officials were Klansmen, and opposition was so weak that Klansmen sometimes ran against one another.[18] Politicians elected with Klan support typically promised to appoint Klan-friendly men to office. An Indiana grand jury investigation of corruption revealed written evidence: the mayor of Indianapolis wrote that "in return for the support of D. C. Stephenson, in the event that I am elected . . . I promise not to appoint any personal [sic] . . . without they first have the endorsement of D. C. Stephenson."[19]

In contrast to contemporary claims that Klan strength lay in rural and small-town America, it racked up many victories in cities. In 1922 the Klan already controlled several city governments, including those in Dallas and Fort Worth. Both Portlands—Maine and Oregon—elected Klan mayors, as did many other cities large and small.[20] In Colorado only one city—Colorado Springs—was not controlled by the Klan.[21] In Muncie, Indiana, the mayor, the president of the Board of Education, and the secretary of the YMCA were Klansmen.[22] In smaller towns Klansmen often ruled absolutely. Tillamook, Oregon, for example, between 1924 and 1928, gave Klansmen positions as county sheriff, state representative, superintendent of schools, schools director, city attorney, county clerk, chief clerks of the post offices, principals of both the elementary and high schools, and the majority of city councilmen.[23]

A writer for the *New Republic* wrote in 1927 that a politician who went along was promised "sure election if he lined up and took orders." If you wanted anything done in Indiana, "you went to Stephenson [Grand Dragon of Indiana] first, and afterward or not at all to those who had official power to grant it." Stephenson boasted, "I am the law." He planned to run for president in 1928.[24] This kind of power led one legal historian to argue that the Klan constituted a "parallel government,"[25] but this is misleading, because it worked within existing governmental lines: unlike classic "dual power" situations, where a nonstate organization such as a labor union gains a legitimacy equivalent to that of the state, the Klan actually took over state and municipal governments. It did this entirely legally, through the ballot. Its members not only ran candidates but also got out the vote. "There was not a Catholic elected," a victorious Klan candidate for a judgeship gloated.[26]

Most of these voters either respected or feared antagonizing the Klan. Many others, no doubt, simply had no objection to Klan power.

IN THE KLAN'S POLITICAL CAMPAIGNS, its rank-and-file members were required only to vote right. But it also conducted economic campaigns that called on members to shop right, by refusing to patronize "alien" businesses.[27] Most of us would call these campaigns boycotts. The Klan, however, denied that it was boycotting, apparently considering the term pejorative: "The Klansmen do not boycott, as a matter of principle, but they are concentrating patronage with their friends."[28] Local chapters, such as that in the small town of Noblesville, Indiana, chose to list the "right" enterprises rather than the targets of their boycotts.[29] At least one Klavern leader read aloud an updated list of "right" and "alien" stores at every meeting.[30] Given the patriotic status of the colonists' Tea Party boycott, this fear of the term is surprising, but it may be that 1920s Klansmen associated it with labor unions. Leery for whatever reason about using the term "boycott," Klavern leaders instructed members to recommend Klan businesses to the general public but not to explain the bases for their recommendations.[31] In a secondary economic tactic, the Klan attempted to remove "aliens" from jobs, especially professional and government jobs, wherever it had influence over employers.[32] Often a direct demand was unnecessary; a straightforward question to an employer, such as "Where does Mr. Smith go to church?," would deliver the message.

Two motives underlay these economic strategies: disadvantaging Klan enemies—people of color, Catholics, Jews, and those of Orthodox faith—and securing customers and jobs for its members. The Klan had long functioned like a Rotary Club, as a site of networking and mutual aid among businesspeople, but also as a site of tips about jobs. Labeling their economic warfare program "vocational Klanishness," Klan leaders named it one of the four duties of members. This duty called for "constant and earnest exercise . . . in the realm of one's business or professional life," and it was expounded at greater length and with greater emphasis than were the other three duties.[33]

The national Klan set up an "intelligence bureau," under the personal authority of Evans, to gather and report information on boycott targets.[34] It announced a plan to publish a directory of Klan businesses, to be printed by the TWK (Klanspeak for Trade with Klansmen) Publishing Company in Washington. Each copy was to come with a TWK placard to be placed in a window and thereby identify the store.[35] This national directory never materialized; only a few local and state Klans actually managed to produce one, including one in Oregon. Word of mouth seems to have been the most common way to identify businesses to avoid, although many could be identified as Catholic or, especially, Jewish by their names.

"Right" shops identified themselves through a variety of signals: displaying American flags in designated spots or posting signs with patriotic slogans such as "100% American," just "100%," or "TWK." Klanspeople pressured businesses to advertise in Klan papers. Many businesses complied, thereby announcing that one's business was "right": for example, "Liberty Bell Coffee is a 100% American brew."[36] Thirteen of the thirty-nine pages in a program booklet produced for a July 4 Klonvocation in Elmira, New York, were devoted to small-business advertisements.[37] Many stores announced their Klannishness by changing the spelling of their names: Kountry Kitchen, Kwik Kar Wash, etc. Smaller locations often lacked enough "Gentile" stores, so Klan publications advertised to attract them. Lawton, Oklahoma, for example, appealed for a "right" clothing store and bookstore; Fredericksburg, Missouri, for a "cleaning and pressing establishment."[38]

Boycotting also served to recruit new members, because a merchant could not display that he was "right" without Klan approval. An Oregon Klavern created a "solicitation committee" with a list of 125 local businessmen "eligible" to join. When it urged members to patronize a barber who was a member, a second barber asked to join immediately afterward.[39] "Right" storeowners in turn coerced their employees to join. Many of these entrepreneurs were not so much ardent Klan supporters but rather people under pressure, or just playing it safe. Many non-Klan members honored these boycotts, whether from agreement or anxiety about retribution. This was one of many ways in which Klan strength rested on the passive acquiescence of nonmembers.

Boycotters occasionally threatened stores that did not comply. Some left "calling cards" at "alien" shops, in the form of dead animals. The owners of one dry goods store were invited to join the Klan on the condition that they fire their one black employee.[40] When the head of the Fuller Brush Company denounced the KKK, a Klan boycott forced him to recant a month later.[41]

Klanswomen were the foot soldiers of the boycott campaigns. WKKK leader Daisy Barr emphasized repeatedly that her members should shop only at "right" stores. Because this form of activism appeared to many women as housewifery and neighborliness, akin to telling a friend about a sale, many of those who boycotted did not recognize it as political activism. Kathleen Blee remarked that "no one I interviewed saw the economic power of the Klan as a political act. None saw it as an act of violence."[42]

The Indiana WKKK, possibly the country's strongest, set up an ambitious boycott machine. It selected point people in each county who then organized groups beneath them, forming a ladder that pushed information rapidly through the state. Republican Committeewoman Vivian Wheatcraft of the WKKK labeled these groups "poison squads of whispering women" because of their ability to spread negative opinions about "alien" businesspeople and "mischievous" stories about Klan enemies. She bragged that her "skirted lieutenants" formed a network through which she could communicate any "gossip" beneficial to the Klan—don't shop here, do shop there—throughout the state within twelve hours.[43] These networks also functioned to bring women together, thereby extending intra-Klan connections and building organizational loyalty. "Poison squads" soon appeared in other states as well.[44]

In locations where small enterprises dominated, the boycotts succeeded in driving some—there is no way to estimate how many—out of business. No doubt greater harm occurred in smaller towns, where shopping habits were more visible and community pressure greater. The most common and effective campaigns focused on Jewish-owned establishments, in keeping with one of the Klan's key premises about Jews, that they cheated their customers. Like much of the Klan's racial ideology, this anti-Semitic slur was taken on faith among many non-Klan Christians.

Former Klanswomen interviewed by Kathleen Blee told of Jewish professionals and merchants, people who had experienced cordial relations with their community for decades, who lost businesses, went into bankruptcy, and fled.[45] As one woman told her, "The one Jew . . . he became part of the community. He went to church dinners and everything. . . . [But then] people didn't go to his store." Simon Rosenthal of Tipton, Indiana, a former fire chief who had personally raised the funds to build a city park, had to close his clothing store. An organization to defend Greek Americans, the American Hellenic Educational Progressive Association (AHEPA), arose in 1922 in response to Klan campaigns against Greek-owned enterprises, notably confectioneries and restaurants. It reported that Greek-owned stores that had once taken in $500–$1,000 a day were earning as little as $25 after the boycott began.[46] One Klavern boycotted a Catholic-owned grocery even though both its men's and women's Klan meetings were held in a room above the store.[47] Anti-Klan newspapers were particularly vulnerable because the Klan could force advertisers to withdraw; the *Portland Telegram* was forced out of business due to the Klan-spread "news" that it had been purchased by the archbishop.[48]

It was much harder, of course, to make a dent in big businesses. The Klan tried boycotts directed at large department stores, which were mostly Jewish owned. The strong Oregon Klan tried to get its supporters not to shop at the Meier & Frank department store, but it faced a formidable opponent: founded in 1857, Meier & Frank also owned a prominent and popular radio station, and in the 1920s its department stores made it the largest retailer west of the Mississippi. The Klan even tried, also in vain, to eject Julius Meier from the board of the planned 1925 State Expo.[49] (In 1930 he was elected governor as an independent.) Nor did the boycotts have much effect on other corporate business, such as the A&P, condemned by the Klan.[50] The Klan was ambitious—and deluded—enough to try mounting a boycott of Mormon businesses and publishing a directory of pro-Klan enterprises in Salt Lake City, but neither succeeded—the LDS Church was too powerful.[51]

Hollywood, of course, was a doubly important target for a major boycott, as it was both Jewish and immoral. The Klan had long denounced "filthy fiction" that "submerged" young people "in a sea of sensuality and sewage."[52] But the movies were more seductive by orders of magnitude. Naturally the Klan opposed showing films on Sunday, but as movies grew more popular, it took on the whole film industry. Using conspiracy allegations, as usual, the Klan alleged that Hollywood's Jews operated a deliberate plot to destroy American morals. Klanspeople understood that the movies both reflected and legitimated erotic license—to indulge in petting, parking in cars, wearing suggestive clothing. Members were instructed to boycott not only Charlie Chaplin's films but scores of other silent movies, including the 1923 *Bella Donna* (in which a white woman falls in love with an Egyptian—"a disgrace to the white race"), the 1924 *Manhandled* with Gloria Swanson, and Samuel Goldwyn's 1925 *A Thief in Paradise*. The 1930s Klan, though a small remnant of its predecessor, sued Warner Bros. over Humphrey Bogart's 1937 *Black Legion*, demanding $100,000 in damages and an additional $500 for every time the film showed. (Its plot: a hardworking machinist loses a promotion to a Polish-born worker and is seduced into joining the secretive Black Legion, which intimidates foreigners through violence. And one of its screenwriters was Jewish.) It lost the case but gained publicity.[53]

Perhaps needless to say, these film boycotts got little traction, so the Klan developed its own film production company, Cavalier Moving Picture Company. Under Charles Lewis Fowler, who had headed the Klan's failed Lanier University, it produced two films: *The Toll of Justice* and *The Traitor Within*. Both offered defensive plots, positioning the Klan as the innocent target of evildoers who falsely blamed its members for their own crimes (in line with its consistent rhetorical assumption of a victim position). *The Toll* appropriated the plot of a popular 1919 Mary Pickford film, *Heart o' the Hills*, in which the star herself donned Klan robes and became a night rider who outed the real villain; but in the Klan film this gender-bending was corrected and a male night rider became the hero. Klan films only infrequently gained showings in movie theaters and were more often shown in public school auditoriums, churches, and large Klan meetings, free to the public.[54] After being fired by Hiram Evans, Edward Clarke launched in 1924 a more ambitious film company that, he hoped, would contest the big studios for market share; it failed, but only after he allegedly embezzled $200,000 from it.[55] Neither of these businesses lasted; filmmaking was extremely costly, requiring significant investments in production, and could not do without paying customers. Besides, Klan films could not even begin to compete with Hollywood's—in part because what the Klan considered immoral was a major part of Hollywood's attraction.

The Klan was equally unsuccessful in its attacks on jazz, blues, and other "immoral" music. The story of the Gennett recording company illustrates. Founded in Indiana in 1917, Gennett was one of the first studios to put out both black and white music, in what was then a segregated production and distribution system. While Okeh Records dominated in producing black music in the East, Gennett ruled in the West. It produced recordings of some of the greatest jazz stars of the era, including the New Orleans Rhythm Kings, Hoagy Carmichael, Jelly Roll Morton, Louis Armstrong, and Bix Beiderbecke. But Gennett also had a cash business, making recordings to order. The Klan was its customer. Ignoring the fact that the owners were Italian Catholics, Hiram Evans used Gennett to record inspirational speeches, and Klan groups recorded hymns and patriotic songs at Gennett studios. Contrariwise, the engineer who worked with recordings of Louis Armstrong was a Klansman.[56] (In the 1950s and 1960s, a revived Klan, then more confined to the South, condemned rock 'n' roll and black music, again to no avail.)

The Klan's frequent hectoring and threatening to penalize members who did not comply with the commercial boycott suggests that embargoing "alien" enterprises was never totally successful. Klavern minutes included denunciations of members who were un-Klannish in their shopping habits. For example, "Klansman Tull was seen buying meat at the Dutchman's shop. . . . Klansman Kenneth McCormick still eats at Herman's lunch counter."[57] Klan leaders issued dire warnings: "Any Klansman, or Klanswoman, who in any way patronizes an enemy of our righteous cause will have to answer for it."[58] Klaverns promised to publish the names of the disloyal shoppers. Such threats against Klanspeople do not seem to have been carried out, however, and many continued to patronize stores they liked regardless of ownership.[59] Moreover, many Klanswomen resisted boycott instructions coming from male Klan leaders, perhaps out of loyalty to a store they had long patronized or whose prices were lowest. Thus the *Imperial Night-Hawk* published accusations such as "That suit of clothes you are wearing, did you buy it from a Klansman?"[60]

Some boycott targets fought back. In Maine a counterboycott of Klan businesses emerged. In Marion City, Ohio, the Knights of Columbus retaliated by constructing a market building that housed a variety of shops. But there the Klan emerged victorious: a boycott forced it to close, and the Klan then purchased the building, allowing in only Protestant shops.[61]

The second front in the economic war, aiming to get Catholics, Jews, and blacks fired and replaced with "right" employees, was only sporadically successful. Large enterprises typically would not, or could not afford to, comply. When the La Grande, Oregon, Klavern tried to oust the Catholic CFO of a local bank, for example, it was told that his departure would mean a loss of $50,000 to the bank, no doubt anticipating a withdrawal of "alien" funds, and claimed that this would sink the bank. The Klavern backed off this demand, though it continued to ask members to move their money to another bank.[62]

The Klan's economic warfare probably had mixed and limited

results. But the boycott also had indirect consequences, because it sent the message that opposing the Klan was unsafe. So too threats against workers and employees who were not "right" must have created anxiety and caution. The economic boycott thus supplemented the mass pageants, the cross-burnings, and the political campaigns in communicating the Klan's strength and discouraging opposition. A message of this kind had the muscle to preclude resistance, particularly among those who preferred the safety of conformity, like Sinclair Lewis's Babbitt, or who wished to remain neutral and to stay out of politics. The Ku Klux Klan practiced a two-sided strategy: working not only to attract members and followers but also to quiet others who might have objected to its goals.

Form F-306 165M 8-8-21

IMPERIAL PALACE

INVISIBLE EMPIRE

Knights of the Ku Klux Klan

(Incorporated)

AEGIS OF THE
IMPERIAL WIZARD

Dear Sir:

We have been requested by one of your personal friends to get in touch with you, and inform you of this organization. And, in view of this request, we are sending you this form. When we receive this with all the questions below properly answered by you and if same is satisfactory we will impart to you the information your friend desires you to have. Without delay you will fill in, sign and return. You will find stamped envelope enclosed for this purpose.

Very truly yours,

KNIGHTS OF THE KU KLUX KLAN,

By_____

1. Is the motive prompting your inquiry serious? _____
2. What is your age? _____
3. What is your occupation? _____
4. Where were you born? _____
5. How long have you resided in your present locality? _____
6. Are you married, single or widower? _____
7. Were your parents born in the United States of America? _____
8. Are you a gentile or jew? _____
9. Are you of the white race or of a colored race? _____
10. What educational advantages have you? _____
11. Color of eyes? _____ Hair? _____ Weight? _____ Height? _____
12. Do you believe in the principles of a PURE Americanism? _____
13. Do you believe in White Supremacy? _____
14. What is your politics? _____
15. What is your religious faith? _____
16. Of what church are you a member (if any)? _____
17. Of what religious faith are your parents? _____
18. What secret, fraternal orders are you a member of (if any)? _____
19. Do you honestly believe in the practice of REAL fraternity? _____
20. Do you owe ANY KIND of allegiance to any foreign nation, government, institution, sect, people, ruler or person? _____

I most solemnly assert and affirm that each question above is truthfully answered by me and in my own handwriting and that below is my real signature.

Signed_____

Inquirer

Business Address_____ Residence Address_____

Telephone No._____ _____

Date_____19____ Telephone No._____

N. B.—If space above is not sufficient to answer question, then make your answer on the other side of this sheet. Number the answer to correspond with the question.

PRINTED BY THE KU KLUX PRESS

Petition for citizenship in the Klan.

(Ian Brabner/Rare Americana.com)

Chapter 10

CONSTITUENTS

IN THE LAST FEW DECADES, HISTORIANS HAVE PRO-
vided somewhat more precision about the class position and occupations of Klansmen. (Much less is known about Klanswomen.)
They have compared Klan membership lists to census information
about occupations, and thereby estimated the class composition of
the movement. The consensus among these scholars is that small
businessmen, lower middle-class employees, and skilled workers constituted the majority of members in most locations. Robert Johnston,
who studied Portland, Oregon's Klan members, elaborated that finding by using the category "middling" people, those at the intersection
of the middle and the working class.[1] That finding points to a more
dynamic view of Klansmen's class position: considering how it was
constructed.

Doing that requires thinking of Klanspeople's social class as a process, just as we have come to understand racial categories as a process. The category "white" changed over time, especially in the period
between the mass migration starting in the 1880s and the 1920s. In
the Northeast, for example, the Irish, Italian, and eastern European
Jewish immigrants were not typically considered white by earlier immigrants; by the 1920s these newer immigrants had become white. (The

Klan could be seen as an oppositional reaction to this expansion of whiteness, by its efforts to limit "right" citizenship to a narrower group.)

Class identity is also a process. Occupations, standards of living, and social standing were in flux in 1920s America, with some people moving downward and others upward. Admittedly, evidence of Klanspeople's mobility in either direction would require information we do not have. It would be useful to know not only members' occupations but how long they had held them, how they defined their class position, and what class aspirations they held. Evidence of that kind is unlikely to be found.

But we can ask, what did a person stand to gain by joining? The Klan had a few rich members, but on the whole the rich had little to gain from membership.[2] The very poor could not afford it. "Middling" people, by contrast, often had much to gain. Few of the Klan's national leaders were born wealthy; they became rich at the expense of their members. The boycotts could promote economic success by shoring up some businesses at the expense of others. The opportunity to earn a commission by recruiting new members attracted some. The connections made through the Klaverns could lead to jobs, customers, investment opportunities. Sinclair Lewis noticed this, writing in *Elmer Gantry* of "the new Ku Klux Klan, an organization of the fathers, younger brothers and employees of the men who had succeeded and became Rotarians."

Class identities, aspirations, and insecurities were not, however, only economic. In many areas Klan membership brought prestige, perhaps more in the North and West than in the South. Recognizing this shows how off-base were eastern liberal stereotypes of Klanspeople as backward, bored small-town dwellers. Klansmen were often ambitious, and not only economically. In bringing community status, Klan membership could not only advantage those on the way up but also offer compensatory status to those stuck in one social level or even on the way down.

Moreover, local Klans typically brought lower-middle-class people together with skilled workers, as Robert Johnston found in studying Portland. In the process, the Klan helped redefine "middle class" so as to bring in men who did manual labor. Its emphasis on patriotism, religious affiliation, temperance, and sexual morality made membership a marker of respectability, and thus helped some working-class members become middle-class. That status required not only constructing a personal identity with these attributes of respectability but also being seen by others as middle-class.[3] (Precisely because respectability was fundamental in building the Klan, when it was ruptured by scandals the Klan went into free fall.) This was as true of women as of men. Joining was often a sign of ambition. One could become middle-class by being treated as an equal through the brotherhood and sisterhood of local Klan groups.

Prestige could be equally important to those who already considered themselves middle-class. Historian Arno Mayer's argument about the European petite bourgeoisie of this interwar period—that it was the most insecure and status-conscious of all social strata—fits the Klan well.[4] Masses of immigrants intensified that insecurity. Those newcomers, no less ambitious than the native-born, threatened a dominance that many white native-born Protestants considered a form of social property. This anger at displacement, blamed on "aliens," sometimes rested on actual experience but more often on imagination and fear stoked by demagoguery. We know this because the Klan flourished in locations with few "aliens," and many local leaders were prosperous.

In this process of reclassifying working-class people as middle class, the Klan contributed to shaping that new, broader class identity. Klan spokesmen confirmed that spreading identity, paradoxically, in its claim that its adherents came from "all walks of life," that its "100% Americans" transcended class. It might seem that the Klan was contradicting that claim when it boasted of representing the "best" citizens, but that boast could also be read as a statement that the middle class *was* "best." For example, while more than three-quarters of Oakland, California, members lived in the affluent outer areas and suburbs of the city, often in Berkeley and Piedmont, many got there through upward mobility.

For example, Klan Klaliff William H. Parker, starting as a real estate agent and insurance salesman, became a key developer of Oakland's new upscale residential areas, and first president of the East Oakland Consolidated Clubs, an organization dedicated to getting improved service for the new neighborhoods. He soon became city commissioner of streets.[5] Thus in examining the Klan's class base, we once again confront the need to see the class *trajectory* of its members.

Still, the Klan's contemporary opponents who labeled it a populist group, representing people who were losing out, or unsophisticated and ill-educated, were mistaken. Some Klaverns included a community's most influential people; in California's six largest cities, for example, Klansmen constituted "a veritable 'Who's Who' of local and county officials."[6] Whether their status was new or old, many Klansmen belonged to a distinctly upper middle class, often managers, businessmen, or professionals. Membership lists included engineers, chemists, physicians, pharmacists, dentists, accountants, schoolteachers, artists, and veterinarians. Gutzon de la Mothe Borglum, the noted sculptor who designed the carved faces on Mount Rushmore, was a member.[7] In Oregon members included numerous attorneys, owners of big farms, a prominent automobile dealer, and officials of the telephone company, Standard Oil, and the Southern Pacific Railroad.[8] Moreover, these data include only members; if Klan sympathizers could be counted, we might very well see more upscale men. No study has yet examined class differences within the Klan, so we do not know if its officers were of higher status than its rank and file. Research on that question could be productive.

Still, most studies agree that the majority of Klanspeople came from the "middling" classes and that white-collar and low-professional employees, along with small businessmen, were overrepresented among Klansmen.[9] In Chicago, 61 percent were in white-collar occupations.[10] Historian Robert A. Goldberg classified 71 percent of Denver Klan members as high and middle nonmanual workers, as compared to 41 percent of all Denver men.[11] Samples of membership lists from Colorado, Montana, Ohio, Pennsylvania, and Tennessee show, for example, that Klansmen had slightly higher rates of literacy than their peers. But studies of state and local Klans make generalization more difficult. In Oregon, one of the strongest Klan states, literacy was nearly universal, so that measure does not apply. In one location Klansmen were more likely to be heads of household than were their peers, but in most locations Klan and non-Klan men were equal in this regard. In some locations Klansmen were more likely than other residents to own their own homes, but in some locations they were not.[12] The Oregon Klans showed great local variation, including variation in what counts as "middling," as for example in Tillamook, where dairy farm owners dominated.[13]

While labeling Klansmen "middling," "white-collar," or "petit bourgeois" tells us little, other characteristics provide more information. A large proportion were members of other fraternal orders, especially Masons. Kleagles, the Klan's traveling recruiters, always approached Masons first when entering a new town, and Klan advertisements often specified "Masons preferred," a designation that served also to imbue the Klan with the Masons' prestige.[14] Men already socialized to the advantages and pleasures of fraternities were ready to join a new one. In a Michigan county, for example, 73 percent of Klansmen also belonged to other fraternal orders, the majority to the Masons and Odd Fellows, and 46 percent of Klanswomen likewise.[15] It bears repeating that the Klan was no more discriminatory than most fraternal orders, which were racially, religiously, and gender-wise exclusionary.[16]

An occupational breakdown tells us more about the groups most attracted by the Klan. The single largest group were small businessmen, including farmers, and their employees, typically white-collar employees. Employees' participation is not surprising, since they were likely to share employers' values, to be subject to employers' pressure, to want employers' approval, or to enjoy participating in a fraternity alongside their employers.[17]

The second-largest group, proportional to their numbers in the population, was probably ministers, particularly among Klan officers. Among the estimated forty thousand Protestant ministers who were members, many became Exalted Cyclopses and Grand Dragons. Many more who were not members praised the Klan in sermons or revivals and allowed Klanspeople to use their churches; their captive audiences made them particularly valuable to the Klan. Accomplished orators, Klan ministers preached at big Klonvocations and became traveling Klan lecturers.[18] The Klan's denunciations of non-Protestants naturally appealed to ministers, but it also helped that men of the cloth could join without paying dues.[19] Ministers, like others, could earn from Klecktokens through their influence on others. If the ministers could not be enticed by personal gain, it was hard for them to refuse the frequent Klan donations to their churches.

When David Curtis Stephenson took over as Indiana Grand Dragon, he criticized the previous focus on recruiting prominent citizens and looked toward employees in the law-and-order business. He knew what he was doing: lawmen and their families joined in large numbers, not only in Indiana but throughout the country.[20] Police chiefs and sheriffs were particularly likely to join, which encouraged their subordinates to follow. Often whole police forces were in or allied with the Klan (except, of course, in locations with many Irish Catholics on the force, as in Boston or New York). The Klan's law-and-order orientation and its unquestioning support for law officers invited their allegiance. Klan membership strengthened the "blue line" of "police brotherhood, right or wrong." The Klan-police fit was mutual: professional lawmen enjoyed the support and help of amateur vigilantes, while the amateurs relished the imprimatur of the professionals. Both groups pulsed to the Klan's masculinist beat and to its racial and religious assumptions that it was people of color, Catholics, and Jews who committed crimes.

Plenty of working-class men did join the Klan. Robert and Helen Lynd, in their iconic study of Muncie, Indiana, got the impression that businessmen were early joiners but that after a year or so "the Klan became largely a working class movement."[21] If this trajectory is correct, it supports the conclusion that workers thought Klan membership would bring higher status, aka middle-class identity. In some locations even workers in large-scale industrial operations joined, and while their motives reflected the ambiguity and local diversity of Klan sentiments—sometimes denouncing big money, sometimes proudly advertising wealthy members—they were almost always angry about immigrants.[22] Eighty percent of one Indiana UMW local were Klan members, 50 to 75 percent of another.[23] In Kansas in 1922, railroad workers on strike flocked into the Klan. In Wisconsin, many German American socialists joined the Klan, and John Kleist was elected to the state supreme court as a Klansman on the Socialist Party ticket.[24] In Evansville, Indiana, among those who were "deputized" when the Klan paid off the police, 40 percent were railroad and factory workers, miners, and servants.[25] But in other places workers fought the Klan, and in Oregon, the only district giving Klan candidates less than a two-thirds majority was an area where railroad workers lived.[26] These apparent anomalies remind us of the Klan's great local variation.

The membership evidence demonstrates at the very least that white industrial workers, even those loyal to their unions, had no immunity from bigotry. That blue-collar workers were a minority in the Klan cannot be taken as a sign that their class consciousness made them critical of it. Those workers hostile to the Klan may have been motivated more by ethnic and/or religious identities than by class consciousness, and those who joined may have been motivated by a bandwagon effect or a desire to hobnob with social superiors. It bears repeating, also, that the cost of Klan membership may have kept out many workers.

Still, Klan power rested on the willingness of elites, both political and economic, to go along. "For courts and legislatures . . . are controlled by one power and one alone, in Oklahoma—money, and not the

Klan," charged a writer for the *New Republic*.[27] As a historian summed up the Klan's success in Indiana, "The business-first crowd held the fort, with organized labor on the run, the 'yellow-dog' contract nailed to factory doors."[28] The Klan advanced no reforms that could help workers, farmers, or small-business people, let alone those who were struggling.

Sociologist Kathleen Blee analyzed the characteristics of Klans-women (in a small Indiana group), the only scholar to do so, although she could not compare their demographics to those of their town. Her findings match what we know about Klansmen, with a few surprises. Only 16 percent were probably single—they had no "Mrs." in front of their names, as was customary then. But even that small proportion of single women was higher than in the general population (10 percent).[29] Of the 84 percent who were or had been married, few had husbands also in the Klan (Blee could find only five); this might suggest women's independent initiative and support for Klan values. Most surprising is the fact that a quarter of the women worked for wages, a higher figure than the overall 15 percent of white women, including immi-grants, who were wage-earners in 1920. (The rate for African Ameri-can women was double that, 30 percent, but of course they were not eligible to be in the Klan.) Of those whose occupations could be found, 28 percent were professionals or business owners, while 33 percent of their husbands were. An astounding 44 percent worked full-time in politics, as party officials, officeholders, or paid staff for the WKKK; however, it seems likely that more information was available about these than about the other Klanswomen, so the actual proportion of paid political operatives was probably smaller. Less surprising is the fact that the majority belonged to other organizations, especially the women's auxiliaries of the fraternal societies.[30] This information comes from a very small sample in one state, but it matches what we know about the men. The information also suggests something quite logical:

that women who were inclined toward community activism and comfortable with public visibility joined the Invisible Empire.

The Ku Klux Klan, then, attracted just enough class diversity that it could claim to represent "middle America." Its community- and identity-building served to construct a collective political subject that simultaneously denied class differences, asserted a class position—middle-class—and repudiated class conflict. Its recruitment, rituals, and celebrations functioned, or tried, to obscure class differences within the Klan. It claimed to represent all "right" Americans. By defining those in restricted racial, ethnic, religious, and ideological terms, it contributed both to myths of classlessness and to today's notion of a vast middle class that includes all except the very rich and the very poor. And it helped some to become middle-class while broadening that label in such a way as to dilute its content.

KKK pageant, 1925. (*Library of Congress Prints and Photographs Division, Washington, DC* [*LC-F81-36625*])

Chapter 11

LEGACY: DOWN BUT NOT OUT

IN THE LATE 1920S, THE KLAN WANED IN INFLUENCE and membership fell almost as rapidly as it had arisen. By 1927 Klan membership had shrunk from several million to about 350,000. Leaders' profiteering—gouging members through dues and the sale of Klan paraphernalia, not to mention criminal embezzlement—grew harder for members to ignore. Power struggles among leaders produced splits and even rival Klans under different names, such as the Allied Protestant Americans and the Improved Order of Klansmen. Rank-and-file resentment transformed the Klan's already high turnover into mass shrinkage as millions of members either failed to pay dues or formally withdrew.

Worse, scandals exposing its leaders' crimes, hypocrisy, and misbehavior hit both local and national newspapers. In Oregon, dentist Ellis O. Willson was twice convicted for raping his secretary and killing her while attempting to perform an abortion. Philip Fox, editor of the *Imperial Night-Hawk*, was sentenced to life imprisonment for killing his rival, William S. Coburn. Imperial Wizard Hiram Evans attempted to stanch the bleeding from Fox's crime by calling it a "personal affair."[1] In Indiana, Klan member Governor Ed Jackson was indicted for bribery, the officers of the state's major Klan bank were indicted for embezzlement and grand larceny, and a Klan minister was accused of crimes "so sensational that persons who heard the sordid details were loath to believe they were true."[2]

Klan vigilantism evoked protests and occasional arrests, and once its brazenness forced even the FBI's J. Edgar Hoover, hardly known for his liberalism, to act. (This case was in the South, where Klan violence was far greater than in the North.) The anti-Prohibition governor of Louisiana discovered in 1922 that Klansmen were not only intercepting his mail and monitoring his phone calls but had killed two of his allies. Examination of the corpses showed that they had been tortured, but Klan-supporting juries refused to convict the accused. Hoover sent FBI agents to investigate. With a chutzpah that reflected their naïveté, Klansmen warned that they would "take care" of the federal agents. Pressed by the governor, Hoover charged eighteen Klan operatives with conspiracy, but once again the jury refused to convict. So he tackled the Klan at an angle: as it had done in charging Al Capone with tax evasion, the FBI prosecuted Klan leader Edward Clarke for violating Prohibition and the Mann Act (which criminalized taking an unmarried woman across state lines for "immoral purposes").[3]

At a more mundane level, merchants frequently complained that the Klan did not pay its bills, no doubt partly because its leaders' megalomania led to extravagant expenditures and unrealistic projects.[4] Supposedly loyal officials betrayed their Klan backers, refusing to meet demands regarding patronage appointments. Oregon's Governor Pierce, no doubt receiving some anti-Klan pressure, refused to appoint the Klan's favored candidate as secretary of the Oregon State Board of Control, a position desirable because the occupant could collect bribes, or "commissions," from businesses contracted with the state government.[5]

The Klan's final undoing was Indiana Grand Dragon Stephenson's conviction for kidnapping, raping, and murdering his secretary, an over-the-top scandal covered widely in the national press. Always one

of the least disciplined of Klan leaders, Stephenson provided an irresistible subject for journalists and writers; the first biography appeared
just a few years after his trial, in 1927. [6] His hypocrisy is stunning. He
drank heavily and entertained lavishly, with Klan money; on one gig
he sailed Lake Erie on his yacht accompanied by a senator, several
congressmen, and a large group of state-level politicians. He would
often go directly from heading a Klan parade to "private orgies of dis-
sipation." His lieutenants kept their complaints in-house, sworn to
Klan secrecy and no doubt bought off by the spoils that Stephenson
distributed to his loyalists. [7] Soon after he assumed power in Indiana,
rumors of immorality began to circulate, not only about his drinking
but also about sexual assaults. One woman who survived an encoun-
ter with him at the Kokomo Klonvocation, described in this book's
opening, called him "a beast when he is drunk." He pled guilty to
indecent exposure when caught with his pants down in his Cadillac
with another young woman. In January 1924, he tried to force himself
on a manicurist whom he had summoned to his hotel room. Later
that year yet another woman told police investigators that during a
party at his house, he locked her in a room, knocked her down, bit
her, and attempted to rape her. (His biting was not only spooky but
also a repeated behavior, suggesting serious derangement.) Imperial
Wizard Hiram Evans, alarmed but anxious to avoid negative publicity, had Stephenson tried by a Klan tribunal, which found him guilty
and called for his expulsion from the Klan. But his Indiana power
base apparently made it impossible for Evans to oust him. Stephenson
responded defiantly and continued to rule the Klan in Indiana, trans-
forming it de facto into an autonomous organization.

The crime that led to his conviction was not only violent but bizarre.
Madge Oberholtzer met Stephenson at a party for Indiana governor
and Klansman Edward L. Jackson. They dated. On March 15, 1925,
he telephoned, well after 10:00 p.m., to say that he simply must see her

and sent his chauffeur to pick her up. He then forced her to accompany him to Chicago and, once in a closed compartment on the train, attacked her. She was literally chewed all over her body, bleeding from several wounds. Then he dragged her into a hotel, refusing to get her medical help. Like so many other women at the time, she felt permanently ruined by what had happened to her; among other traumas, she would have been unmarriageable. Stephenson allowed her to go to a drugstore when she said she needed rouge, but instead she purchased tablets of bichloride of mercury, then used to treat syphilis despite its extreme toxicity, and swallowed six of them. She became deathly ill. Again refusing to get medical treatment for her, he delivered her to her mother's house in Indianapolis, where she died, slowly and in agony. Stephenson was convicted of second-degree murder. His conviction, despite the fact that she voluntarily poisoned herself, reflected a bitter truth of the time: that a jury assumed that her violation made her permanently "ruined" and thus caused her suicide.

The Stephenson scandal was a last straw for many Klanspeople. Members found it hard to ignore their leaders' corruption and sinful hypocrisy. For some, the hocus-pocus rituals may have lost their initial thrill. Many deserted, or simply did not pay dues. Politicians who once complied with the Klan's every wish now abandoned it; Stephenson had counted on a pardon from the governor he had worked to elect, and was no doubt outraged that the governor ran for cover, so he had to serve out his full sentence. With some regional variation, by 1927 the Klan was but a small fraction of its peak size.

Some scholars and contemporary observers have seen the 1920s northern Klan as a failure because it was short-lived and because its campaigns against Catholics and Jews did not manage to confine them to second-class citizenship. But transience is common to most social movements. Moreover, the Klan declined in part because it had triumphed in several respects. State eugenics laws, providing for forcible sterilization of those of "defective stock," spread to thirty states, and those labeled defective were typically the poor and people of color. The biggest Klan victory was immigration restriction, and Imperial Wizard Evans repeatedly claimed credit for its passage.[8] The Johnson-Reed Act of 1924, named for Washington Klansman Albert Johnson in the House and Pennsylvania's David Reed in the Senate, ensconced into law the Klan's hierarchy of desirable and undesirable "races" by assigning quotas for immigrants in proportion to the ethnicity of those already in the United States in 1890. (This meant that the immigrant quota for the UK, Ireland, and Germany constituted 70 percent of the total allowed.[9]) The quotas radically restricted the inmigration of some of the world's most desperate people, including notably Jews in eastern Europe and Russia. The act also turned the previous exclusions of Chinese and Japanese into an across-the-board exclusion of all Asians, including South Asians.[10] This racial discrimination in immigration continued until 1965. Certainly Klanspeople were not alone responsible, but Klan propaganda surely strengthened racialized anti-immigrant sentiment both in Congress and among the voters. Its anti-immigrant influence shows today in opposition to the admission of refugees, in the deportation even of long-term residents, and in calls to end birthright citizenship, despite the fact that it was, ironically, almost uniquely American.[11]

The biggest Klan victory was equally consequential but less tangible: it influenced the public conversation, the universe of tolerable discourse. It increased the intensity and spread of bigoted speech and, occasionally, action. True, the Klan did not invent bigotry. Sometimes ebbing, sometimes flowing, white racism had appeared as soon as Europeans arrived on this continent. But the Klan spread, strengthened, and radicalized preexisting nativist and racist sentiments among the white population. In reactivating these older animosities it also relegitimated them. However reprehensible hidden bigotry might be, making its open expression acceptable has significant additional impact. Stigmatizing bigoted talk conveys the message that it is shameful. Moreover, silent bigotry exerts less influence on others. Similarly, vigilantism works to legitimate not only violence but also justifications for it, especially the claim that threats from people of the wrong religion or race require the action of private citizens. Then, when courts acquit vigilantes, as they did so often in the 1920s—and virtually always in the South—the vigilantes' self-justifications become yet more acceptable.

The influence of the Klan's mandatory patriotism, defining righteous Americanism ideologically and repressively, also reappeared in later decades. True, Klan ideology never made anti-Communism as important a cause as its bigotry, although Imperial Wizard Hiram Evans explicitly conflated "Liberalism" with "the Bolshevist platform." The Klan consistently branded dissent as dangerous, even treasonous. Its anti-immigrant discourse included attacks on "foreign ideas," a "steady flood" of which was being spread—"always carefully disguised as American."[12] Its major tool for suppressing dissent, however, was its unqualified, ever-reiterated boasting of American superiority. This obligatory patriotism was expressed symbolically, visually, in the mass pageants with their extravagant displays, and literally in speeches and texts asserting that "right" Americans were the chosen people, that the American governmental system was the most perfect on earth, that profit-seeking was the grounds of American greatness.

Propounding an expurgated and often fictional rendition of American history confirmed these values. In their efforts to rewrite textbooks so as to place themselves in the tradition of the founding fathers, and to teach a false and ahistorical notion of what these eighteenth-century liberals thought, Klanspeople taught that "true" Americanness required adherence to an ideology. Similar demands of history textbooks continue today. The Klan's version of Americanism was recapitulated, in slightly altered form, by McCarthyism, the domestic face of the Cold War; when it tried to define dissent as unAmerican, it was carrying on this part of the Klan's legacy. That version of ideological patriotism has reappeared periodically, as a value system in which being a loyal American requires conformity to a political ideology. Condemning dissent from this ideology as dangerous prefigured Red-baiting directed against causes as disparate as civil rights and "progressive education."

The longest-term force behind the Klan's decline was, of course, the increasing integration of Catholics and Jews into American politics, culture, and economy.[13] The allegedly inassimilable Jews assimilated and influenced the culture, both high-brow and low-brow. The alleged vassals of the pope began to behave like other immigrants, firm in their allegiance to America. This process of Americanization integrated diverse immigrants into the industrial and commercial organization of work and leisure.

That integration then forced the Klan to search for new allies. One example: in the 1930s, many Klanspeople enthusiastically supported a *Catholic* radio personality, the racist and virulently anti-Semitic priest Charles Coughlin (known on the air as Father Coughlin). His weekly broadcasts, said to reach thirty million listeners, slandered President Roosevelt and praised Hitler, Mussolini, and Hirohito. Some Klanspeople also supported the German American Bund (*Amerikadeutscher Bund*), a group organized at the direction of Nazi Deputy Führer Rudolf Hess. Attempting to maintain a patriotic veneer, the Bund carried American flags and claimed George Washington as the first fascist. Both Coughlin and the Bund were openly anti-Semitic but not anti-Catholic. Ultimately some Klan groups even discarded their traditional anti-Semitism. As with most racisms, the Klan's bigotry was fungible, and it backed off from targeting groups that gained in political power and social prestige. If the Klan had continued in its early 1920s strength, it might have identified different targets or redefined its categories of "true" and "false" Americans.

By contrast, the Klan never gave up its hatred for people of color.

As African Americans moved northward and westward, as more Latin American and East Asian immigrants arrived, the latter-day Klan shifted toward a simpler, purer racial system, with two categories: white and not white. In the South the Klan neither modulated its anti-black racism nor allowed it to recede as the group's primary focus. The twenty-first-century North is by no means free of the Klan's genuflection to whiteness, as Aryan Nations and other white supremacist groups carry on the Klan's tradition. Some of these groups even continue to unite white supremacy with the "right" religion, as the Klan did—for example, in groups such as the Christian Defense League, the Posse Comitatus, and the Christian Identity movement. As one leader put it, "Christianity for the Aryan is race— and race is Christianity."[14]

Of the Klan's six ancestors—the first Ku Klux Klan, nativism, temperance, fraternalism, Christian evangelicalism, populism— only some remain influential today. Only a few Americans would reinstate Prohibition, and support for continued prohibition of marijuana is waning. Membership in fraternal orders declined steeply after 1950. The Klan itself survives, with some five thousand to eight thousand members, but they belong to independent local groups without a disciplining national organization.[15] "Ku Klux Klan" is now a term so besmirched that even those who agree with the organization's principles might hesitate to identify with it; avoiding this stigmatized association was a major motive in the rise of the 1950s White Citizens Councils. But other groups promoting bigotry, nativism, and Christian evangelicalism continue. What is different is that these activists no longer have a single organization to unite them. The lack of unity reflects the fact that fewer people unite all these causes: for example, not all those who fear immigration are evangelicals, not all evangelicals are nativists or racists, not all bigots are hostile to immigration.

IF UNDERSTANDING THE ORIGINS of the 1920s Klan required looking backward to its progenitors, our understanding of its appeal and its ideology may also benefit from a glance at developments outside the United States and in later decades. I have tried to show the 1920s Klan in its historical context, but I cannot empty my consciousness of later history, notably, the fascisms of Italy and Nazi Germany. Today the fascist label is appearing again, not only in the United States but throughout Europe, as right-wing parties gain power, threatening democratic processes and abolishing civil liberties.

Several historians have classified the 1920s Klan and today's right-wing populism as part of a fascist family.[16] There are good reasons to avoid the subject of fascism, not only because it is so inflammatory but also because its variants are numerous. Moreover, the label has been applied so loosely, to condemn everything from the US government to feminism, that it often works as a panicky pejorative without specific content. As a result, some scholars have suggested abandoning the term altogether. I find it still useful, however, if only because it requires recognizing that right-wing movements come in many forms and contents. They are different enough to make a generic, universal definition of fascism impossible. Umberto Eco, in his 1995 essay "Ur-Fascism," argues that "fascism had no quintessence." It was "a fuzzy totalitarianism, a collage . . . a beehive of contradictions. . . . The fascist game can be played in many forms." Historian Robert Paxton agrees; in his article "The Five Stages of Fascism," he writes that we cannot identify fascism "by its plumage."[17] For all these reasons, applying that label to the 1920s Ku Klux Klan would be unproductive. Noting the overlap between the KKK and various avatars of fascism can, however, be illuminating.

The 1920s Klan was not a uniquely American phenomenon. It was part of a group of movements around the globe that have come

to be called right-wing populisms, fascism one of them. It was growing throughout central and eastern Europe just as the second Klan
arose, and is reawakening today. Similar movements avoid the fascist label but share its modalities, especially hostility to immigrants.[18]
These movements often co-opt grievances associated with the Left,
notably economic inequality, but typically blame foreigners, racial minorities, and cosmopolitan, liberal elites. These movements also share
patterns of thought and rhetoric, such as conspiracy-mongering, apoc-
alyptic narratives, anti-intellectualism, and intense nationalism, often
called "patriotism."[19] If generic populism calls on "ordinary people" to
struggle against a powerful and undemocratic elite, right-wing populism defines that elite enemy as an alliance between politicians and
liberal, professional-class urbanites.

Luckily the 1920s Klan appeared in a country with long-imbedded
electoral procedures. It also strategized that respectability and legality
were its most productive route to power; it did not plan a coup. While
American federalism helped it gain power in the state, it also impeded its
potential as a national force.

The Klan's reliance on demagogic speakers to mobilize people and
intensify political emotions was characteristically fascist. All populisms find ways to arouse masses of people and to forge them into a
political constituency that can challenge elites. But the demagogic orators of the Klan and right-wing populisms used their orators and slo-
ganeers almost exclusively to stimulate anger at minority groups. They
used outrageously false and/or exaggerated claims to ratchet up fears
that "aliens" were threatening morals, law and order, political control,
"family values," "American values," and, not least, jobs. Like European
fascists, the Klan produced spectacular, choreographed pageants to
intensify members' pride in belonging to the master race and to arouse
nonmembers' desire to become part of it. We might call these events
visual demagoguery. In speeches, writings, and performances, the Klan
stirred men with metaphors of war and thereby stimulated vigilantism.

Similarly, like fascism and especially its Nazi version, the Klan promulgated a racialized nationalism: it conflated the "nation" with a master "race," that is, "Nordics."[20] Sinclair Lewis warned that should fascism come to the United States, it would appear as patriotic and entirely American. In his 1935 novel *It Can't Happen Here*, the fictional fascist senator Berzelius Windrip promises "'to make America a proud, rich land again.'"[21] That concept of national destiny fueled hostilities even toward neighbors, even those who had long been part of Klanspeople's communities (a process that replicated on a smaller scale the power of tribal nationalisms to transform neighbors into enemies, as in the former Yugoslavia, even into targets of genocide, as in Rwanda).

Unlike Nazism and Italian fascism, however, the KKK did not bring large-scale capital into supporting its hypernationalism. The Klan also differed from German and Italian fascists, as well as today's conservative populists, by melding nationalism with religion.[22] This gave it several advantages: it intensified self-righteousness among its supporters and turned "aliens" into sinners. Sin was a powerful category for Christians: it not only justified keeping aliens out but also validated the dominance of "right" Americans.

The Klan's nationalist arguments rested on appeal to tradition, a glorious tradition, another theme common to right-wing populisms. The "tradition" Klan leaders referenced was largely a fiction, as traditions often are in popular understanding. One example is the Klan's claim that the early United States was a homogeneously Protestant nation, when in fact non-Protestants had been part of the country since its origin. Traditionalists of all political stripes have often called for a return to a postulated golden age that never existed. But in fascist ideologies, this "tradition" became a destiny; the Klan view of America's destiny paralleled fascist conceptions of Italian destiny and Nazi conceptions of Germanic destiny. The Klan, however, outdid the European fascists in the authority it cited for this destiny: not only the "founding fathers" but also God himself.

Like all social movements, the Klan provided to members, at least temporarily, the satisfactions of belonging to a like-minded community, and this was no small part of its temporary success. All social movements generate group loyalty, of course, and all draw a border between members and outsiders, a border especially clearly demarcated in fraternal orders. But not all create intense aversion to those outside the group. The Klan tried to divide people between the pure and the impure, the godly and the ungodly, patriots and traitors. Eschewing nuance, these binaries raised a particularly high wall separating the righteous from the wicked. There are resemblances here not only to fascists but also to religious believers for whom individuals outside the faith are infidels, either susceptible to conversion or damned. The Klan's emphasis on chastity and sobriety demanded more of its members than did most fascists. This moral high-mindedness resembles that of some more recent evangelical leaders; in offering a righteous identity and thereby attracting converts, leaders build not only their organization but also their personal power and wealth. There is a considerable chink in this wall of morality, however: since many cannot or will not conform to these stringent norms of purity, hypocrisy ensues, and when exposed, creates scandals that damage the cause.

Not all populisms challenge the dominant economic form of organization. Those on the democratic end, like the 1890s Populists, have frequently called for regulating the ability of the wealthy to "rig" the system, while those on the conservative end have not usually challenged the ruling power structure. In its economic values, the Klan was wholly conservative. Klanspeople respected the rich. The middle-class identity promoted by the Klan honored the profit motive (which insulated its profiteering leaders from criticism for a time). These values then confirmed the belief that America offered economic opportunity to everyone. That ideology might seem to contradict its assertions that "aliens" were stealing jobs from "right" Americans, but that accusation was largely rhetorical, as there were few areas of Klan strength in which immigrants were competing with the native-born for jobs. One might call this claim about unfair competition from "aliens" a grievance to be taken seriously but not literally, to use a twenty-first-century phrase.

What economic complaints the Klan articulated always took the form of racial and religious prejudices. Klan anti-Semitism closely resembled the Nazi version. Jews were not only swindlers but, due to their tribal conspiracies, blocked honest competition. Klan anti-Semitism differed from mainstream anti-Semitism only in intensity; condemning Jews for their commercial success by branding them cheaters and money-grubbers was a popular slur of the time, to the extent that "Jewing" referred to ruthless haggling over prices. The pecuniary stereotype of Jews served both to veil the pecuniary dishonesty and profiteering of non-Jews, notably Klan officials themselves, and to deflect criticism from the inequities imbedded in the economy. Klan discourse, unlike that of the Nazis, did not often blame Jews for Communism, an argument that would become a regular feature of Father Coughlin's fascism in the 1930s. Anti-Communism appeared occasionally in Klan propaganda but was never a major theme in the North. If it had been, it would have yielded the contradiction so common in Europe, accusing Jews both of Communism and predatory capitalism.

By contrast, Klan anti-Catholicism was, in the main, uniquely American. As in its anti-Semitism, the Klan charged Catholics with unfair competition, alleging that the pope's emissaries helped them take over police forces, newspapers, and big-city governments. These allegations then bled into the Klan's anger at the entire "political class," despite its own ambition to become that political class.

Condemning Jews and Catholics while honoring "right" Americans for the same practices speaks to the Klan's demand that supporters accept its allegations on faith. Because the Klan was a religious as well as a nationalist organization, the beliefs required of its members were all the more obligatory. Challenging its truths constituted treason or heresy or both. The emphasis on faith as opposed to evidence-driven inquiry both reflected and fed suspicion of science, especially evolutionary theory. That suspicion strengthened its hostility to intellectuals in general. Klan doctrine was impregnable to disproof. Its discursive mode—anecdotal, testimonial—resisted challenge. In this respect the KKK was authoritarian, even as it denounced Catholics for their subservience to papal authority. Klan anti-intellectualism protected it from skeptics. In this respect it differed from European fascisms, which, partly because they were less religiously narrow, did not typically display hostility to science. What Umberto Eco wrote of fascist ideology—"There can be no advancement of learning. Truth has been already spelled out once and for all"—actually fits the Klan better than it describes European fascism.[23]

Some scholars have labeled fascist and populist movements irrational, as in the analyses of historian Richard Hofstadter and sociologists Joseph Gusfield, William Kornhauser, and Neil Smelser in the 1960s. The Klan did not engage in the characteristic fascist romanticization of violence. Moreover, the status-anxiety diagnoses that dominated social-movement scholarship in the 1960s characterize social movements as products of psychological strain or tension and therefore not rational pursuits of concrete goals. These conclusions mirrored those of 1920s critics of the Klan. Behind the "irrationality" accusation lies an assumption equating emotion, especially fear and anger, with irrationality. Anger and especially indignation, "the morally grounded form of anger" in sociologist James Jasper's definition, can be not only rational but also justified.[24] But mass emotion can be rational even if it rests on false beliefs. The Klan's drive to maintain the supremacy of white Protestants was a perfectly rational expression of what many of its members conceived as their interest. So were its strategies for achieving that goal. Even the Klan's appeal to fear was a rational means to build mass support. So it becomes important to distinguish emotionality from irrationality.

Among the Klan's emotional appeals, gendered messages to men had particular power. Like European fascism, the Klan supplied a way for members to confirm manliness at a time when its content was shifting. As more men became white-collar workers, as more small businesses lost out to chains, as the political supremacy of Anglo-Saxons became contested, as more women reached for economic and political rights, alternative ways for men to enact manliness became especially magnetic, even stimulating vigilante violence. Fascism is distinguished not only by its ideologies, which are often incoherent, but also through its visual symbolism and its aggressive mobilizations. The Klan similarly organized performances of masculinity and male bonding through uniforms, parades, rituals, secrecy, and hierarchical military ranks and titles. A study of today's Minutemen, a group that patrols the southern US border to keep Latin Americans out, described their motives in phrases that fit the Klan: they long for "male spaces, spaces where they can carry guns and be soldiers at war."[25] Klanspeople trafficked in warlike discourse; manliness was strength, womanliness weakness. This binary was hardly exclusive to the Klan; it pervaded the United States. As with its racism, the Ku Klux Klan merely offered an intensified version. Its excitatory rhetoric both reflected and elicited a yearning for action. To be manly was to fight; not to fight was to be weak. All this was fundamental to fascism, and the Nazis used it in violent, even sadistic attacks on and humiliations of its "aliens." The northern Ku Klux Klan rarely did that. Klan leaders realized that they could gain more from electoral than from martial action. True, there was vigilantism, but its scale was tiny compared to the Nazis' violence. The northern Klan stopped far, far short of Storm Trooper behavior.

In the South, by contrast, precisely the area that 1920s Klan leaders sought to decenter, vigilantism remained the Klan's core function. It constituted a strategic terrorism directed at African Americans. Once legal segregation was challenged, the 1950s and 1960s White Citizens Councils (the organizations that opposed school desegregation) responded by establishing ostensibly private—and therefore legal—segregated schools. In their inflammatory rhetoric, ratcheting up fears about the losses of white privilege, the councils could be seen as revivals of 1920s Klaverns.

In the north, however, part of the Klan's genius lay in enabling men to imagine themselves warriors even as they behaved peaceably. For most Klansmen the hierarchy, the rituals, and the uniformed parades were metaphorically, not literally, militaristic. But the metaphor was essential. Like most other right-wing populisms, the Klan could not survive a peace treaty or even an armistice with its enemies. It needed a sense of danger to thrive. Klanspeople had to visualize themselves as soldiers defending against threats, and in doing so created belief in those threats. Right-wing populisms often produce this doubled effect.

Women were also aroused by the Klan's warlike rhetoric. To presume that women were not avid participants in the Klan's militaristic performances is to replicate Victorian assumptions about women's moral superiority. They did not need to be vigilantes to like vigilantism. But women's energy for promoting the Klan produced tension. Klansmen and Klanswomen both honored a family ideal that confined women to their homes, but in practice Klanswomen rejected it. As the sisters organized Klan groups, the brothers had to accept them as co-soldiers, if of subordinate rank. Despite the ideology that men's roles included protecting women, most Klansmen, like most other men, must have known perfectly well that womanly delicacy and passivity were myths. Klansmen exploited and depended on millions of hours of labor by Klanswomen and the even more numerous Klan wives. These women not only made the mass Klonvocations possible but also socialized children into Klan values, performed charitable work in the Klan's name, cast votes for Klan candidates, and promoted boycotts against "alien" merchants. Klansmen liked to imagine Klanswomen's roles as merely supportive, an illusion that Klanswomen frequently punctured. They often insisted on autonomy, influence, and a wider range of activity. This contradiction—that women's activism often defied the domesticity they appeared to endorse—appears in many conservative movements. Second to no men in their bigotry, Klanswomen seem often to have militated for equality within the organization (although the scarcity of research limits the available evidence). Kathleen Blee's study of Klanswomen illustrates this contradiction, as do historical studies of other conservative and fascist women.[26]

The Ku Klux Klan's bigotry and rabble-rousing were typical of fascism, but its official political values were not: the Klan ostensibly favored democracy. In Klan propaganda it was the Catholic enemy who sought to impose authoritarian rule. By excluding "aliens" through the allegation that they could not be loyal citizens, the Klan could support majority rule, because white Anglo-Saxon Protestants were still a majority in the United States. For example, the Klan supported the many state constitutional amendments allowing voters to initiate referendums. This kind of democracy—a *herrenvolk* democracy, democracy of the privileged—would effectively disenfranchise the rest of the population, leaving them without protection from discrimination. The journalist Dorothy Thompson, who spent years covering Nazi Germany, and lived through the 1920s heyday of the Klan, pointed out that "no people ever recognize their dictator in advance. He never stands for election on the platform of dictatorship. He always represents himself as the instrument [of] the Incorporated National Will. . . . When our dictator turns up you can depend on it that he will be one of the boys, and he will stand for everything traditionally American."[27]

The Klan's vision of majoritarian or plebiscitary democracy was not entirely the opposite of authoritarianism. Democracy seemed a safe bet for Klanspeople because, in the 1920s, they could hardly imagine a United States in which "right" Americans would not be a majority. In this respect the Klan differed sharply from today's right-wing populisms, when such a loss of majority threatens.

The Klan's electoral work illustrates, perhaps, its greatest divergence from fascism: it sought ideological hegemony but planned to achieve it without fundamental changes to the political rules of American democracy. The KKK was a political machine and a social movement, not an insurrectionary vanguard. It is quite possible that in the 1920s a majority of American citizens shared Klan values. This context illuminates also the Klan's contrast with today's right-wing populist movements, which are often distinctly oppositional, because they face an America in which liberal values have to some degree taken root in the majority of the population. For the majority, segregation and discrimination are wrong, freedom of speech is widely endorsed, racism is a pejorative term, and tens of millions of those the Klan considered "aliens" are respected citizens. True, these values are neither universal nor entirely secure, and many who enunciate them in principle violate them in practice. But today's right-wing populists, even as they can win elections, face majorities who reject their values.

Every such movement arises also from specific local and national contexts, and all are different. But they share characteristics, as a particular but recognizable type of conservatism. Illiberal in their suspicion of dissent and the rights of minority groups, clinging to fictive images of their nations as homogeneous and destined to be so, resentful of cultural elites yet accepting the dominance of economic elites, they direct anger at big-city cosmopolitans and at groups outside their imagined homogeneity. In the United States these movements and their populist, racist, demagogic, and incitatory orientation are a continuing part of our history, if sometimes dormant. The Klannish spirit—fearful, angry, gullible to sensationalist falsehoods, in thrall to demagogic leaders and abusive language, hostile to science and intellectuals, committed to the dream that everyone can be a success in business if they only try—lives on.

APPENDIX 1:
A GLOSSARY OF SOME
KLAN TITLES

Alien—nonmember of the Klan and/or someone not a white native-born Protestant

Exalted Cyclops—head of a Klavern

Grand Goblin or Grand Dragon—head of one of the nine domains for purposes of recruitment

Imperial Kleagle—supervisor of Grand Goblins
Imperial Klonsel—national lawyer for the Klan
Imperial Wizard—national head of the Klan
Invisible Empire—the whole Klan

King Kleagle—head of recruitment for a region, under a Grand Goblin
Klabee—treasurer
Kladd—conductor, in charge of initiating new members
Klaliff—Vice Cyclops
Klarogo—guard of a Klavern's "inner room"
Klavern—local chapter

Kleagle—recruiter, under a King Kleagle

Klecktoken—initial joining fee

Klexter—outer guard at a Klavern meeting

Kligrapp—administrative officer of a Klavern

Klokan—head of a committee to investigate potential members

Klokard—traveling lecturer or representative of national Klan

Klonklave—weekly meeting of a Klavern

Klonverse—weekly meeting of a province

Klonversation—event at which new members were "naturalized"

Klonvocation—national or regional public event

Kloran—Klan bible, setting out rules and procedures

Klorero—large Klan gathering

Kludd—chaplain

Naturalization—installing new members, who were then no longer aliens

Night-Hawk—courier and custodian of props; in charge of new recruits prior to naturalization

Terrors—the officers of a Klavern

APPENDIX 2:
KLAN EVALUATION
OF US SENATORS, 1923

State	Evaluation
ALABAMA	Two Democrats, Underwood, reactionary, and Heflin, progressive.
ARIZONA	Ashurst, progressive Democrat; Cameron, Old Guard Republican.
ARKANSAS	Robinson and Caraway, Progressive Democrats.
CALIFORNIA	Both Republicans, Johnson listed as progressive with a question mark, and Shortridge a machine man.
COLORADO	Has Adams—a recently appointed Democrat, and Phipps, Old Guarder.
CONNECTICUT	Brandegee and McLean—both reactionary Republicans.
DELAWARE	Bayard, untested Democrat, and Ball, a machine Republican.
FLORIDA	Fletcher and Trammell, both Democrats, the latter more progressive.

From the *Fiery Cross,* Michigan State edition, December 13, 1923, as reproduced in Rory McVeigh, *The Rise of the Ku Klux Klan: Right-Wing Movements and National Politics* (Minneapolis: University of Minnesota Press, 2009), figure 12.

State	Evaluation
GEORGIA	Has Harris and George, good Democrats.
IDAHO	Borah is an outstanding progressive, and Gooding a "me too" Republican.
ILLINOIS	Two machine Republicans, McCormick and McKinley.
INDIANA	Ralston is a progressive Democrat; Watson has been a Republican machine leader.
IOWA	Has Cummins, Republican reactionary, and Brookhart, who is his own boss.
KANSAS	Curtis as a machine leader, with Capper somewhat on the fence.
KENTUCKY	Stanley, progressive Democrat on most issues; Ernst, colorless Old Guarder.
LOUISIANA	Ransdell and Broussard, both very conservative Democrats.
MASSACHUSETTS	Lodge is the dean of Republican reactionaries, with Walsh a progressive Democrat.
MARYLAND	Has Bruce, an untried Democrat, and Weller of the Republican Old Guard.
MAINE*	Both Fernald and Hale are Republican regulars.
MICHIGAN	Ferris is a progressive Democrat and Couzens, an independent Republican.
MINNESOTA	Both Shipstead and Johnson are ultra progressive.
MISSISSIPPI	Has Harrison and Stephens, good Democrats.
MISSOURI	Reed is an able Democrat, while Spencer will do anything the Old Guard machine thinks best.
MONTANA	Walsh and Wheeler, both able Democrats with the latter a real independent.

* Incorrect alphabetization in original.

State	Evaluation
NEBRASKA	Has two Republican progressives—Norris and Howell.
NEVADA	Pittman is a progressive Democrat and Oddie an Old Guard Republican.
NEW HAMPSHIRE	Both Moses and Keyes are regular Republicans.
NEW JERSEY	Edwards is an untested Democrat and Edge a reactionary Republican.
NEW MEXICO	Has a progressive Democrat in Jones, with Bursum a machine Republican.
NEW YORK	Has Copeland, a liberal Democrat, and Wadsworth, Old Guard.
NORTH CAROLINA*	Simmons is an able, progressive Democrat, with Overman, also of that party, but conservative.
OHIO	Has two regular Republicans—Willis and Fess.
OKLAHOMA	Checks itself, Owen being a liberal Democrat and Harreld a machine Republican.
OREGON	Both Republicans, with McNary a wobbler and Stanfield dependable from the Old Guard point of view.
PENNSYLVANIA	Has two Old Guarders—Pepper and Reed.
RHODE ISLAND	Gerry is a progressive Democrat and Colt a Republican regular.
SOUTH CAROLINA	Two Democrats—Smith and Dial, with the former more liberal.
SOUTH DAKOTA	Both Republicans, with Norbeck having progressive leanings and Sterling in the camp of the regulars.
TENNESSEE	Has two Democrats—Shields and McKellar, the latter progressive.

* There is no entry for North Dakota.

State	Evaluation
Texas	Both Democrats, Sheppard being a dependable progressive, with Mayfield, a new senator, said to be in that camp.
Utah	King is a fighting, independent Democrat, with Smoot an expert Republican machinist.
Vermont	Has one Republican—Greene—and a vacancy due to the death of Dillingham.
Virginia	Swanson and Glass are good Democrats.
Washington	Has Dill, a progressive Democrat, and Jones, a sometimes independent Republican.
West Virginia	Neeley is an average Democrat, and Elkins a completely colorless Old Guarder.
Wisconsin	LaFollette is an outstanding liberal leader, with Lenroot a regular.
Wyoming	Has one of the highest class Democrats in Kendrick and an Old Guard wheel horse in Warren.

A partial decoding of the identifications used in these evaluations: A Democrat is usually someone the Klan considered a reliable supporter of its program; so is a progressive. Republicans, especially if labeled Old Guard, machine, or regular, could not be counted on; similarly with liberals. Note that Democrats are never characterized as "machine." But some Republican senators were considered favorable to the Klan, especially if labeled progressive or independent. Punctuation as in original.

NOTES

Introduction: "100% Americanism"

1. Craig Fox, *Everyday Klansfolk: White Protestant Life and the Ku Klux Klan in 1920s Michigan* (East Lansing: Michigan State University Press, 2012), 195; Richard Melching, "The Activities of the Ku Klux Klan in Anaheim, California, 1923–1925," *Southern California Quarterly* 56, no. 2 (Summer 1974): 182; Kathleen Blee, *Women of the Klan* (Berkeley: University of California Press, 1991), 136.

2. In 1923, the Ku Klux Klan offered to purchase this university for $175,000, planning to expand it to the size of Purdue University and devote it to the instilling of Americanism. In fact, the Klan was never able to raise the money, and in 1925 Valparaiso was purchased by the Lutheran Church—Missouri Synod and Evangelical Lutheran Church in America.

3. Leonard J. Moore, *Citizen Klansmen: The Ku Klux Klan in Indiana* (Chapel Hill: University of North Carolina Press, 1991), 99.

4. Reliable figures on the second Klan's membership are unavailable. Estimates of its size ranged from one million to ten million members. The lower figures are probably the most reliable, as both pro- and anti-Klan people exaggerated its size, and members left the Klan as often as new people joined.

5. Arnold S. Rice, *The Ku Klux Klan in American Politics* (New York: Haskell House, 1972), 367.

6. Alberto Melucci, *Challenging Codes: Collective Action in the Information Age* (New York: Cambridge University Press, 1996), 40, quoted in Kathleen Blee and Ashley Currier, "Character Building: The Dynamics of Emerging Social Movement Groups," *Mobilization* 10, no. 1 (February 2005): 129.

7. Charles Tilly defined social movements as a series of contentious performances, displays, and campaigns by which ordinary people make collective claims on others in his *Social Movements, 1768–2004* (Boulder, CO: Paradigm Publishers,

2004). Sidney Tarrow defined a social movement as "collective challenges [to elites, authorities, other groups, or cultural codes] by people with common purposes and solidarity in sustained interactions with elites, opponents and authorities" in his *Power in Movement: Collective Action, Social Movements and Politics* (Cambridge: Cambridge University Press, 1994). John McCarthy and Mayer Zald defined a social movement as "a set of opinions and beliefs in a population which represents preferences for changing some elements of the social structure and/or reward distribution of a society" in their "Resource Mobilization and Social Movements: A Partial Theory," *American Journal of Sociology* 82, no. 6 (May 1977): 1217–18.

8. Coincidentally, the Klan also claimed the Boston Tea Party as an honored ancestor, naming it the first recorded Klan meeting.

Chapter 1. REBIRTH

1. Maxim Simcovitch, "The Impact of Griffith's 'Birth of a Nation' on the Modern Ku Klux Klan," *Journal of Popular Film* 1, no. 1 (Winter 1972): 45–54. Simcovitch makes the film largely responsible for the revival of the Klan.

2. Quoted in William Keylor, "The Long-Forgotten Racial Attitudes and Policies of Woodrow Wilson," *Professor Voices*, March 4, 2013, http://www.bu.edu/ professorvoices/2013/03/04/the-long-forgotten-racial-attitudes-and-policies -of-woodrow-wilson/.

3. The "Protocols" forgery appeared first in Russian in 1903 as Протоколы сионских мудрецов and is still widely available online. Klan editors would later gather the *Dearborn Independent* articles into a four-volume book, *The International Jew*. Robert Michael, *A Concise History of American Antisemitism* (New York: Rowman & Littlefield, 2005), 139.

4. Simmons falsely claimed to have studied medicine at the University of Alabama. William Peirce Randel, *The Ku Klux Klan: A Century of Infamy* (New York: Chilton, 1965), 183.

5. Rice, *The Ku Klux Klan in American Politics*, 20.

6. *Dawn*, a publication of the Chicago Klan, October 21, 1922, quoted in John Mack Shotwell, "Crystallizing Public Hatred: Ku Klux Klan Public Relations in the Early 1920s" (MA thesis, University of Wisconsin–Madison, 1974), 33.

7. Part of his appeal was calling for support for the war. Quotation from Wyn Craig Wade, *The Fiery Cross: The Ku Klux Klan in America* (New York: Simon & Schuster, 1987), 147, 150.

8. Winfield Jones, *Knights of the Ku Klux Klan* (New York: Tocsin Publishers, 1941), 82.

9. William G. Shepherd, "Ku Klux Koin," *Collier's*, July 21, 1928, 8–9, 38–39.

10. Frank Bohn, "The Ku Klux Klan Interpreted," *American Journal of Sociology* 30, no. 4 (January 1925): 395; Craig Strain, "Shearith Israel Renovates 'All South-

ern' Lanier University (1981)," *Virginia-Highland Voice*, January 1981, http://vahi
.org/shearith-israel-renovates-all-southern-lanier-university-1981/. Ironically, the
Lanier building later became a synagogue.

11. Charles O. Jackson, "William J. Simmons: A Career in Ku Kluxism," *Georgia
Historical Quarterly* 50, no. 4 (December 1966): 353–54.

12. William Loren Katz, *The Invisible Empire: The Ku Klux Klan Impact on History*
(Washington, DC: Open Hand Publishing, 1986), 79. The contract is reprinted in
Jones, *Knights of the Ku Klux Klan*, 228–30.

13. Jackson, "William J. Simmons," 353–54.

14. Quoted in Randel, *The Ku Klux Klan*, 187.

15. Henry P. Fry, *The Modern Ku Klux Klan* (Boston: Small, Maynard, 1922),
37–51.

16. Stanley Frost, *The Challenge of the Klan* (New York: Bobbs-Merrill, 1924), 1.

17. Randel, *The Ku Klux Klan*, 191.

18. Bohn, "The Ku Klux Klan Interpreted," 391.

19. Jones, *Knights of the Ku Klux Klan*, 141. That a social movement could be a
business may seem eccentric today but was fundamental to the KKK's organization, as we will see in chapter 4.

20. Katz, *The Invisible Empire*, 79; Rice, *The Ku Klux Klan in American Politics*,
chapter 1; Randel, *The Ku Klux Klan*, 195.

21. Thomas R. Pegram, *One Hundred Percent Americanism: The Rebirth and
Decline of the Ku Klux Klan in the 1920s* (Chicago: Ivan R. Dee, 2011), 17.

22. William D. Jenkins, *Steel Valley Klan: The Ku Klux Klan in Ohio's Mahoning
Valley* (Kent, OH: Kent State University Press, 1990), 7; Richard K. Tucker, *The
Dragon and the Cross: the Rise and Fall of the Ku Klux Klan in Middle America*
(Hamden, CT: Archon Books, 1991), 93–94.

23. Fry, *The Modern Ku Klux Klan*, 31–32; Shepherd, "Ku Klux Koin," 9.

24. Edgar Allen Booth, *The Mad Mullah of America* (Columbus, OH: B. Ellison,
1927), 39, and a memo of August 22, 1925, reproduced on 232-A; Jones, *Knights
of the Ku Klux Klan*, 142.

25. Minutes of LaGrande, Oregon, Klavern, December 5, 1955, in *Inside the
Klavern: The Secret History of a Ku Klux Klan of the 1920s*, ed. David A. Horo-
witz (Carbondale: Southern Illinois University Press, 1999), 99; Hiram Wesley
Evans, "The Klan's Fight for Americanism," *North American Review* 223, no. 830
(March–May 1926): 33; Rice, *The Ku Klux Klan in American Politics*, 10–11.

26. M. William Lutholtz, *Grand Dragon: D. C. Stephenson and the Ku Klux
Klan in Indiana* (West Lafayette, IN: Purdue University Press, 1991); Karen
Abbott, "'Murder Wasn't Very Pretty': The Rise and Fall of D. C. Stephenson,"
Smithsonian.com, August 30, 2012, http://www.smithsonianmag.com/history/
murder-wasnt-very-pretty-the-rise-and-fall-of-dc-stephenson-18935042/#7oEO
a8oGSP2emP4L.99.

27. Todd Tucker, *Notre Dame vs. the Klan: How the Fighting Irish Defeated the Ku*

Klux Klan (Chicago: Loyola Press, 2004), 95; Alva W. Taylor, "What the Klan Did in Indiana," *New Republic*, November 16, 1927, 330–31; Moore, *Citizen Klansmen*, 14.

28. Newell G. Bringhurst, "The Ku Klux Klan in a Central California Community: Tulare County During the 1920s and 1930s," *Southern California Quarterly* 82, no. 4 (Winter 2000): 376; Blee, *Women of the Klan*, 168, 170; Kathleen Blee, speaking on NPR, http://www.npr.org/sections/npr-history-dept/2015/03/19/390711598/when-the-ku-klux-klan-was-mainstream.

29. Rebecca McClanahan, *The Tribal Knot* (Bloomington: Indiana University Press, 2013), chapter 12; also in Rebecca McClanahan, "Klan of the Grandmother," *Southern Review* 32, no. 2 (Spring 1996): 344–62.

30. Randel, *The Ku Klux Klan*, 191; John T. Kneebone, "Publicity and Prejudice: The New York World's Exposé of 1921 and the History of the Second Ku Klux Klan," Virginia Commonwealth University *Scholars Compass*, 2015, http://scholars compass.vcu.edu/cgi/viewcontent.cgi?article=1014&context=hist_pubs.

31. US House of Representatives, 67th Congress, Committee on Rules, *Hearings on the Ku Klux Klan* (Washington, DC: GPO, 1921).

32. Quoted in Charles Alexander, "Kleagles and Cash: The Ku Klux Klan as a Business Organization, 1915–1930," *Business History Review* 39, no. 3 (Autumn 1965): 354. Shepherd, in "Ku Klux Koin," claims that Georgia congressman William David "Wee Willie" Upshaw, who had been elected in 1919 with Klan votes, called for hearings because he figured that the publicity would help the Klan.

33. Llewellyn Nelson, "The Ku Klux Klan for Boredom," *New Republic*, January 14, 1925, 196–98; Taylor, "What the Klan Did in Indiana," 330–32; John Grierson, untitled review, *American Journal of Sociology* 31, no. 1 (July 1925): 114–15; Bohn, "The Ku Klux Klan Interpreted," 385–407; Kenneth T. Jackson, *The Ku Klux Klan in the City, 1915–1930* (Chicago: Ivan R. Dee, 1967), xiii; Wade, *The Fiery Cross*, 140; John Moffatt Mecklin, *The Ku Klux Klan: A Study of the American Mind* (New York: Harcourt, Brace, 1924); Frank Tannenbaum, *Darker Phases of the South* (New York: G. P. Putnam's Sons, 1924).

34. Francis Butler Simkins, *A History of the South* (New York: Knopf, 1963), 545–46.

35. Malcolm M. Willey, untitled review, *American Journal of Sociology* 28, no. 3 (November 1922): 353–54; Rice, *The Ku Klux Klan in American Politics*; Randel, *The Ku Klux Klan*.

36. Sinclair Lewis, *Babbitt* (New York: Harcourt, Brace, 1922), 30.

37. The nine cities were Atlanta, Chicago, Dallas, Denver, Detroit, Indianapolis, Knoxville, Memphis, and Portland, Oregon. Jackson, *The Ku Klux Klan in the City*, 236.

38. Barron H. Lerner, "In a Time of Quotas, a Quiet Pose in Defiance," *New York Times*, May 25, 2009.

39. Michael, *A Concise History of American Antisemitism*, 128, 134–35, 138.

40. C. Vann Woodward, *Tom Watson: Agrarian Rebel* (New York: Macmillan, 1938), 426, 473.

41. Bohn, "The Ku Klux Klan Interpreted," 403.

42. Linda Gordon, *The Moral Property of Women: A History of Birth Control Politics in America* (Urbana and Chicago: University of Illinois Press, 2002), chapter 6; William F. Pinar, *The Gender of Racial Politics and Violence in America: Lynching, Prison Rape, and the Crisis of Masculinity* (New York: Lang, 2001), 577.

Chapter 2. ANCESTORS

1. Some claim that the term "Invisible Empire" emerged from Confederate General Robert E. Lee's polite request to keep his support for the nascent Klan "invisible." Others see it as a reference to the secrecy surrounding the original hooded fraternity. Kristofer Allerfeldt, "Invisible Empire: An 'Imperial' History of the KKK," *Imperial and Global Forum*, July 7, 2014, https://imperialglobalexeter.com/2014/07/07/invisible-empire-an-imperial-history-of-the-kkk/.

2. Kathleen Blee distinguishes between conservative and right-wing movements, but I am not at all sure that the distinction holds up with respect to the Klan. Kathleen M. Blee and Kimberly A. Creasap, "Conservative and Right-Wing Movements," *Annual Review of Sociology* 36 (2010): 269–86.

3. Fox, *Everyday Klansfolk*. Masking in public was also banned in several localities, including some in Vermont, with no negative impact on the Klan. Interview with Maudine Neill by Mark Greenberg, 1988, Vermont Historical Society, *Green Mountain Chronicles*, http://vermonthistory.org/research/research-resources-online/green-mountain-chronicles/the-k-k-k-in-vermont-1924.

4. The Know Nothings had been particularly strong in Oregon, which the Ku Klux Klan considered its "blue ribbon" state. Charles Easton Rothwell, "The Ku Klux Klan in the State of Oregon" (BA thesis, Reed College, 1924), 86.

5. Carol Medlicott, "Constructing Territory, Constructing Citizenship: The Daughters of the American Revolution and 'Americanisation' in the 1920s," *Geopolitics* 10, no. 1 (2005): 99–120.

6. The oath can be found at http://historymatters.gmu.edu/d/5351/.

7. Evans, "The Klan's Fight for Americanism," 55; "Immigrants Pouring In," *Searchlight* (KKK newspaper), March 25, 1922, 4.

8. I often call the Klan bigoted rather than racist because most readers today would not consider Catholics or Jews a "race." But Jews had long been both a religion and an ethnicity, and in the 1920s "race" was an unusually pliable term, often applied to an identity we would today consider an ethnicity, such as "the Irish race." The "race" label has been shaped and reshaped to serve the interests of those who deploy it.

9. Minutes in Horowitz, *Inside the Klavern*, 137.

10. Thomas R. Pegram, "Hoodwinked: The Anti-Saloon League and the Ku Klux Klan in 1920s Prohibition Enforcement," *Journal of the Gilded Age and Progressive Era* 7, no. 1 (January 2008): 91; Moore, *Citizen Klansmen*, 191; FBI, *The Ku Klux Klan, Section I: 1915–1944* (Washington, DC: US DOJ, FBI, July 1957), 21. For one example, top Klan organizer Edward Young Clarke had been a fund-raiser for the Anti-Saloon League.

11. Pegram, "Hoodwinked," 91.

12. Noel Gist, "Secret Societies: A Cultural Study of Fraternalism in the United States," *University of Missouri Studies* 15, no. 4 (October 1940): 42. My interpretation of fraternalism is primarily indebted to Mary Ann Clawson, *Constructing Brotherhood: Class, Gender, and Fraternalism* (Princeton, NJ: Princeton University Press, 1989).

13. Quoted in Lynn Dumenil, *Freemasonry and American Culture, 1880-1930* (Princeton, NJ: Princeton University Press, 1984), 122.

14. Fox, *Everyday Klansfolk*, 121.

15. Kristofer Allerfeldt, "Jayhawker Fraternities: Masons, Klansmen and Kansas in the 1920s," *Journal of American Studies* 46, no. 4 (2012): 1035–53.

16. Bringhurst, "The Ku Klux Klan in a Central California Community," 376. See also Kathleen Blee and Amy McDowell, "The Duality of Spectacle and Secrecy: A Case Study of Fraternalism in the 1920s US Ku Klux Klan," *Ethnic and Racial Studies* 36, no. 2 (2013): 249–65,

17. Quoted in Robert A. Goldberg, "The KKK in Madison, 1922–1927," *Wisconsin Magazine of History* 58, no. 1 (Autumn 1974): 33.

18. Shawn Lay, "Imperial Outpost on the Border: El Paso's Frontier Klan No. 100," in *The Invisible Empire in the West: Toward a New Historical Appraisal of the Ku Klux Klan of the 1920s*, ed. Shawn Lay (Urbana: University of Illinois Press, 2004), 74.

19. The Know Nothings were one such fraternal order, secret, just like the KKK. Gist, *Secret Societies*.

20. Mark Paul Richard, "'This Is Not a Catholic Nation': The KKK Confronts Franco-Americans in Maine," *New England Quarterly* 82, no. 2 (June 2009): 289.

21. Bringhurst, "The Ku Klux Klan in a Central California Community," 373.

22. Evans, "The Klan's Fight for Americanism," 48; Hiram Wesley Evans and Israel Zangwill, *Is the Ku Klux Klan Constructive or Destructive?* (Girard, KS: Haldeman-Julius, 1924).

23. John Scopes had violated a Tennessee law banning the teaching of evolution; although he was convicted, defense attorney Darrow embarrassed prosecutor Bryan by exposing the absurdity of some of his beliefs in the literal truth of the Bible.

24. Charles Postel, *The Populist Vision* (New York: Oxford University Press, 2007).

25. David M. Chalmers, *Hooded Americanism: The History of the Ku Klux Klan* (Durham, NC: Duke University Press, 1987), 193.

Chapter 3. STRUCTURES OF FEELING

1. Raymond Williams, a great British social and cultural critic, first used this phrase in his 1954 *A Preface to Film*, then elaborated it in his later books *The Long Revolution* and *Marxism and Literature*. He uses "structure of feeling" as a concept that argues for the material reality of culture and employs the term "feeling" in order to "emphasize a distinction from more formal concepts of 'world view' or 'ideology.'. . . We are talking about characteristic elements of impulse, restraint, and tone; specifically affective elements of consciousness and relationships: not feeling against thought, but thought as felt and feeling as thought: practical consciousness of a present kind, in a living and interrelating continuity. We are then defining these elements as a 'structure': as a set, with specific, internal relations, at once interlocking and in tension." Williams, *Marxism and Literature* (Oxford: Oxford University Press, 1977), 132.

2. Arlie Russell Hoshschild, *The Managed Heart: Commercialization of Human Feeling* (Berkeley: University of California Press, 1983).

3. Judge John J. Jeffery, "The Klan and the Law," *Watcher on the Tower* (a Washington State Klan paper), October 29, 1923, 2, quoted at http://depts.washington.edu/civilr/kkk_wot.htm.

4. "The Negro—His Relation to America," *Kourier Magazine* (a KKK publication), January 1926, 17–19.

5. "Quotations from 'White America,'" *Kourier Magazine*, August 1927, 31, quoted in Robert S. Lynd and Helen Merrell Lynd, *Middletown* (New York: Harcourt, Brace, 1929), 483.

6. Lynd and Lynd, *Middletown*, 483. I have no reason to think these figures were accurate.

7. R. H. Sawyer, *The Truth About the Invisible Empire Knights of the Ku Klux Klan* (Portland, OR: Knights of the Ku Klux Klan, 1922); Allen Safianow, "The Klan Comes to Tipton," *Indiana Magazine of History* 95, no. 3 (1999): 203–31.

8. Quoted in Tucker, *The Dragon and the Cross*, 5.

9. Shotwell, "Crystallizing Public Hatred," 41–42.

10. *Maine Klansman*, December 6, 1923, 3, quoted in Richard, "'This Is Not a Catholic Nation,'" 292.

11. Evans and Zangwill, *Is the Ku Klux Klan Constructive or Destructive?*, 10.

12. Alma White, *The Ku Klux Klan in Prophecy* (Zarephath, NJ: Good Citizen, 1925), chapter 4.

13. Robert J. Neymeyer, "In the Full Light of Day: The Ku Klux Klan in 1920s Iowa," *Palimpsest* 76, no. 2 (Summer 1995): 61.

14. Evans, "The Klan's Fight for Americanism," 39.

15. Quoted in Rob Kroes, "Signs of Fascism Rising: A European-Americanist Looks at Recent Political Trends," unpublished manuscript, courtesy of Marilyn B. Young.

16. Radio stations included WTRC in Brooklyn, New York, later moved to Virginia as WTFF and WJSV (initials standing for *The Fellowship Forum*, a Klan stealth publication, and then for James S. Vance, its publisher). See James Snyder, "WJSV History," http://dcmemories.com/wjsv/WJSVHistory.html.

17. Evans, "The Klan's Fight for Americanism," 49.

18. Lynd and Lynd, *Middletown*, 483–84.

19. Alma White, *Guardians of Liberty*, 3 vols. (Zarephath, NJ: Pillar of Fire, 1943), 1:72.

20. James Martin, SJ, "The Last Acceptable Prejudice?" quoted in Andrew Greeley, *An Ugly Little Secret: Anti-Catholicism in North America* (Kansas City: Sheed Andrews and McMeel, 1977), and at http://www.americamagazine.org/issue/281/article/last-acceptable-prejudice; Lyman Beecher, *A Plea for the West* (Cincinnati: Truman & Smith, 1835), https://archive.org/details/pleaforwest00beec; Mark S. Massa, SJ, "Anti-Catholicism in the United States," *Oxford Research Encyclopedia*, http://americanhistory.oxfordre.com/view/10.1093/acrefore/9780199329175.001.0001/acrefore-9780199329175-e-316.

21. Thomas M. Conroy, "The Ku Klux Klan and the American Clergy," *Ecclesiastical Review* 70 (1924): 53.

22. White, *Guardians of Liberty* 2:112.

23. Elsie Thornton in Alabama Ku Klux Klan Newsletter, June 1926, quoted in ibid.

24. Robert V. Hunt Jr., "The Fundamentalist–Ku Klux Klan Alliance: A Colorado Study (1921–1926)," *Journal of the West* 38, no. 4 (October 1999): 87.

25. Quoted in Blee, *Women of the Klan*, 87.

26. Lynd and Lynd, *Middletown*, 482.

27. Helen Jackson, *Convent Cruelties; or, My Life in a Convent* (Detroit: Helen Jackson, 1919); White, *Guardians of Liberty* 2:97–98; also circulating were copies of Maria Monk's *Awful Disclosures of the Hotel Dieu Nunnery of Montreal*, originally published in 1836 in Montreal.

28. White, *Guardians of Liberty* 2:102.

29. Quoted in Maudean Neill, *Fiery Crosses in the Green Mountains: The Story of the Ku Klux Klan in Vermont* (Randolph Center, VT: Greenhills Books, 1989), 25.

30. *A Pseudo 'Ex-nun' Thwarted: The Case of Helen Jackson vs. 'Ypsilanti Press'* (St. Louis, MO: Central Bureau, Central Verein, 1921); Jackson, *Convent Cruelties*; David. B. Tyack, "The Perils of Pluralism: The Background of the Pierce Case," *American Historical Review* 74, no. 1 (October 1968): 85; Norman Fredric Weaver, "The Knights of the Ku Klux Klan in Wisconsin, Indiana, Ohio and Michigan" (PhD diss., University of Wisconsin, 1954), 160; interview with Maudine Neill by Mark Greenberg, 1988, for *Green Mountain Chronicles*, Vermont Historical Society, at http://vermonthistory.org/research/research-resources-online/green-mountain-chronicles/the-k-k-k-in-vermont-1924; Blee, *Women of the Klan*, 89–91; Fox, *Everyday Klansfolk*, 57; John T. McGreevy, *Catholicism and American Free-*

dom (New York: W. W. Norton, 2004), 147; Hunt, "The Fundamentalist–Ku Klux Klan Alliance," 88.

31. Jeff LaLande, "'Beneath the Hooded Robe': Local Politics, Opportunism, and the Ku Klux Klan in Jackson County, Oregon, 1921–23" (MA thesis, University of Oregon, 1992), 21.

32. Safianow, "The Klan Comes to Tipton."

33. *Imperial Night-Hawk*, August 29, 1923.

34. Evans, "The Klan's Fight for Americanism," 46–47.

35. George Estes, *The Roman Catholic Kingdom and the Ku Klux Klan* (Troutdale, OR: Geo. Estes, 1923), 6–8.

36. White, *The Ku Klux Klan in Prophecy*, chapter 12, pp. 89–91.

37. Sawyer, *The Truth About the Invisible Empire*.

38. White, *The Ku Klux Klan in Prophecy*, 52.

39. Sarah Elizabeth Doherty, "Aliens Found in Waiting: Women of the KKK in Suburban Chicago, 1870–1930" (PhD diss., Loyola University Chicago, 2012), 87.

40. Hiram Evans, quoted in George S. Clason, *Catholic, Jew, Ku Klux Klan: What They Believe, Where They Conflict* (Chicago: Nutshell Publishing, 1924), 31.

41. Quoted in Tom Rice, "Protecting Protestantism: The Ku Klux Klan vs. the Motion Picture Industry," *Film History* 20, no. 4 (2008): 370–71, 374. Also Tom Rice, "'The True Story of the Ku Klux Klan': Defining the Klan Through Film," *Journal of American Studies* 42, no. 3 (December 2008): 475; Melissa Ooten, *Race, Gender and Film Censorship in Virginia, 1922–1965* (Boulder, CO: Lexington Books, 2015), 90; Alma White, *Heroes of the Fiery Cross* (Zarephath, NJ: The Good Citizen, 1928), 10.

42. Bohn, "The Ku Klux Klan Interpreted," 388.

43. Quoted in Shotwell, "Crystallizing Public Hatred," 48.

44. Jeffrey Herf, *Reactionary Modernism: Technology, Culture and Politics in Weimar and the Third Reich* (Cambridge: Cambridge University Press, 1984).

45. Minutes, December 5, 1955, in Horowitz, *Inside the Klavern*, 34.

46. Mecklin, *The Ku Klux Klan*, 101.

47. The Klan liked this quote and used it often: Michael W. Schuyler, "The Ku Klux Klan in Nebraska, 1920–1930," *Nebraska History* 66 (1985): 250; Wade, *The Fiery Cross*, 248; Lynd and Lynd, *Middletown*, 483.

48. Quoted by John F. McClymer in "Passing from Light into Dark," *Journal for Multimedia History* 4 (2003), http://www.albany.edu/jmmh/vol4/passing/passing1.html.

49. White, *The Ku Klux Klan in Prophecy*, chapter 6.

50. Clason, *Catholic, Jew, Ku Klux Klan*, 30.

51. Hiram Evans, quoted in ibid., 30–31.

52. White, *Heroes of the Fiery Cross*, 33; White, *The Ku Klux Klan in Prophecy*, 53.

53. Rice, "Protecting Protestantism," 371.

54. Michael Barkun, *Religion and the Racist Right: The Origins of the Christian Identity Movement* (Chapel Hill: University of North Carolina Press, 1994).

55. Evans, "The Klan's Fight for Americanism," 60; Robert Singerman, "The Jew as Racial Alien: The Genetic Component of American Anti-Semitism," in *Anti-Semitism in American History*, ed. David A. Gerber (Urbana: University of Illinois Press, 1986), 118. The Khazars were a Turkic, not Mongolian, group who had established a powerful state (a khanate) that dominated the area from the Volga-Don steppes to the eastern Crimea and the northern Caucasus in the years 650–965 and were reputed to have converted to Judaism.

56. White, *The Ku Klux Klan in Prophecy*, 27.

57. White, *Heroes of the Fiery Cross*, 186 and chapter 2; quotation from Rev. C. C. Curtis of Vancouver, Washington, speaking in Auburn, Oregon, in David Norberg, "Ku Klux Klan in the Valley: A 1920s Phenomena [*sic*]," White River Valley Museum, *White River Journal*, January 2004, http://www.wrvmuseum.org/journal/journal_0104.htm.

58. Quoted in Paul L. Murphy, "Sources and Nature of Intolerance in the 1920s," *Journal of American History* 51, no. 1 (June 1964): 72n35.

59. The illustration, an etching, is by Rev. Branford Clarke, a prolific Klan artist, and appears in White, *The Ku Klux Klan in Prophecy*, 74. Clarke immigrated from England and became minister of a Brooklyn Klan church in 1921; Lynn S. Neal, "Christianizing the Klan: Alma White, Branford Clarke, and the Art of Religious Intolerance," *Church History* 78, no. 2 (June 2009): 358.

60. Herbert Kaufman, "Scum o' the Melting-Pot," *McClure's Magazine*, March/April 1920, 7.

61. Evans, "The Klan's Fight for Americanism," 40.

62. Alberto Brandolini, an Italian computer programmer, developed this "law," also known as the BAP, bullshit asymmetry principle, based on Nobel Prize–winning economist Daniel Kahneman's *Thinking, Fast and Slow* (New York: Random House, 2011).

63. Jack Z. Bratich, *Conspiracy Panics: Political Rationality and Popular Culture* (Albany: SUNY Press, 2008), 98–100; Jovan Byford, *Conspiracy Theories: A Critical Introduction* (Basingstoke: Palgrave MacMillan, 2015), 25–27.

64. White, *Heroes of the Fiery Cross*, 116–18, 144.

65. Ibid.

66. Evans quoted in McClymer, "Passing from Light into Dark."

67. Hunt, "The Fundamentalist–Ku Klux Klan Alliance," 86.

68. Conroy, "The Ku Klux Klan and the American Clergy," 55.

69. These fears and longings provide rich material for psychoanalytic interpretation.

70. Wade, *The Fiery Cross*, 176–77. The same idea appears in White, *Heroes of the Fiery Cross*, 14.

71. White, *Guardians of Liberty* 2:96–97.

72. White, *The Ku Klux Klan in Prophecy*, 74; Neal, "Christianizing the Klan," 352.

73. White, *Heroes of the Fiery Cross,* chapter 7.

74. Kenneth Burke, quoted in M. Elizabeth Weiser, *Burke, War, Words* (Columbia: University of South Carolina Press, 2008), 58. The Klan also used the Babel reference to condemn immigration; for example, *Imperial Night-Hawk*, August 29, 1923.

75. Republican motherhood is a historians' label for the belief, in the American revolutionary era, that mothers should instill republican ideals in their children. Mothers should thus be custodians of civic virtue responsible for upholding the morality of their husbands and children. Linda K. Kerber originally argued this in her *Women of the Republic: Intellect and Ideology in Revolutionary America* (Chapel Hill: University of North Carolina Press, 1980), introduction.

76. Evans, "The Klan's Fight for Americanism," 39.

77. Estes, *The Roman Katholic Kingdom and the Ku Klux Klan,* 6.

78. Rice, *The Ku Klux Klan in American Politics,* 20.

79. I would love to know how the fertility rates of Klanswomen compared with those of other women in the same locations.

Chapter 4. RECRUITMENT, RITUAL, AND PROFIT

1. Ronald G. Fryer Jr. and Steven D. Levitt, "Hatred and Profits: Getting Under the Hood of the Ku Klux Klan," working paper 13417, National Bureau of Economic Research, September 2007, 9.

2. Clarke to E. C. Mickey of Charleston, South Carolina, August 23, 1920, in Du Bois Papers, series 1A, General Correspondence, at University of Massachusetts–Amherst Special Collections. The travels of this letter gave me some perverse pleasure: it ended up in the archives of W. E. B. Du Bois, likely because Mr. Mickey was indeed an elite of Charleston but, unbeknownst to the Klan, an African American and a regular correspondent of Du Bois's.

3. Jones, *Knights of the Ku Klux Klan,* 112.

4. Knights of the Ku Klux Klan, Department of Realms, *Klan Building: An Outline of Proven Klan Methods for Successfully Applying the Art of Klankraft in Building and Operating Local Klans* (Atlanta, 1925), 4.

5. Randel, *The Ku Klux Klan,* 193; Fox, *Everyday Klansfolk,* 17.

6. Rice, *The Ku Klux Klan in American Politics,* 18–19; Wade, *The Fiery Cross,* 193; Fox, *Everyday Klansfolk,* chapter 1.

7. Alexander, "Kleagles and Cash," 361. This article details many other profitable Klan schemes.

8. Ibid., 360; Fryer and Levitt, "Hatred and Profits," 11.

9. Conroy, "The Ku Klux Klan and the American Clergy," 50; Jackson, *The Ku Klux Klan in the City,* 212.

10. Neill interview, http://vermonthistory.org/research/research-resources-online/green-mountain-chronicles/the-k-k-k-in-vermont-1924.

11. Weaver, "The Knights of the Ku Klux Klan," 6–7, 44–45; Safianow, "The Klan Comes to Tipton."

12. Quoted in Dana M. Caldemeyer, "Conditional Conservatism: Evansville, Indiana's Embrace of the Ku Klux Klan," *Ohio Valley History* 11, no. 4 (Winter 2011): 18.

13. California Knights of the KKK, "The Klan in Action: A Manual of Leadership and Organization for Officers of Local Klan Committees," mimeo, author's possession, n.d.; KKK, *Klan Building*, 4. This research assignment was not wholly different from one used by the Nazis in developing local groups. William Allen describes how the Nazis in Northeim charged admission fees to speeches and then tracked attendance on different topics so as to fine-tune their appeal to match local response; *The Nazi Seizure of Power: The Experience of a Single German Town, 1922–1945* (New York: Franklin Watts, 1965), 29. I am grateful to Judith Vichniac for alerting me to this practice.

14. Bohn, "The Ku Klux Klan Interpreted," 399.

15. Doherty, "Aliens Found in Waiting," passim.

16. Caldemeyer, "Conditional Conservatism," 21.

17. Carlos M. Larralde and Richard Griswold del Castillo, "San Diego's Ku Klux Klan, 1920–1980," *San Diego Historical Society Quarterly* 46, nos. 2–3 (2000), http://www.sandiegohistory.org/journal/2000/april/klan/; Mark Paul Richard, "'Why Don't You Be a Klansman?' Anglo-Canadian Support for the Ku Klux Klan Movement in 1920s New England," *American Review of Canadian Studies* 40, no. 4 (December 2010): 509, 513; McClymer, "Passing from Light into Dark."

18. Jackson, *The Ku Klux Klan in the City*, 181, 237, 281; Conroy, "The Ku Klux Klan and the American Clergy," 50.

19. Shepherd, "Ku Klux Koin."

20. The following description is from Knights of the Ku Klux Klan, *Handbook*, author's possession, n.d.; McClanahan, "Klan of the Grandmother."

21. Elaine Frantz Parsons, "Costume and Performance in the Reconstruction-Era Ku Klux Klan," *Journal of American History* 92, no. 3 (December 2005): 811–36.

22. KKK, *Klan Building*, 11; Robert Neymeyer, "The Ku Klux Klan of the 1920s in the Midwest and West: A Review Essay," *Annuals of Iowa* 51, no. 6 (Fall 1992): 625–33.

23. My interpretation of secrecy was influenced by Allen Hunter, who explained and led me to Georg Simmel, "The Sociology of Secrecy and of Secret Societies," *American Journal of Sociology* 11, no. 4 (January 1906): 441–98.

24. The following description is from the Kloran.

25. For whatever reason, different Klan documents gave different sets of names; Chester L. Quarles, *The Ku Klux Klan and Related American Racialist and Antisemitic Organizations: History and Analysis* (Jefferson, NC: McFarland, 1999), 65–66.

26. I assume that using the term "naturalization" was a deliberate appropriation of, and inversion of, the name for the legal process of acquiring citizenship which the Klan, of course, opposed for non-WASP immigrants.

27. Blee, *Women of the Klan*, 38.

28. The songs included "Battle Hymn of the Republic" and "The Star-Spangled Banner" on the patriotic side and "Whiter than Snow," "In the Cross of Christ I Glory," and "Blest Be the Tie That Binds" on the religious side; WKKK, *Musiklan* (Little Rock, AR, n.d.).

29. This is but an abbreviated summary of a much more detailed set of instructions given in the Kloran.

Chapter 5. SPECTACLES AND EVANGELICALS

1. Neymeyer, "In the Full Light of Day," 56–63.

2. Rice, "'The True Story of the Ku Klux Klan,'" 481.

3. This description is a composite, based on descriptions in Weaver, "The Knights of the Ku Klux Klan," 157–58; Guy B. Johnson, "A Sociological Interpretation of the New Ku Klux Movement," *Journal of Social Forces* 1, no. 4 (May 1923): 440–45; Moore, *Citizen Klansmen*, 76ff; Blee, *Women of the Klan*, 128, 135, 166; Tucker, *The Dragon and the Cross*, 50; Robert Coughlan, "Konklave in Kokomo," in *The Aspirin Age, 1919–1941*, ed. Isabel Leighton (New York: Simon & Schuster, 1949); combined with descriptions of other similar Klan mass picnics.

4. Elizabeth Dorsey Hatle and Nancy M. Vaillancourt, "One Flag, One School, One Language: Minnesota's KKK in the 1920s," *Minnesota History* 61, no. 8 (Winter 2009–10): 365.

5. Schuyler, "The Ku Klux Klan in Nebraska," 236.

6. Jackson, *The Ku Klux Klan in the City*, 97; William Vance Trollinger Jr., "The University of Dayton, the Ku Klux Klan, and Catholic Universities and Colleges in the 1920s," *American Catholic Studies* 124, no. 1 (Spring 2013): 7–8; Chris Rhomberg, "White Nativism and Urban Politics: The 1920s Ku Klux Klan in Oakland, California," *Journal of American Ethnic History* 17, no. 2 (Winter 1998): 46; *Matawan Journal*, August 31, 1923, https://pediaview.com/openpedia/History_of_the_Ku_Klux_Klan_in_New_Jersey#cite_note-10.

7. Linton Weeks, "When the KKK Was Mainstream," *History Dept.*, March 19, 2015, http://www.npr.org/sections/npr-history-dept/2015/03/19/390711598/when-the-ku-klux-klan-was-mainstream.

8. Quoted in Fox, *Everyday Klansfolk*, 195; Trollinger, "The University of Dayton, the Ku Klux Klan," 8.

9. In honor of his journey, Chicago renamed Seventh Street as Balbo Drive. In an additional gesture of generosity, Mussolini plundered a Roman column, dating from the second century AD, from a portico near the Porta Marina of

Ostica Antica, the ancient port city of Rome, and shipped it to Chicago, where it was erected in front of the Italian pavilion of the Century of Progress fair in 1934.

10. *Klan Komment*, 1923, quoted in American Social History Project and Center for History and New Media, George Mason University, *Who Built America? From the Great War of 1914 to the Dawn of the Atomic Age in 1946*, CD-ROM (New York: Worth, 2000).

11. Citizens League of Dallas, "The Klan and Its Propaganda Methods," 1922, http://americainclass.org/sources/becomingmodern/divisions/text1/colcommentary klan.pdf, 7–8.

12. Newspaper accounts quoted in Fox, *Everyday Klansfolk*, 179.

13. Schuyler, "The Ku Klux Klan in Nebraska," 238.

14. *Imperial Night-Hawk*, August 29, 1923.

15. Donna Troppoli, "The Invisible Boardwalk Empire: The Ku Klux Klan in Monmouth County During the 1920s," *GardenStateLegacy.com*, June 2015, http://gardenstatelegacy.com/files/The_Invisible_Boardwalk_Empire_Troppoli _GSL28.pdf.

16. Felix Harcourt, "Invisible Umpires: The Ku Klux Klan and Baseball in the 1920s," *Journal of Baseball History and Culture* 23, no. 1 (Fall 2014): 3–6.

17. Baseball commissioner Herrmann seemed willing, but that date was already taken. Cottrell, *Two Pioneers*, 7–8.

18. Goldberg, "The KKK in Madison," 32–33, 38.

19. A Wisconsin King Kleagle began his work in 1920 with a private meeting on a Coast Guard cutter in the Milwaukee River, able to do this, no doubt, because of one or more Klan supporters in the Coast Guard. Chalmers, *Hooded Americanism*, 191; quotations from Goldberg, "The KKK in Madison," 34, 38. Image from yearbook in Timothy Messer-Kruse, "Memories of the Ku Klux Klan Honorary Society at the University of Wisconsin," *Journal of Blacks in Higher Education* 23 (Spring 1999): 83; Melching, "The Activities of the Ku Klux Klan in Anaheim, California"; Timothy Messer-Kruse, "The Campus Klan of the University of Wisconsin: Tacit and Active Support for the Ku Klux Klan in a Culture of Intolerance," *Wisconsin Magazine of History* 77 (Autumn 1993): 2.

20. Doherty, "Aliens Found in Waiting," 124–25.

21. Fox, *Everyday Klansfolk*, 165–69.

22. Ibid., 168–74; Neill interview, http://vermonthistory.org/research/research -resources-online/green-mountain-chronicles/the-k-k-k-in-vermont-1924.

23. Doherty, "Aliens Found in Waiting," 125; Neill interview, http://vermonthistory .org/research/research-resources-online/green-mountain-chroniclesthe-k-k-k-in -vermont-1924.

24. Kelly J. Baker, *Gospel According to the Klan: The Ku Klux Klan's Appeal to Protestant America, 1915–1930* (Lawrence: University Press of Kansas, 2011); Wade, *The Fiery Cross*, 178.

25. White, *The Klan in Prophecy*, 25.

26. Quoted in Richard, "'This Is Not a Catholic Nation,'" 291.

27. These included, for example, the Assemblies of God, Southern Baptists, Independent Baptists, Black Protestants, African Methodist Episcopal, African Methodist Episcopal Zion, Church of Christ, Churches of God in Christ, Lutheran Church—Missouri Synod, National Baptist Church, National Progressive Baptist Church, Nondenominational, Pentecostal denominations, and the Presbyterian Church in America; some conservative members and reform movements within such mainline denominations as the Episcopal Church in the USA, the Presbyterian Church (USA), and the United Methodist Church also consider themselves evangelicals.

28. Charles C. Alexander, *The Ku Klux Klan in the Southwest* (Norman: University of Oklahoma Press, 1995), 85; Wade, *The Fiery Cross*, 178. I should note that some historians confuse "fundamentalist" with "evangelical."

29. Robert Moats Miller, "A Note on the Relationships Between the Protestant Churches and the Revived Ku Klux Klan," *Journal of Southern History* 33, no. 3 (August 1956): 355–68; Shawn Lay, "Hooded Populism: New Assessments of the Ku Klux Klan of the 1920s," *Reviews in American History* 22, no. 4 (December 1994): 670.

30. Lay, "Hooded Populism, 670.

31. Alexander, *The Ku Klux Klan in the Southwest*, 85; Wade, *The Fiery Cross*, 176–77.

32. Robert Alan Goldberg, *Hooded Empire: The Ku Klux Klan in Colorado* (Urbana: University of Illinois Press, 1981); "The Ku Klux Klan," http://bio.suny orange.edu/updated2/creationism/CREATIONISM/evolution/2_klan.htm; Susie Cunningham Stanley, *Feminist Pillar of Fire: The Life of Alma White* (Cleveland, OH: Pilgrim Press, 1993), 88; Wade, *The Fiery Cross*, 171.

33. Melching, "The Activities of the Ku Klux Klan in Anaheim, California," 176, 181.

34. Edward Clarke, letters of March 23, April 7, and April 9, 1921, reproduced in Randel, *The Ku Klux Klan*, 198–99.

35. Sessions, "The K.K.K. in Vermont Through 1927."

36. Blee and McDowell, "The Duality of Spectacle and Secrecy."

37. Schuyler, "The Ku Klux Klan in Nebraska," 239.

38. Wade, *The Fiery Cross*, 176–77.

39. Daniel Cady, "A Battle Transplanted: Southern California's White Churches, Black Press, and the 1920s Ku Klux Klan," *Journal of the West* 48, no. 2 (Spring 2009): 50–57; Richard Allen Loomis, "A Narrative Interpretation of the 1920s Ku Klux Klan in Oregon" (PhD diss., Fuller Theological Seminary, 2000), 276ff.; Doherty, "Aliens Found in Waiting," 127; LaLande, "'Beneath the Hooded Robe,'" 19.

40. Tom Sitton, "The 'Boss' Without a Machine: Kent K. Parrot and Los Angeles Politics in the 1920s," *Southern California Quarterly* 65, no. 4 (Winter 1985): 381.

41. Matthew Avery Sutton, "Uncovering Aimee Semple McPherson's Demons in 21st Century Evangelicalism," *History News Network*, May 27, 2007, http://history newsnetwork.org/article/38391.

42. Wade, *The Fiery Cross*, 176–77.

43. Glenn Feldman, *Politics, Society, and the Klan in Alabama, 1915–1949* (Tuscaloosa: University of Alabama Press, 1999).

Chapter 6. VIGILANTISM AND MANLINESS

1. Malcolm X with Alex Haley, *The Autobiography of Malcolm X* (New York: Grove Press, 1965), chapter 1.

2. David A. Horowitz, "Order, Solidarity, and Vigilance: The Ku Klux Klan in La Grande, Oregon," in Lay, *The Invisible Empire in the West*, p. 190.

3. Quoted in Lawrence J. Saalfeld, *Forces of Prejudice in Oregon, 1920–1925* (Portland, OR: Archdiocesan Historical Commission, 1984), 23; LaLande, "'Beneath the Hooded Robe,'" 30.

4. Messer-Kruse, "The Campus Klan of the University of Wisconsin," 4; Goldberg, "The KKK in Madison," 31–44.

5. Nancy MacLean, *Behind the Mask of Chivalry: The Making of the Second Ku Klux Klan* (New York: Oxford University Press, 1994), 161.

6. Jenkins, *Steel Valley Klan,* 26; Jerry Wallace, "The Ku Klux Klan Comes to Kowley Kounty, Kansas: Its Public Face, 1921–22," in *Celebrate Winfield History 2012* (Winfield, KS: Cowley County Historical Society, 2012), 11.

7. The New Jersey Klan *Recorder* did so throughout 1925, 1926, and 1927. Tyreen A. Reuter, "African-Americans and the Ku Klux Klan in 1920s Metuchen," http://www.jhalpin.com/anonymous/mehs/MetuchenKlan.pdf.

8. Schuyler, "The Ku Klux Klan in Nebraska," 244.

9. B. Johnson, "John Barleycorn Must Die! The War Against Drink in Arkansas, 1920–1950," Little Rock, Arkansas, Old State House Museum exhibit, formerly available at http://www.oldstatehouse.com/exhibits/archive/john-barleycorn/1920-1950.asp.

10. Clason, *Catholic, Jew, Ku Klux Klan*, 58.

11. Hunt, "The Fundamentalist–Ku Klux Klan Alliance," 87.

12. David J. Hanson, "KKK and WCTU: Partners in Prohibition," *Alcohol Problems and Solutions*, https://www.alcoholproblemsandsolutions.org/ku-klux-klan-kkk-wctu-partners-prohibition; Pegram, "Hoodwinked," 98–104.

13. *Fiery Cross,* June 20, 1924, quoted in Pegram, "Hoodwinked," 97.

14. Minutes in Horowitz, *Inside the Klavern*, 53, 88.

15. Chris Gavaler, "The Ku Klux Klan and the Birth of the Superhero," *Journal of Graphic Novels and Comics* 4, no. 2 (2013): 191–208.

16. Evans, "The Klan's Fight for Americanism," 18; Goldberg, "The KKK in Madison," 38.

17. Norberg, "Ku Klux Klan in the Valley."

18. *Outlook*, January 30, 1924, 184, quoted in Rothwell, "The Ku Klux Klan in the State of Oregon," 56.

19. Wilhelm Reich, *Listen, Little Man!* (New York: Farrar, Straus & Giroux, 1974).

20. Quoted in Marion Monteval (believed to be a pseudonym), *The Klan Inside-Out* (Claremore, OK: Monarch Publishing, 1924), 122–23.

21. Bohn, "The Ku Klux Klan Interpreted," 398.

22. Ibid., 399.

23. Shawn Lay, *Hooded Knights on the Niagara: The KKK in Buffalo, New York* (New York: NYU Press, 1995), 71, 74; Chalmers, *Hooded Americanism*, 213; Caldemeyer, "Conditional Conservatism," 6; John Zerzan, "Rank-and-File Radicalism Within the KKK of the 1920s," *Anarchy* 37 (Summer 1993): 48–53, and at http://theanarchistlibrary.org/library/john-zerzan-rank-and-file-radicalism-within-the-ku-klux-klan-of-the-1920s.pdf.

24. Reuter, "African Americans and the Ku Klux Klan in 1920s Metuchen."

25. Booth, *The Mad Mullah*, 37.

26. Brooks R. Blevins, "The Strike and the Still: Anti-Radical Violence and the Ku Klux Klan in the Ozarks," *Arkansas Historical Quarterly* 52, no. 4 (Winter 1993): 410.

27. Christopher Cocoltchos, "The Invisible Empire and the Search for Orderly Community: The Ku Klux Klan in Anaheim, California," in Lay, *The Invisible Empire in the West*, 114; Tucker, *The Dragon and the Cross*, 83.

28. Caldemeyer, "Conditional Conservatism," 16.

29. Alfred L. Brophy, "Norms, Law, and Reparations: The Case of the Ku Klux Klan in 1920s Oklahoma," *Harvard BlackLetter Law Journal* 20 (2004): 37.

30. Quoted in Malcolm Clark Jr., "The Bigot Disclosed: 90 Years of Nativism," *Oregon Historical Quarterly* 75, no. 2 (June 1974): 155.

31. Quoted in Neill, *Fiery Crosses in the Green Mountains*, 30.

32. Hunt, "The Fundamentalist–Ku Klux Klan Alliance," 86.

33. Blee, *Women of the Klan,* offers an example on 87.

34. Richard, "'This Is Not a Catholic Nation,'" 301.

35. Hunt, "The Fundamentalist–Ku Klux Klan Alliance," 86.

36. Wallace, "The Ku Klux Klan Comes to Kowley Kounty, Kansas," 13.

37. The last is an example of the notion of vagrancy, and the use of vagrancy law, widely employed in the South to control the movements of people of color; in the southern world of segregation, vagrancy law gave police wide discretion to charge a person of color on the streets.

38. Wallace, "The Ku Klux Klan Comes to Kowley Kounty, Kansas," 13–14; LaLande, "'Beneath the Hooded Robe,'" 3, 24–26; Eckard Vance Toy, "The Ku Klux Klan in Oregon: Its Character and Program" (MA thesis, University of Oregon, 1959), 70–73; Max Price, "The Oregon Ku Klux Klan: A Failed Attempt at Creating a Homogeneous State" (unpublished paper, Pacific University, 2011), 25.

39. Larry O'Dell, "Ku Klux Klan," in *Encyclopedia of Oklahoma History and Culture*, www.okhistory.org/publications/enc/entry.php?entry=KU001; Allerfeldt, "Jayhawker Fraternities," 1049.

40. National Humanities Center, "Becoming Modern: America in the 1920s," http://americainclass.org/sources/becomingmodern/divisions/text1/colcommentary klan.pdf.

41. Minutes in Horowitz, *Inside the Klavern*, 88.

42. Trolinger, "The University of Dayton, the Ku Klux Klan," 2, from the *Dayton Daily News*.

43. Ibid., 1–2.

44. Tucker, *Notre Dame vs. the Klan*, 103–4. Tucker believes that the killings were instigated by Evans in his feud with Stephenson.

45. Hunt, "The Fundamentalist–Ku Klux Klan Alliance," 85, 87.

46. Sam Guerre, "The 1922 Ku Klux Klan Inglewood Raid," *South Bay History*, March 15, 2014, at http://blogs.dailybreeze.com/history/2014/03/15/the-1922-ku -klux-klan-inglewood-raid/; Monteval, *The Klan Inside-Out*, 97.

47. Benjamin Herzl Avin, "The Ku Klux Klan, 1915–1925: A Study in Religious Intolerance" (PhD diss., Georgetown University, 1952), 226–27; Bringhurst, "The Ku Klux Klan in a Central California Community," 369; interview with V. Wayne Kenaston Jr., quoted in Larralde and Griswold del Castillo, "San Diego's Ku Klux Klan"; William D. Carrigan and Clive Webb, *Forgotten Dead: Mob Violence Against Mexicans in the United States, 1848–1928* (New York: Oxford University Press, 2013), 148, 150.

48. Thomas H. Heuterman, *The Burning Horse: The Japanese-American Experience in the Yakima Valley, 1920–1942* (Cheney: Eastern Washington University Press, 1995), 95–108.

49. Quoted in Alexander, *The Ku Klux Klan in the Southwest*, 60.

50. Clark, "The Bigot Disclosed," 154–58.

51. Cocoltchos, "The Invisible Empire," 112.

52. Trolinger, "The University of Dayton, the Ku Klux Klan," quotations on 7.

53. Goldberg, "The KKK in Madison," 34, 36, 40–41.

54. Hatle and Vaillancourt, "One Flag, One School, One Language," 361.

55. Caldemeyer, "Conditional Conservatism."

56. Moore, *Citizen Klansmen*, 123; Weaver, "The Knights of the Ku Klux Klan," 260; Allen Safianow, "'You Can't Burn History': Getting Right with the Klan in Noblesville, Indiana," *Indiana Magazine of History* 100, no. 2 (June 2004): 124; Caldemeyer, "Conditional Conservatism," 11, 16.

57. Rhomberg, "White Nativism and Urban Politics," 44.

58. "The Anti-Klan Fighters of the 1920s," *Daily Kos*, January 21, 2015, formerly available at http://www.dailykos.com/story/2015/1/21/1358986/-The-anti-Klan -fighters-of-the-1920-s. New Jersey was not fertile ground for the Klan, but because Alma White's headquarters were there, the Klan could not stay away.

59. Harry Baujan, quoted in Trollinger, "The University of Dayton, the Ku Klux Klan," 7.

60. Tucker, *Notre Dame vs. the Klan.*

61. Richard, "'This Is Not a Catholic Nation,'" 297.

62. Norberg, "Ku Klux Klan in the Valley."

63. Tucker, *Notre Dame vs. the Klan*, 152–55, 131–34; Evans, "The Klan's Fight for Americanism," 62; "The Anti-Klan Fighters of the 1920s."

64. *Imperial Night-Hawk*, August 29, 1923; Tucker, *Notre Dame vs. the Klan.*

65. Jenkins, *Steel Valley Klan.*

66. Schuyler, "The Ku Klux Klan in Nebraska," 245; Trevor Griffey, "The Ku Klux Klan in Washington State, 1920s," *Seattle Civil Rights & Labor History Project*, http://depts.washington.edu/civilr/kkk_intro.htm.

67. Canadians also joined the Ku Klux Klan bandwagon in the 1920s, even in Francophone Canada. A Montreal Klan group burned Catholic buildings in Quebec in 1922. Other groups formed in Ontario, Nova Scotia, New Brunswick, and Newfoundland, but the movement was particularly strong in the west. There the Klan targeted Catholic immigrants and French Canadians. Five provinces enacted legislation prohibiting bilingual instruction in the schools. At the same time, expatriate Protestant Canadians in New England were admitted to a Klan auxiliary, the Royal Riders of the Red Robe. Richard, "'Why Don't You Be a Klansman?'"; Richard, "'This Is Not a Catholic Nation.'"

68. Caldemeyer, "Conditional Conservatism," 8, 12–13, 17, 19; Goldberg, "The KKK in Madison," 38.

69. Minutes in Horowitz, *Inside the Klavern*, 19; Horowitz, "Order, Solidarity," 195–96; Zerzan, "Rank-and-File Radicalism Within the Ku Klux Klan of the 1920s."

70. Virginia Durr, quoted in Zerzan, "Rank-and-File Radicalism Within the Ku Klux Klan of the 1920s."

71. Franklin Folsom, *Impatient Armies of the Poor: The Story of Collective Action of the Unemployed, 1808–1942* (Niwot: University Press of Colorado, 1991), 267.

72. Bringhurst, "The Ku Klux Klan in a Central California Community," 390.

73. My interpretation of vigilantism is influenced by my earlier study, *The Great Arizona Orphan Abduction* (Cambridge, MA: Harvard University Press, 1999).

74. As they did in the action documented in *The Great Arizona Orphan Abduction.*

Chapter 7. KKK Feminism

1. My interpretation of women's Klans is deeply indebted to Kathleen Blee and Nancy MacLean. For examples from other countries, see Paola Bacchetta and Margaret Power, eds., *Right-Wing Women: From Conservatives to Extremists Around the World* (New York: Routledge, 2002).

2. Leila J. Rupp and Verta A. Taylor, *Survival in the Doldrums: The American Women's Rights Movement, 1945 to the 1960s* (New York: Oxford University Press, 1987); Maureen Honey, "Gotham's Daughters: Feminism in the 1920s," *American Studies* 31, no. 1 (1990): 25–40.

3. Walter Lippmann, *A Preface to Morals* (New York: Macmillan, 1929), chapter 4.

4. Blee, *Women of the Klan,* 65ff.

5. Groups included the White American Protestants, Grand League of Protestant Women, Ladies of the Cu Clux Clan, Ladies of the Golden Den, Hooded Ladies of the Mystic Den, Puritan Daughters of America, and Ladies of the Invisible Empire (of which more below). Blee, *Women of the Klan,* 28.

6. Quoted in Wendy Rielly Thorson, "Oregon Klanswomen of the 1920s: A Study of Tribalism, Gender, and Women's Power" (MA thesis, Oregon State University, 1997), 68.

7. Blee, *Women of the Klan,* 125.

8. Founded in 1891, this was originally an auxiliary to the male Order of United American Mechanics.

9. Doherty, "Aliens Found in Waiting," 17.

10. *New York Times,* September 21, 1921.

11. Quoted in Blee, *Women of the Klan,* 22.

12. Quoted in Wade, *The Fiery Cross,* 162.

13. Doherty, "Aliens Found in Waiting," 17.

14. A right-wing anti-feminist screed on the web today accuses Tyler of seizing power in the Klan by falsely accusing Grand Dragon Simmons of "improprieties" and replacing him with her "paramour." David R. Usher, "Feminism: Today's Women's Ku Klux Klan," *World Net Daily,* October 31, 2014, http://www.wnd.com/2014/10/feminism-todays-womens-ku-klux-klan/.

15. My discussion of Barr is primarily from Dwight W. Hoover, "From Quaker to Klan 'Kluckeress,'" *Indiana Magazine of History* 87, no. 2 (June 1991): 171–95, data on 187; and Steven J. Taylor, "Misc Monday: A Ku Klux Quaker?" *Historic Indianapolis,* September 28, 2015, http://historicindianapolis.com/misc-monday-a-ku-klux-quaker/.

16. Quoted in Hoover, "From Quaker to Klan 'Kluckeress,'" 171–72, from *Papers Read at the Meeting of Grand Dragons, Knights of the Ku Klux Klan, at Their First Annual Meeting Held at Asheville, North Carolina, July 1923,* 135.

17. These profits came to light from a suit against Barr by the WKKK.

18. Holiness is a sectarian movement rooted in Wesleyan Methodism. Its central tenet is the call for a second work of grace, aka entire sanctification, following a first salvation. This second salvation cleanses the sanctified person of even the temptation to sin and therefore allows a fully holy life. The holiness churches thereby deny the doctrine of original sin.

19. *New York Times* obituary, "Bishop Alma White, Preacher, Author; Founder of Pillar of Fire Dies at 84—Established Several Schools and Colleges," June 27, 1946.

20. Blee, *Women of the Klan*, 75. White herself claimed that she had created sixty-one churches. Some one-third to one-half of Methodists followed holiness beliefs in the 1890s. Vinson Synan, *The Holiness-Pentecostal Tradition: Charismatic Movements in the Twentieth Century* (Grand Rapids, MI: Wm. B. Eerdman Publishers, 1971).

21. Biographical information and this quotation are from Alma Bridwell White, *The Story of My Life and the Pillar of Fire* (Zarephath, NJ: Pillar of Fire, 1935), Vol. I, quotation 223–24.

22. Pentacostalism is a Protestant renewal movement that places special emphasis on a direct personal experience of God through baptism with the Holy Spirit.

23. "Fundamentalist Pillar," *Time*, July 8, 1946.

24. Quoted in Merrit Cross, "Alma Bridwell White," in Edward T. James, ed., *Notable American Women* (Cambridge, MA: Belknap Press of Harvard University Press, 1971), 3:581–83.

25. "Bishop v. Drink," *Time*, December 18, 1939; "The Pillar of Fire Mission," *Christian Science Monitor*, May 21, 1920, quoted in https://en.wikipedia.org/wiki/Pillar_of_Fire_International#cite_note-17.

26. Cross, "Alma Bridwell White."

27. Lately Thomas, *Storming Heaven: The Lives and Turmoils of Minnie Kennedy and Aimee Semple McPherson* (New York: William Morrow, 1970), 32.

28. White, *Heroes of the Fiery Cross*, 187; White, *The Ku Klux Klan in Prophecy*, 187.

29. Alma Bridwell White, "America—the White Man's Heritage," *Good Citizen*, August 1929.

30. The books are *The Ku Klux Klan in Prophecy*; *Klansmen: Guardians of Liberty*; and *Heroes of the Fiery Cross*. She republished them as a three-volume set as late as 1943 under the title *Guardians of Liberty*.

31. White, *The Ku Klux Klan in Prophecy*; White, *Heroes of the Fiery Cross*.

32. Alma Bridwell White, *Woman's Chains* (Zarephath, NJ: Good Citizen, 1943). She also produced a periodical with the same name. Stanley, *Feminist Pillar of Fire*, 111–14.

33. White, *Guardians of Liberty*, I, 121; White, *Heroes of the Fiery Cross*, 173.

34. The Colorado Federation of Women's Clubs, Colorado State Federation of Garden Clubs, and Women's Club of Denver.

35. Blee, *Women of the Klan*, 26, 167.

36. Its list included Bishop William F. Anderson, Judge George W. Anderson, Bishop Benjamin Brewster, Professor Irving Fisher, Doctor David Starr Jordan, Rabbi Henry Levi, Bishop Francis J. McConnell, William A. Neilson, Dean Roscoe Pound, Rev. Harold E. B. Speight, and William Allen White. In forming the list, it implicitly signed on to the New York State Lusk Committee's report, published as *Revolutionary Radicalism: Its History, Purpose and Tactics with an Exposition and Discussion of the Steps Being Taken and Required to Curb It.*

The Joint Legislative Committee to Investigate Seditious Activities, popularly known as the Lusk Committee, was formed in 1919 by the New York state legislature to investigate individuals and organizations in the state suspected of sedition.

37. Helen Tufts Bailie, "Our Threatened Heritage: A Letter to the DAR by a Member," April 5, 1928, http://womhist.alexanderstreet.com/milit/doc20.htm.

38. *New York Times*, September 13, 1921, quoted in Jackie Hill, "Progressive Values in the WKKK," *Constructing the Past* 9, no. 1, article 6 (2008): 24, http://digital commons.iwu.edu/cgi/viewcontent.cgi?article=1014&context=constructing.

39. Richard, "'Why Don't You Be a Klansman?'" 513.

40. Blee, *Women of the Klan*, 140.

41. Thorson, "Oregon Klanswomen," 4.

42. Richard, "'Why Don't You Be a Klansman?'" 513.

43. Blee, *Women of the Klan*, 31, 59ff.; Richard, "'Why Don't You Be a Klansman?'"

44. Quoted in MacLean, *Behind the Mask of Chivalry*, 114–15.

45. Minutes in Horowitz, *Inside the Klavern*, 59.

46. *Western American*, quoted in Thorson, "Oregon Klanswomen," 38.

47. McClanahan, "Klan of the Grandmother." We don't know if she was ever admitted.

48. WKKK Constitution; WKKK Kloran; quotation from Kelli R. Kerbawy, "Knights in White Satin: Women of the Ku Klux Klan" (MA thesis, Marshall University, 2007), 66.

49. Aware that he was losing power, Simmons had set up the Kamelia as a rival to the WKKK, but it failed to gain momentum.

50. Quoted in Kerbawy, "Knights in White Satin," 57–58.

51. Ibid, 57; Thorson, "Oregon Klanswomen," image on 42.

52. Thorson, "Oregon Klanswomen," 32.

53. Blee, *Women of the Klan*, 32.

54. Quoted in ibid., 50–51. I am indebted to India Cooper for finding the original source of this line; the Klan writer seems to have taken this phrase from a book touting patriotism, Francis Trevelyan Miller's *America, the Land We Love* (New York: W. T. Blaine, 1916), 468.

55. *Western American*, quoted in Thorson, "Oregon Klanswomen," 21.

56. Doherty, "Aliens Found in Waiting," 103; Blee, *Women of the Klan*, 120.

57. Fox, *Everyday Klansfolk*, 96.

58. *Western American*, quoted in Thorson, "Oregon Klanswomen," 5.

59. Mary Beth Slusar, "Multi-Framing in Progressive Era Women's Movements: A Comparative Analysis of the Birth Control, Temperance, and Women's KKK Movements" (PhD diss., Ohio State University, 2010), 117.

60. McClanahan, "Klan of the Grandmother."

61. Betty Jo Brenner, "The Colorado Women of the Ku Klux Klan," *Denver Inside and Out: Colorado History* 16 (2011): 64; Blee, *Women of the Klan*, 140.

62. Blee, *Women of the Klan*, 31, 34.

63. Thorson, "Oregon Klanswomen," 20, 23.

64. *New York Times*, April 1, 1925.

65. A photograph of Sanger with Klanspeople—men as well as women—circulates widely, especially online, but it is a fake that pastes a well-known image of Sanger onto an image of Klanspeople. Opponents of reproductive rights frequently put out "fake news" about Sanger, birth control, and Planned Parenthood, the successor organization to Sanger's Birth Control League.

66. Quoted in Blee, *Women of the Klan*, 24.

67. McClanahan, "Klan of the Grandmother."

68. Quoted in Kerbawy, "Knights in White Satin," 721.

69. Association of Georgia Klans, "The Charitable Works of the Ku Klux Klan," http://associationofklanskkkk.weebly.com/activities-from-1915-1944.html.

70. Norberg, "Ku Klux Klan in the Valley."

71. Blee, *Women of the Klan*, 140–44; Brenner, "The Colorado Women of the Ku Klux Klan," 65; Doherty, "Aliens Found in Waiting," 136.

72. Blee, *Women of the Klan*, 158–59; Thorson, "Oregon Klanswomen," 23.

73. Blee, *Women of the Klan*, 161, 166–67.

74. *New York Times*, May 11, 1925, quoted in Hill, "Progressive Values in the WKKK," 25.

75. Goldberg, "The KKK in Madison," 36.

76. Minutes in Horowitz, *Inside the Klavern*, 90.

77. Letters to the Athens, Georgia, Klan that Nancy MacLean uncovered showed that white women looked to the Klan as a paragovernmental force that could discipline these violent and irresponsible men. MacLean, "White Women and Klan Violence in the 1920s: Agency, Complicity and the Politics of Women's History," *Gender and History* 3, no. 3 (Autumn 1991): 285–303; Gordon, *The Great Arizona Orphan Abduction*; Katz, *The Invisible Empire*.

78. Minutes in Horowitz, *Inside the Klavern*, 37–38.

79. Knights of the KKK, "The Obligation of American Citizens to Free Public Schools," author's possession, n.d.

80. Wade, *The Fiery Cross*, 258–59.

81. Blee, *Women of the Klan*, 128.

82. Kerbawy, "Knights in White Satin," 721; Hill, "Progressive Values in the WKKK," 27.

Chapter 8. Oregon and the Attack on Parochial Schools

1. See Matt Novak, "Oregon Was Founded as a Racist Utopia," *American Renaissance*, January 21, 2015, http://www.amren.com/news/2015/01/oregon-was-founded-as-a-racist-utopia/; and "Kali Ma Beer and the Oregon Ku Klux

Klan," *Hindu Human Rights*, May 11, 2012, http://www.hinduhumanrights.info/kali-ma-beer-and-the-oregon-klu-klux-klan/.

2. *Oregon Voter: Magazine of Citizenship for Busy Men and Women*, March 4, 1922, 4; Frances Paul Valenti, "The Portland Press, the Ku Klux Klan, and the Oregon Compulsory Education Bill: Editorial Treatment of Klan Themes in the Portland Press in 1922" (MA thesis, University of Washington, 1993), 65–67, 88; Clark, "The Bigot Disclosed," 168; Jackson, *The Ku Klux Klan in the City*, 203.

3. Kimberley Mangun, "'As Citizens of Portland We Must Protest': Beatrice Morrow Canaday and the African American Response to D. W. Griffith's 'Masterpiece,'" *Oregon Historical Quarterly* 107, no. 3 (Fall 2006): 382–91; Eckard V. Toy, "The Ku Klux Klan in Oregon," in *Experiences in a Promised Land: Essays in Pacific Northwest History*, ed. G. Thomas Edwards and Carlos A. Schwantes (Seattle: University of Washington Press, 1986), 271.

4. Robert D. Johnston, in his *The Radical Middle Class: Populist Democracy and the Question of Capitalism in Progressive Era Portland, Oregon* (Princeton, NJ: Princeton University Press, 2003), attributed the election upset to "the peculiar form of class alliance between small business owners and skilled workers" (223).

5. Chalmers, *Hooded Americanism*, 86; Tyack, "The Perils of Pluralism," 85; Rothwell, "The Ku Klux Klan in the State of Oregon."

6. Toy, "The Ku Klux Klan in Oregon," 271; Valenti, "The Portland Press, the Ku Klux Klan," 68, 75.

7. Figures differ. See Eckard Toy, "Ku Klux Klan," *Oregon Encyclopedia*, https://oregonencyclopedia.org/articles/ku_klux_klan/#.V7lwZj4rI6U; Chalmers, *Hooded Americanism*, 88; Mangun, "'As Citizens of Portland We Must Protest,'" 395; and Eckard V. Toy Jr., "The Ku Klux Klan in Tillamook, Oregon," *Pacific Northwest Quarterly* 53, no. 2 (April 1962): 61.

8. Toy, "The Ku Klux Klan in Oregon," 271; Norberg, "Ku Klux Klan in the Valley."

9. Quoted in Johnston, *The Radical Middle Class*, 225.

10. Trevor Griffey, "Luther I. Powell, Northwest Ku Klux Klan Organizer," chapter 2 in "The Washington State Klan in the 1920s," *Seattle Civil Rights & Labor History Project*, 2007, http://depts.washington.edu/civilr/kkk_powell.htm.

11. *Oregon Voter*, March 4, 1922, 4.

12. *Oregon Voter*, March 25, 1922, 5.

13. Saalfield, *Forces of Prejudice*, 40; Rothwell, "The Ku Klux Klan in the State of Oregon," 130ff. Baker claimed his proudest accomplishment was running IWW "subversives" out of town; "Worst Mayors Ever," *Portland Mercury*, October 19, 2012, http://www.portlandmercury.com/portland/worst-mayors-ever/Content?oid=7320289.

14. Johnston, *The Radical Middle Class*, 245.

15. *Western American*, quoted in Thorson, "Oregon Klanswomen," 23; Jackson, *The Ku Klux Klan in the City*, 209.

16. Annie McLain, "Unmasking the Oregon Klansman: The Ku Klux Klan in Astoria, 1921–1925" (unpublished paper, Pacific University, 2003), https://www.pacificu.edu/sites/default/files/documents/Annie%20McLain.pdf.

17. R. H. Sawyer, "Ku Klux and Jews," *Oregon Voter*, April 15, 1922, 16.

18. Michael Barkun, *Religion and the Racist Right: The Origins of the Christian Identity Movement* (Chapel Hill: University of North Carolina Press, 1994), 22–26.

19. Quoted in Saalfeld, *Forces of Prejudice*, 23.

20. Authorities made immediate use of the new law, arresting Socialist Party members for selling copies of the *Western Socialist* less than a week after the law took effect.

21. Linda Tamura, *The Hood River Issei: An Oral History of Japanese Settlers in Oregon's Hood River Valley* (Urbana: University of Illinois Press, 1993), 88ff; William Toll, "Black Families and Migration to a Multiracial Society: Portland, Oregon, 1900–1924," *Journal of American Ethnic History* 17, no. 3 (Spring 1998): 40, 57.

22. Finn J. D. John, "Corruption, Hypocrisy Brought Down Ku Klux Klan in 1920s," *Yamhill Valley NewsRegister*, June 6, 2013.

23. Marjorie R. Stearns, "The History of the Japanese People in Oregon" (MA thesis, University of Oregon, 1937), quoted in Toy, "The Ku Klux Klan in Oregon," 281.

24. Quoted in William Toll, "Progress and Piety: The Ku Klux Klan and Social Change in Tillamook, Oregon," *Pacific Northwest Quarterly* 69, no. 2 (April 1978): 39, 77; Jackson, *The Ku Klux Klan in the City*, 204.

25. Thomas H. Heuterman, "Bifurcation: How the Wapato, Washington, *Independent* Covered Japanese in the Yakima Valley, 1920–1942," AEJMC Minorities and Communication Division working paper, 1987, 12; John, "Corruption, Hypocrisy Brought Down Ku Klux Klan."

26. Quoted in Larralde and Griswold del Castillo, "San Diego's Ku Klux Klan," at www.sandiegohistory.org/journal/2000/april/klan.

27. Ibid.

28. Ibid., from an interview with Galarza.

29. McLain, "Unmasking the Oregon Klansman."

30. Jackson, *The Ku Klux Klan in the City*, 198–99.

31. Ibid., 208–9.

32. *Oregon Journal*, June 16, 1922, quoted in Saalfeld, *Forces of Prejudice*, 66–67; M. Paul Holsinger, "The Oregon School Bill Controversy, 1922–1925," *Pacific Historical Review* 37, no. 3 (1968): 330.

33. Lyman Beecher, *A Plea for the West* (Cincinnati: Truman & Smith, 1835), https://archive.org/details/pleaforwest00beec.

34. Quoted in Fox, *Everyday Klansfolk*, 151.

35. I suspect that, like ALEC today, Klan leaders drafted legislation that friendly state legislators could introduce.

36. Rory McVeigh, *The Rise of the Ku Klux Klan: Right-Wing Movements and National Politics* (Minneapolis: University of Minnesota Press, 2009), 125.

37. Allerfeldt, "Jayhawker Fraternities," 1051; "bagful of bolshevism" quoted in Fox, *Everyday Klansfolk*, 61; Knights of the Ku Klux Klan, "The Obligation of American Citizens to Free Public Schools," n.d., author's possession. The conservative condemnation confirms that the national Klan in this period did not focus on a threat from Communism.

38. Johnston, *The Radical Middle Class*, 122–23; Rod Farmer, "Power to the People: The Progressive Movement for the Recall, 1890s–1920," *New England Journal of History* 57, no. 2 (Winter 2001): 59–83. U'Ren was also successful in making Oregon the first state to conduct a presidential primary and to institute proportional representation.

39. The federation, originally established during World War I, declared itself "an instrument to counteract the strength of corporate power in Oregon," thus recalling the anti-elitist stream in this movement. Exalted Cyclops Frederick L. Gifford was elected its director. Chalmers, *Hooded Americanism*, 85.

40. Some leading Oregon Masons claimed that the schools bill was "foisted" upon them by the Klan. Tyack, "The Perils of Pluralism," 77; Valenti, "The Portland Press, the Ku Klux Klan"; Holsinger, "The Oregon School Bill Controversy," 329–30; Jackson, *The Ku Klux Klan in the City*, 205; Saalfield, *Forces of Prejudice*, 74.

41. Edward Clarke, quoted in Holsinger, "The Oregon School Bill Controversy," 329.

42. Quoted in ibid., 330; Saalfield, *Forces of Prejudice*, 72.

43. Testimony of a "Klan Victim" from North Judson, Indiana, http://www.iub .edu/~imaghist/for_teachers/mdrnprd/Klan/klanvictimmemory.html.

44. Quoted in Jackson, *The Ku Klux Klan in the City*, 205. Baker, *Gospel According to the Klan*, 92–95; Eckard V. Toy, "Robe and Gown: The Ku Klux Klan in Eugene, Oregon, During the 1920s," in Lay, *The Invisible Empire in the West*, pp. 160ff.

45. The following summary of Oregon elections and legislative action is from Holsinger, "The Oregon School Bill Controversy."

46. Loomis, "A Narrative Interpretation of the 1920s Ku Klux Klan in Oregon," 16.

47. Toy, "The Ku Klux Klan in Oregon," 277.

48. Emily Pellegrini, "The Fool of the Family: Nativism and the Ku Klux Klan in Oregon's 1922 Election" (BA thesis, University of Oregon, 2014), 45–46.

49. Robert R. McCoy, "The Paradox of Oregon's Progressive Politics: The Political Career of Walter Pierce," *Oregon Historical Quarterly* 110, no. 3 (Fall 2009): 399.

50. Quoted in Pellegrini, "The Fool of the Family," 55, 57, from *Oregon Voter*, April 22, 1922, 8.

51. *Oregon Voter*, June 17, 1922; Saalfield, *Forces of Prejudice*, 27.

52. Quoted in Saalfield, *Forces of Prejudice*, 27. Banker Robert E. Smith of Lumberman's Trust was also an ardent supporter of the schools bill; ibid., 67.

53. Toy, "The Ku Klux Klan in Oregon," 280–81.

54. Pellegrini, "The Fool of the Family," 62, 65.

55. Jackson, *The Ku Klux Klan in the City*, 207; Johnston, *The Radical Middle Class*, 231–33.

56. *New York Times*, April 1, 1924.

57. Holsinger, "The Oregon School Bill Controversy," 338–39.

58. Ibid., 336; Saalfield, *Forces of Prejudice*, 72; Goldberg, "The KKK in Madison," 36.

59. Weaver, "The Knights of the Ku Klux Klan," 165–67; Hatle and Vaillancourt, "One Flag, One School, One Language," 367.

60. Wade, *The Fiery Cross*, 248–49; Tyack, "The Perils of Pluralism," 91.

61. Minutes in Horowitz, *Inside the Klavern*, 25, 27, 80; Toy, "Robe and Gown," 170ff. No data on firings are available, but we know, for example, that from April to July 1924, the Anaheim, California, city council was systematically dismissing its non-Klan city employees and replacing them with Klanspeople, and in Madison Klanspeople tried to intimidate public school teachers by calling and asking their religion. Cocoltchos, "The Invisible Empire," 111; Goldberg, "The KKK in Madison," 37.

62. Wade, *The Fiery Cross*, 248–49; Tyack, "The Perils of Pluralism," 91.

63. *Western American*, quoted in Thorson, "Oregon Klanswomen," 25, 32.

64. Blee, *Women of the Klan*, 25.

65. Thorson, "Oregon Klanswomen," 40–44.

66. Besides LOTIE, these included Kamelia, Queens of the Golden Mask, League of Protestant Women, Puritan Daughters of America, and American Women.

67. The following summary of this episode is from Thorson, "Oregon Klanswomen," chapter 4, taken in turn from Lem Dever, *Confessions of an Imperial Klansman* (Portland, OR: n.p., 1924); but since Dever was not present, we know that he was repeating, or embellishing, what the women told him.

68. Today we do not think of organizations such as LOTIE as commodities, but the fact that Davis did is entirely consistent with the Klan's understanding of the whole enterprise as a business and not necessarily more egregious than Evans's insistence on merger, because both plans were intended to increase Klan leaders' profits.

69. Thorson, "Oregon Klanswomen," 68, 72.

70. Ibid., 26–27.

71. "Tales from the Grubby End: The Ku Klux Klan in Newburg," *Portland Tribune*, July 16, 2014, http://portlandtribune.com/pt/11-features/227348-90225-tales-from-the-grubby-end-the-ku-klux-klan-in-newberg.

72. In the 1920s, however, as I argued in earlier work, progressive women operated within the same contradiction: leaders were the exception, and domestic-

ity remained the standard for the majority of women. Linda Gordon, *Pitied but Not Entitled: Single Mothers and the History of Welfare* (New York: Free Press, 1994).

Chapter 9. POLITICAL AND ECONOMIC WARFARE

1. Goldberg, "The KKK in Madison," 38; White, *The Ku Klux Klan in Prophecy*, 121–22; Rory McVeigh, "Structural Incentives for Conservative Mobilization: Power Devaluation and the Rise of the Ku Klux Klan, 1915–1925," *Social Forces* 77, no. 4 (June 1999): 1461–96; Katz, *The Invisible Empire*, 99.

2. Mae N. Ngai, *Impossible Subjects: Illegal Aliens and the Making of Modern America* (Princeton, NJ: Princeton University Press, 2004), 48, 288n97.

3. *Imperial Night-Hawk*, August 29, 1923. The proposal represented the Klan's assumption that it could be as influential as those of the US Congress Immigration Commission of 1911, also known as the Dillingham Commission, whose report formed one of the first official governmental arguments for immigration restriction.

4. Wade, *The Fiery Cross*, 196–97; Feldman, *Politics, Society, and the Klan in Alabama*, 24.

5. Tucker, *The Dragon and The Cross*, 54; Allerfeldt, "Jayhawker Fraternities," 1042.

6. MacLean, *Behind the Mask of Chivalry*, 18.

7. Weaver, "The Knights of the Ku Klux Klan," 308–11; Tucker, *The Dragon and the Cross*, 103, 116.

8. Minutes in Horowitz, *Inside the Klavern*, 27.

9. G. W. Price to "esteemed Klansman," September 10, 1922, in Monteval, *The Klan Inside-Out*, 202.

10. Quoted in Rhomberg, "White Nativism and Urban Politics," 44.

11. The following description of the convention is taken from Robert K. Murray, *The 103rd Ballot* (New York: Harper & Row, 1976).

12. In another sign of the Klan's mainstream character, the Republican platform shared with the Democratic support for immigration restriction.

13. Quoted in Garland S. Tucker III, "Lessons from the Ultimate Contested Convention," *National Review*, April 9, 2016, http://www.nationalreview.com/article/433875/contested-convention-historical-precedent-good-and-bad.

14. Quoted in Jack Shafer, "1924: The Wildest Convention in U.S. History," *Politico*, March 7, 2016, http://www.politico.com/magazine/story/2016/03/1924-the-craziest-convention-in-us-history-213708.

15. Peter Carlson, "The Battle Brawl of 1924," *Washington Post*, March 4, 2008, http://www.washingtonpost.com/wp-dyn/content/article/2008/03/03/AR2008030303277.html.

16. Murray, *The 103rd Ballot*; Garland S. Tucker III, "The Ultimate 'Messy' Convention: The 1924 Democratic Convention," Calvin Coolidge Presidential Foundation blog, July 22, 2016, https://coolidgefoundation.org/blog/the-ultimate-messy-convention-the-1924-democratic-convention/.

17. Schuyler, "The Ku Klux Klan in Nebraska," 252.

18. Price, "The Oregon Ku Klux Klan"; Toy, "The Ku Klux Klan in Tillamook, Oregon," 63.

19. Quoted in Tucker, *The Dragon and the Cross*, 89.

20. Toll, "Progress and Piety," 79; McLain, "Unmasking the Oregon Klansman"; Schuyler, "The Ku Klux Klan in Nebraska," 252.

21. Hunt, "The Fundamentalist–Ku Klux Klan Alliance," 87.

22. W. E. B. Du Bois, "The Shape of Fear," *North American Review*, June 1926.

23. Toll, "Progress and Piety." Kansas was another location of great Klan power; see Charles William Sloan Jr., "Kansas Battles the Invisible Empire," *Kansas History: A Journal of the Central Plains* 40, no. 3 (Autumn 1974): 393–409, https://www.kshs.org/p/kansas-historical-quarterly-kansas-battles-the-invisible-empire/13247.

24. Charles O. Jackson, "William J. Simmons: A Career in Ku Kluxism," *Georgia Historical Quarterly* 50, no. 4 (December 1966): 331; Tucker, *The Dragon and the Cross*, 2.

25. Brophy, "Norms, Law, and Reparations," 25.

26. Quoted in Caldemeyer, "Conditional Conservatism," 19; Wade, *The Fiery Cross*, 165, 196; McGreevy, *Catholicism and American Freedom*, 185; Chalmers, *Hooded Americanism*, 210; Fryer and Levitt, "Hatred and Profits," 27; Richard, "'Why Don't You Be a Klansman?'"; Pegram, "Hoodwinked," 96, 115; Rhomberg, "White Nativism and Urban Politics," 39–55.

27. Scholars have not been able to examine this activism closely, likely because it happened so diffusely and was therefore not visible enough to be reported in newspapers. Another reason for this omission in studies of the Klan may be underestimating women's activism, for they were certainly the main shoppers in most families. Leonard Moore, in his *Citizen Klansman* (92), concludes that the boycotting was mainly ineffective, and he may be right, but we lack evidence.

28. Quoted in Thorson, "Oregon Klanswomen," 22; Minutes in Horowitz, *Inside the Klavern*, 61.

29. Saalfield, *Forces of Prejudice*, 26; Safianow, "'You Can't Burn History,'" 122.

30. David A. Horowitz, "The Klansman as Outsider: Ethnocultural Solidarity and Antielitism in the Oregon KKK," *Pacific Northwest Quarterly* 80, no. 1 (January 1989): 14.

31. Knights of the Ku Klux Klan, "The Practice of Klanishness," Imperial Instructions Document No. 1, 1924, author's possession.

32. Examples in Tyack, "The Perils of Pluralism," 86, 91.

33. The others were physical Klanishness (helping to maintain the health and well-being of Klansmen), social Klanishness (equality among members), and moral

Klanishness. Knights of the Ku Klux Klan, "The Practice of Klanishness"; Minutes in Horowitz, *Inside the Klavern*, 33.

34. McVeigh, *The Rise of the Ku Klux Klan*, 160.

35. Jewish Telegraphic Agency release, October 27, 1924, http://www.jta.org/1924/10/27/archive/klan-starts-nation-wide-boycott-against-jews.

36. Weaver, "The Knights of the Ku Klux Klan," 231ff., offers an example from Columbus, Ohio.

37. Knights and Women of the Ku Klux Klan, "Klorero," Elmira, New York, 1925.

38. *Imperial Night-Hawk*, June 20 and August 15, 1923, quoted in Shotwell, "Crystallizing Public Hatred," 46.

39. Horowitz, "The Klansman as Outsider," 14.

40. Safianow, "'You Can't Burn History,'" 123.

41. Wade, *The Fiery Cross*, 193.

42. Blee, *Women of the Klan*, 150.

43. Ibid., 115; Allerfeldt, "Jayhawker Fraternities," 1048.

44. The practice of reclaiming and revaluing a derogatory term has been characteristic of movements of outsiders and people discriminated against.

45. Her interviews with former Klanswomen yielded stories not only painful but bewildering, revealing an economic violence akin in its suddenness to the ethnic hatreds that broke out in the destruction of Yugoslavia. Blee, *Women of the Klan*, 147ff.

46. Steven Gerontakis, "AHEPA vs. the Ku Klux Klan: Greek Americans on the Path to Whiteness" (senior thesis, University of North Carolina–Asheville, 2012).

47. Blee, *Women of the Klan*, 150; Safianow, "The Klan Comes to Tipton"; Gregory Pappas, "Forgotten History: The Klan vs. Americans of Greek Heritage in an Era of Hate and the Birth of the Ahepa" (senior thesis, University of North Carolina–Asheville, 2012), 19, http://www.pappaspost.com/forgotten-history-the-klan-vs-americans-of-greek-heritage-in-an-era-of-hate-and-the-birth-of-the-ahepa/.

48. Thorson, "Oregon Klanswomen," 22; Saalfield, *Forces of Prejudice*, 72.

49. *Oregon Voter*, January 21, 1922, 12; March 4, 1922, 4.

50. Mecklin, *The Ku Klux Klan*, 168; Brenner, "The Colorado Women of the Ku Klux Klan," 64; Thorson, "Oregon Klanswomen," 5.

51. Larry R. Gerlach, "A Battle of Empires: The Klan in Salt Lake City," in Lay, *The Invisible Empire in the West*, 131.

52. Quoted in MacLean, *Behind the Mask of Chivalry*, 113.

53. Tom Rice, "How the Ku Klux Klan Seized Cinema to Become a Force in America," *The Conversation*, December 8, 2015, https://theconversation.com/how-the-ku-klux-klan-seized-cinema-to-become-a-force-in-america-52030; Rice, "'The True Story of the Ku Klux Klan.'"

54. Melissa Ooten, *Race, Gender, and Film Censorship in Virginia, 1922–1965*

(Boulder, CO: Lexington Books, 2015), 91; Rice, "Protecting Protestantism," 371; Rice, "'The True Story of the Ku Klux Klan.'"

55. Rice, "'The True Story of the Ku Klux Klan,'" 488.

56. Scott Bomboy, "The Klan's Indirect Role in Fostering the Jazz Age," *Constitution Daily*, November 28, 2012, http://blog.constitutioncenter.org/2012/11/the-klans-indirect-role-in-fostering-the-jazz-age/.

57. Minutes in Horowitz, *Inside the Klavern*, 13, 54, 79.

58. *Western American*, quoted in Thorson, "Oregon Klanswomen," 22.

59. For example, Minutes in Horowitz, *Inside the Klavern*, 36.

60. *Imperial Night-Hawk*, June 20 and August 15, 1923, quoted in Shotwell, "Crystallizing Public Hatred," 46.

61. Richard, "'This Is Not a Catholic Nation,'" 293; Bohn, "The Ku Klux Klan Interpreted," 390.

62. Minutes in Horowitz, *Inside the Klavern*, 27; Horowitz, "The Klansman as Outsider," 14.

Chapter 10. CONSTITUENTS

1. Johnston, *The Radical Middle Class*, 237.

2. For example, Charles N. Hurd of Pacific States Telephone and Telegraph; Rothwell, "The Ku Klux Klan in the State of Oregon," 124. Lycurgus Breckenridge Musgrove, coal mining millionaire, was a Klansman and chair of the Anti-Saloon League executive committee, but that was in the South, where conditions were entirely different; Pegram, "Hoodwinked," 105.

3. With the expansion of "welfare" programs, that ideology also redefined "independent." Nancy Fraser and Linda Gordon, "A Genealogy of 'Dependency': Tracing a Keyword of the US Welfare State," *Signs* 19, no. 2 (Winter 1994): 309–36.

4. Arno Mayer, "The Lower Middle Class as Historical Problem," *Journal of Modern History* 47, no. 3 (1975): 409–36.

5. Rhomberg, "White Nativism and Urban Politics," 45, 47.

6. Bringhurst, "The Ku Klux Klan in a Central California Community," 370–71.

7. Tucker, *The Dragon*, 6, 131.

8. LaLande, "'Beneath the Hooded Robe,'" 17.

9. Horowitz, "Order, Solidarity, and Vigilance," 194–95; Goldberg, *Hooded Empire*, 183–86. But white-collar men were not overrepresented in Pennsylvania; see Fryer and Levitt, "Hatred and Profits."

10. Jackson, *The Ku Klux Klan in the City*, 242.

11. Goldberg, "Beneath the Hood and Robe," 195.

12. Fryer and Levitt, "Hatred and Profits"; Holsinger, "The Oregon School Bill Controversy," 328.

13. Toll, "Black Families," 79.

14. Weaver, "The Knights of the Ku Klux Klan," 99.

15. Fox, *Everyday Klansfolk*, 121–22.

16. Moore, *Citizen Klansmen*, 95.

17. Fox, *Everyday Klansfolk*, 125; Rhomberg, "White Nativism and Urban Politics," 45–46.

18. Loomis, "A Narrative Interpretation of the 1920s Ku Klux Klan," 276ff.

19. Pegram, "Hoodwinked," 115; Minutes in Horowitz, *Inside the Klavern*, 72.

20. Toy, "Robe and Gown," 154; Caldemeyer, "Conditional Conservatism," 16.

21. Lynd and Lynd, *Middletown*, 482.

22. Jackson, *The Ku Klux Klan in the City*, table 3.

23. Quoted in Zerzan, "Rank-and-File Radicalism Within the Ku Klux Klan of the 1920s," 52.

24. Chalmers, *Hooded Americanism*, 191.

25. Caldemeyer, "Conditional Conservatism," 12, 17, 19.

26. LaLande, "'Beneath the Hooded Robe,'" 40.

27. Nelson, "The Ku Klux Klan for Boredom," 198.

28. Taylor, "What the Klan Did in Indiana," 330–32.

29. US Decennial Census (1890–2000); American Community Survey (2010).

30. Blee, *Women of the Klan*, 119–22.

Chapter 11. LEGACY: DOWN BUT NOT OUT

1. For example, Minutes in Horowitz, *Inside the Klavern*, 34, 44, 143, 146.

2. Safianow, "The Klan Comes to Tipton," 226; Taylor, "What the Klan Did in Indiana," 330–32.

3. Richard Gid Powers, *Secrecy and Power: The Life of J. Edgar Hoover* (London: Collier Macmillan, 1987), 140; Chalmers, *Hooded Americanism*, 62–63, 105; R. J. Stove, "J. Edgar Hoover and the Ku Klux Klan," *National Observer* 41 (Summer 2001), http://www.nationalobserver.net/2001_summer_109.htm.

4. E.g., attorney Donald G. Hughes to Atlanta Klan headquarters, August 20, 1923, quoted in Monteval, *The Klan Inside-Out*, 113.

5. Minutes in Horowitz, *Inside the Klavern*, 144.

6. Material about Stephenson comes from Booth, *The Mad Mullah*; Taylor, "What the Klan Did in Indiana," 330–32; Lutholtz, *Grand Dragon*; Doug Linder, "The D. C. Stephenson Trial: An Account," 2010, http://law2.umkc.edu/faculty/projects/ftrials/stephenson/stephensonaccount.html; Abbott, "Murder Wasn't Very Pretty."

7. Taylor, "What the Klan Did in Indiana," 330–32.

8. Evans, "The Klan's Fight for Americanism," 42.

9. Pew Research Center, *Hispanic Trends*, "The Nation's Immigration Laws,

1920 to Today," September 28, 2015, http://www.pewhispanic.org/2015/09/28/chapter-1-the-nations-immigration-laws-1920-to-today/.

10. Ngai, *Impossible Subjects*, 37ff.

11. Only 30 of 194 countries, none of them in Europe, grant birthright citizenship.

12. Evans, "The Klan's Fight for Americanism," 41–42.

13. This integration parallels an earlier transition that turned groups seen as nonwhite—such as Jews, the Irish, and Mediterranean peoples—into "whites." The 1920s Klan did not see them as nonwhite but nevertheless viewed them as inferior; it was groups that we might today call "people of color"—those of African, Latin American, and Asian descent—whom the Klan considered nonwhite.

14. Eckard Toy, "'Promised Land' or Armageddon? History, Survivalists, and the Aryan Nations in the Pacific Northwest," *Montana: The Magazine of Western History* 36, no. 3 (Summer 1986): 82.

15. Journalist Nina Rastogi has identified six categories of white supremacist groups today: neo-Nazi, KKK, Christian Identity, racist skinhead, Nordic mystics, and Aryan prison gangs. Nina Rastogi, "The Six Flavors of White Supremacy," *Slate*, May 5, 2009, http://www.slate.com/articles/news_and_politics/explainer/2009/05/the_six_flavors_of_white_supremacy.html.

16. Those who so label it include Robert Paxton, "The Five Stages of Fascism," *Journal of Modern History* 70, no. 1 (March 1998): 12, and Nancy MacLean agrees.

17. Umberto Eco, "Ur-Fascism," *New York Review of Books*, June 22, 1995; Paxton, "The Five Stages of Fascism," 3.

18. Thomas Greven, "The Rise of Right-Wing Populism in Europe and the United States: A Comparative Perspective," a Friedrich-Ebert-Stiftung Perspective, http://www.fesdc.org/fileadmin/user_upload/publications/RightwingPopulism.pdf.

19. Chip Berlet and Matthew N. Lyons, *Right-Wing Populism in America: Too Close for Comfort* (New York: Guildford Press, 2000).

20. Historian Roger Griffin labels as fascist the call for a "re-birth" of an ethnically pure nation, and this fits the Klan exactly if we include a religion requirement. Roger Griffin, "Revolution from the Right: Fascism," in *Revolutions and the Revolutionary Tradition in the West, 1560–1991*, ed. David Parker (London: Routledge, 2000); Griffin, *The Nature of Fascism* (New York: St. Martin's Press, 1991), xi.

21. Michael Mark Cohen, "Buzz Can Happen Here: Sinclair Lewis and the New American Fascism," *New Ohio Review* 20 (Fall 2016): 170.

22. Croatian, Hungarian, Lithuanian, Romanian, Slovakian, and Ukrainian fascisms did incorporate religion.

23. Eco, "Ur-Fascism."

24. James M. Jasper, "Constructing Indignation: Anger Dynamics in Protest Movements," *Emotion Review* 6, no. 3 (2014): 208.

25. Harel Shapiro, *Waiting for José: The Minutemen's Pursuit of America* (Prince-

ton, NJ: Princeton University Press, 2013), quoted by Greg Grandin in his review, "History's Sinkhole," *Nation*, November 11, 2013, 28.

26. For example, Lisa McGirr, *Suburban Warriors: The Origin of the New American Right* (Princeton, NJ: Princeton University Press, 2001); Michelle M. Nickerson, *Mothers of Conservatism: Women and the Postwar Right* (Princeton, NJ: Princeton University Press, 2012); Mary C. Brennan, *Wives, Mothers, and the Red Menace: Conservative Women and the Crusade Against Communism* (Boulder: University Press of Colorado, 2008); Claudia Koonz, *Mothers in the Fatherland: Women, the Family, and Nazi Politics* (New York: St. Martin's, 1987); and Victoria de Grazia, *How Fascism Ruled Women: Italy, 1922–1945* (Berkeley: University of California Press, 1993).

27. Statement of 1935, quoted in Helen Thomas, *Watchdogs of Democracy? The Waning Washington Press Corps and How It Has Failed the Public* (New York: Scribner, 2006), 172.

INDEX

Page numbers in *italics* refer to illustrations.
Page numbers followed by *n* refer to endnotes.

ABOUT THE AUTHOR

Though born in Chicago, Linda Gordon considers Portland, Oregon, her hometown. Educated at Swarthmore College and Yale University, she first became a historian of the Ukraine, examining the origin of the Cossacks and publishing *Cossack Rebellions: Social Turmoil in the Sixteenth-Century Ukraine*. Frustrated by the difficulties of research in the USSR, at a time when access to Russian archives was limited, she happily turned to US history. For the first part of this new career, she wrote about the historical and gendered roots of social policy debates in the United States, publishing three prizewinning books: *The Moral Property of Women*, a history of birth-control politics; *Heroes of Their Own Lives*, about family violence; and *Pitied but Not Entitled: Single Mothers and the History of Welfare*. She then turned toward topics that engaged her West Coast background, and to a narrative mode of exploring historical problems. Part of what made the American West different from the East was its greater racial diversity and complex forms of racism; with this in mind she wrote *The Great Arizona Orphan Abduction* (1999), about a vigilante action against Mexican Americans, which won the Bancroft Prize for best book in US history and the Beveridge Prize for best book on the history of the Western hemisphere. Her 2009 biography of West Coast photographer Dorothea Lange also won the Bancroft Prize, making Gordon one of very few authors ever to win it twice, as well as the *Los Angeles Times* Book Prize for Biography. While working on that book, she discovered some eight hundred never-published Lange photographs of the internment of Japanese Americans during World War II, which had been impounded by the US Army because they were so clearly critical of the internment; Gordon and coauthor Gary Okihiro published a selection of these photographs, along with commentary about the internment, as *Impounded: Dorothea Lange and the Censored Images of Japanese American Internment*. Gordon's most recent book is *Feminism Unfinished: A Short, Surprising History of American Women's Movements*, written with Dorothy Sue Cobble and Astrid Henry.

Gordon taught at the University of Massachusetts Boston, then at the University of Wisconsin–Madison; in 1999 she moved to New York City, where she is now University Professor of Humanities and History at New York University.